LEAN WORLD

LEAN WORLD

The DNA of Success and
The Path to Prosperity

DAVID J. CLIFT

PUBLISHED BY

Lean World

IPSWICH, ENGLAND

Lean World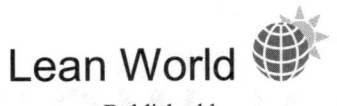

Published by
LEAN WORLD LTD, 2007

LEAN WORLD LTD,
331, Colchester Road,
Ipswich, Suffolk,
United Kingdom, IP4 4SF

www.leanworld.co.uk

1 3 5 7 9 10 8 6 4 2

A catalogue record for this book is
available from the British Library.

ISBN: 978–0–9556131–0–4

Typeset by Rowland Phototypesetting Ltd, Bury St Edmunds, Suffolk
Printed in England by St Edmundsbury Press Ltd, Bury St Edmunds, Suffolk

For *Dawn, Thomas* and *Peter*,
For all their love and support.

My sincere thanks go to a number of dedicated reviewers, who provided invaluable feedback during the course of writing this book. They include *Neil Abbott, Ray Hooper, Roy Hutchinson, John Lindley, Mark Sheasby, Richard Tunnicliffe* and *Ian Watson*. Particular thanks also go to *Richard Tunnicliffe,* of the *CBI, UK* for his encouragement, to *Chief Superintendent Mark Sheasby* and the *West Midlands Police,* for providing control charts demonstrating their successful reduction in crime, and to Joe Davey for the drawn illustrations.

Contents

Preface

The purpose of this book is to uncover the '**DNA of Success**', as well as the '**Path to Prosperity**' and a better world – a '**Lean World**'.

This book explores how to create
- SUCCESSFUL and GROWING enterprises,
- More CONTENTED communities,
- Increased individual WELL-BEING and HAPPINESS,
- A more STABLE and SUSTAINABLE environment,
- . . . a **LEAN WORLD**!

It goes 'back to basics' to determine what roles enterprises will play and what the future world is likely to look like. The book
- Successfully decodes 'THE DNA OF SUCCESS' for enterprises, agencies and governments,
- Identifies the generic MANAGEMENT SYSTEMS necessary for growth and prosperity, and
- Identifies the PRACTICAL STEPS leaders, managers and front-line staff need to take.

It also highlights how ANY enterprise can
- Develop a new and more PROSPEROUS future,
- Create unparalleled FOCUS and MOTIVATION,
- Become as successful as companies like TOYOTA or TESCO in their sector,
- Double their performance in the eyes of their customers whilst also halving costs,

- Release currently UNTAPPED POTENTIAL to deliver what really matters to customers,
- Remove some of the STRESS and FRUSTRATION from everyday life, and
- Create more CONTENTED communities and a more SUSTAINABLE WORLD.

The book provides new insights into the future of enterprise and the world of work. It explores the natural relationships which exist between enterprises, individuals, communities and the environment. It is written for leaders of change, as well as anyone interested or involved in change. However, it also provides essential reading for individuals who feel frustrated or stressed in their daily working lives; having to respond to ever increasing customer demands, whilst being constantly subjected to change initiatives that fail to provide any help whatsoever. It will also provide new perspectives for communities and groups, such as families, local communities, political parties, investment funds, unions, consumer bodies and environmental groups; in fact any-one who wants to create a better, more successful and sustainable future.

The book is essential reading for experienced 'Lean' leaders and practitioners who are looking to widen their understanding and application of 'Lean Thinking'. However, it is just as relevant and important to CEO's, company directors, change agents, managers and front line operational staff with little to no prior understanding of 'Lean Thinking', but looking for fresh ideas as to how they can significantly improve the enterprises they work for. It will help to motivate and create a new genera-tion of leaders, entrepreneurs, managers and operational staff. It will help to revolutionise current perceived wisdom, including enterprise, community and environmental governance and practices. By doing so, it will help to transform the world of work, as well as the wider world as we currently know it. In short, it could create the transformation of the century.

So where do we start? Well, 'Lean' is a philosophy under-pinned by the fundamental belief that success is derived from continually creating more and more value for others, not from simplistic cost reduction exercises. 'Lean' results in fitness, prosperity and growth, and an enterprise working in much closer harmony with their surroundings. 'Lean' focuses on creating value from a customer's perspective; continually removing barriers to delivering value, whilst identifying new ways to create additional value. 'Lean' also successfully harnesses the ingenuity of all staff, unlocking the doors to almost unlimited potential and generating a far more stimulating and rewarding environment to work. Too good to be true . . . absolutely not!

A number of leading enterprises, from both manufacturers and service providers, have begun their journey of discovery and by embracing 'Lean Thinking', are charting a quite different path to prosperity. These enterprises (and their competitors) are both amazed and shocked when they find out what they are capable of achieving - yet they have only just begun! . . . They are growing rapidly and already emerging as leaders in their fields, differentiating themselves, creating more and more value and continually catching up with, or accelerating away from, any competitors. At the same time, new entrants, particularly those embracing the current communication revolution, are also effectively embarking on such a journey from the very outset and achieving meteoric growth and success. They have all, in their own unique way, started to share their path to prosperity into the 21st Century . . . one continually learning and responding to customers demand, as well as the surroundings in which they operate.

By going 'back to basics', decoding the 'DNA of Success' and the 'Path to Prosperity' of enterprises leading the way, this book uniquely uncovers and describes a generic management system – a **Lean World Management System** – one capable of creating sustained success for any enterprise. The book classifies and describes the key components of a successful enterprise, from strategy and direction setting, through to the types of processes required and the outcomes that result. It describes every component of the management system, using plain language and simple day to day examples to illustrate each one. It provides a unique and holistic picture of 21st Century enterprise, explaining how and why activities such as marketing, customer service, provision, procurement and accounting are being re-invented and transformed, forever.

The management system can be applied to any type of enterprise; big or small, local or global, public or private. It can also be used by manufacturers, service providers, charities and government agencies alike. The management system can quickly and easily explain the ingredients of success behind enterprises such as Google, Amazon, eBay and Skype. It is also able to uniquely explain the success and growth of enterprises such as Toyota and Tesco. The book describes, in some detail, how the management system applies to these types of companies and by doing so, starts to uncover in a practical way the real 'DNA of Success'.

Enterprises, embarking down such a path, quickly realise that 'Lean' is not a destination but a journey. The Lean World Management System itself offers a huge leap forward, by providing an overarching system for understanding and managing a 'Lean Enterprise' and by helping enterprises to navigate their way successfully in the 21st Century. Given change is a major activity within any enterprise it should be of little surprise that the approach to steering a new path is contained within the Lean World Management System itself. If this were not the case then enterprises would be unable to stay on course or successfully respond to a changing environment. The navigation system is itself called a **Lean Navigation System**.

All enterprises need to create their own unique management system and their own way – their 'Lean Way'. Change is most effective when it is carried out through an experiential learning process. At the same time, change has to be focused, successful and effective; in an increasingly competitive market, time to successfully implement change and to achieve significant results is an ever decreasing luxury. This is particularly true for enterprises that are highly likely to be, if they are not already, challenged by other competitors following a 'Lean Way' of their own. Because of this, a Lean Navigation System, by its very design, must be able to adapt, respond and continually learn. It needs to prioritise and rapidly implement change, freeing up more resources to create further change. This helps an enterprise to quickly accelerate towards a better and brighter future. The starting gun has already been fired ... and the race is on. Enterprises that are either unwilling or too slow to change from a more 'Traditional Way' are likely to find that they eventually fall by the wayside, as those successfully adopting a 'Lean Way' emerge, develop and prosper. Such a significant change in direction can be extremely challenging for any enterprise. Because of this, **Lean Navigators** are often called upon, particularly in the early stages, to provide guidance and to help introduce a Lean Navigation System. This book describes a Lean Navigation System and highlights a number of ways that key stakeholders, supported by Lean Navigators using **Lean Filters**, help to ensure they are successfully implemented.

The role of a 'Lean Enterprise' goes beyond that of providing more and more value to customers. It also involves operating in harmony with us all as individuals, communities and the environment as a whole. Hence a 'Lean Enterprise' creates more meaningful work for their employees, increased community well-being and a more sustainable environment. They also reduce risk and provide increasing returns for investors. The book therefore explores in more detail the wider relationships between enterprises, communities, the environment and us as individuals. It describes a unique, yet simple, high level system – a **Lean World System** – one capable of exploring and understanding the types of dynamic relationships that exist, whilst highlighting the more holistic role of enterprise.

The book uses the Lean World System to demonstrate some of the additional roles a Lean Enterprise plays, including:

- Reducing much of the frustration and stress currently experienced in daily life, and
- Improving the environment and the sustainability of our planet's resources.

It concludes by taking a wider perspective, exploring progress towards a 'Lean World' and the role technology is starting to play. It also explores what it might mean for us all as individuals and communities in the future.

However, the book starts by going 'back to basics'. It is important that the book begins by defining 'Lean' more precisely and describing both its origin and application. It will explore the principles of 'Lean Thinking', its initial development and continued success within the manufacturing sector, as well as highlighting its ever increasing application in the service sector. The book will also highlight ways to explore the natural dynamics within any system – techniques known as 'Systems Thinking'. The application of these approaches is necessary to ensure enterprises are designed to be responsive and successful in their goals. They are also needed to understand the bigger picture; the dynamics that naturally occur between enterprises and the environment in which they operate.

As you read this book, I hope you also join me and the ever increasing numbers of 'Lean' leaders and practitioners around the world, all stepping forward together and playing a key role in changing our world – for the better.

Part One

Introduction

Chapter 1

What is Lean?

The biggest mistake often made when applying 'LEAN' is to assume it involves 'slimming down' – 'cutting out the fat', 'reducing cost' or 'eliminating waste'. It does not mean this at all. Lean involves 'creating more value' and 'removing the barriers to delivering more value' – this results in 'fitness, prosperity and growth'. It creates 'stability, agility and sustainability' and places customers at the heart of 'innovation' and 'continuous improvement'.

Few companies create long term profitable growth by simply cutting costs. Yet many change activities still fall into the trap of being internally driven and primarily focused on cost reduction (e.g. consolidation, off-shoring and outsourcing). Few change initiatives are truly customer driven, despite the hype. Most customer programmes are focused on trying to improve how a customer, or their order/request, is 'processed', rather than helping to improve the real value they receive. The tremendous success of companies like Toyota are not the result of a cost cutting strategy, but a long term strategy focused on continuous improvement and adding more and more value, as perceived by their customers.

Let's take a different perspective for a moment. Within every species in the animal kingdom, individuals that are very thin are often weak and those that are very large are often slow. Those that survive and most likely to prosper in the long term are those that are lean – strong, fit and agile. To take this one step further let us consider a marathon runner. One may well think becoming a lean marathon runner involves building up muscle and removing body fat. If taken separately, a potential marathon runner could build up their muscle by using weights and remove fat by going on a diet. They may never practice long distance running at all. In reality, successful marathon runners have to practice a great deal to build up their stamina, develop their body as a whole and optimise their level of stored fat. In fact, fat is crucial to balancing the overall level of energy resources available to a runner during the race. Without the right balance, a marathon runner is extremely unlikely to compete effectively and worse still, could suffer significant physical difficulties in pursuit of their goal. Without understanding the system as a whole and being clear of the end goal, the runner could have wrongly chosen to reduce their energy intake and lower their overall body metabolism, without creating any improvement to their fitness or stamina at all. This simple analogy highlights a number of key aspects of Lean; such as being clear about the goal and understanding the system as a whole, not just the individual parts. Others include taking a long term view, learning by doing, adopting continuous improvement and creating sustainable success.

The types of principles outlined above for the marathon runner may be applied to enterprise. Enterprises who view 'Lean' as simply meaning less of everything (e.g. fewer staff, less inventory, minimal resources) tend to find they indirectly destroy their ability to develop, grow and prosper. The responsibility of creating more is often given to one group (e.g. a revenue challenge given to product/marketing teams) whilst the job of using less of everything is given to another group (e.g. cost reduction challenge given to customer services/operational teams). As a result, enterprises risk becoming blinkered from the overall goal; continuously improving the value created from the customer's perspective and removing any barrier (i.e. waste) encountered. In doing so, many traditional enterprises are embarked upon a continual downward spiral, without even realising it. By focusing on creating less value for less cost, they are effectively commoditising their products/services and putting their future existence at risk. 'Lean' is about creating fitness and growth, as well as a more holistic pursuit of goals.

So what is 'Lean'? The word is used by so many people to mean many different things. For instance, it is used to describe programmes focused on 'removing waste', to describe methods (e.g. Quality Circles, Just-in-Time) or to simply describe tools (e.g. Control charts, Kanbans).

The right definition of 'Lean' is crucial to success in a 'Lean World'. First of all, as stated at the beginning, 'Lean' is about creating more, not less – more value, more sustainable growth and development. However, just like the marathon runner, it is about being fit and agile in order to develop and compete successfully. It is about creating more value but at the same time consuming less (e.g. effort) in the process. Customers, communities, shareholders and the environment, determine value. Anything that directly contributes to the creation of value is classed as value adding, everything else is not. This includes any wasted time, energy, resources, space and inventory. However, it also includes wasted intelligence. Staff must not be overburdened in terms of the mental and physical demands placed upon them. At the same time, capability needs to be developed and collective creativity harnessed.

But 'Lean Thinking' is more than this. **'Lean Thinking'** is actually a **Philosophy** – a philosophy of continuous improvement. The future 'Lean World' is therefore all about **'Continuous Improvement'**; Continuous improvement creating **'Complete Success'**. 'Continuous Improvement' involves everyone and constantly explores new ways to deliver more and more value. 'Complete' means for the customer, employee, enterprise, society, shareholder and the environment. 'Success' is determined by the value created for everyone. It is very noticeable that companies employing 'Lean Thinking' as their philosophy are ones that stand out from the crowd. They are generating growth, developing their staff and constantly increasing the level of value they create.

Without applying 'Lean Thinking' as a philosophy, individuals, enterprises and communities will find it difficult to see the opportunities available for everyone to flourish. Conversely, when 'Lean Thinking' is defined and applied correctly, it has the ability to provide 'the DNA of Success' for individuals, communities, enterprise and the environment. It can help improve the overall well-being and happiness of individuals, families and communities – something that is attracting increasing levels of importance in people's lives.

Whilst exploring the 'Lean World', many things may well begin to appear very different and much simpler than initially thought. 'Lean Thinking' has the power to simplify, but also to create new perspectives and deeper insight. It minimises any unnecessary complexity and introduces continual learning. However, 'Lean Thinking' still fundamentally involves adopting a 'Continuous Improvement' philosophy; one uniquely capable of creating wholesale transformation and resulting in sustained success – i.e. growing value and prosperity (See Figure 1.1). Lean creates clarity in terms of its direction, defining 'What' needs to be improved (e.g. Customer Value) and ensuring it becomes the focus of everyone. In contrast, traditional transformation programmes often fail to create sustainable change, despite their large number and diversity. They tend to suffer from a lack of a clear and unambiguous direction, with separate programmes and approaches regularly implemented in relative isolation from each other and with conflicting objectives [1]. They're also driven by a few individuals and rarely understood or embraced by the many.

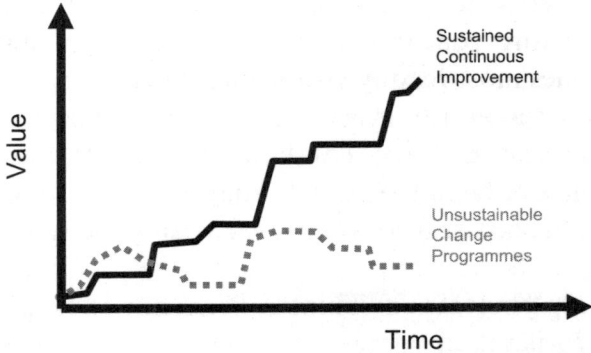

Figure 1.1 Continuous improvement creating transformational change.

Chapter 2

Background

The concept of a Lean World is derived from robust foundations and proven methods. These include philosophies and methods of Lean Thinking and Systems Thinking. Lean Thinking originated from studying the activities of leaders in the Japanese automotive industry; in particular Toyota and the pioneering work of Taiichi Ohno. Toyota also took to heart the teachings of W. Edwards Deming, following his seminars in Japan. Deming brought to the attention of everyone the need for new management practices and became particularly renowned for his pioneering work on Quality [2]. However, his teachings were far more than this. He also highlighted the need for new philosophies and approaches; including i) creating a sense of purpose, ii) adopting continuous improvement and iii) understanding the needs of customers, the nature and flow of work, as well as what makes people 'tick'. By the 1990's, Deming had encapsulated his work into what he called the 'System of Profound Knowledge' [3], an approach not surprisingly intertwined and embedded in Lean Thinking. Lean Thinking therefore provides a powerful set of principles and approaches; ones most readily visible in Toyota.

The dynamic relationships occurring between customers, work teams, individuals and suppliers are also critical to any enterprise. Without a thorough understanding of these, the creation and flow of value across a supply chain cannot be optimised. One element of the 'System of Profound Knowledge', commonly referred to as 'Systems Thinking', is particularly helpful in this regard. Whilst it can successfully help enterprises to understand and align purpose, it also provides an invaluable way of capturing entities and activities and exploring the dynamic relationship between them (called a 'system'). It can provide unique insight into the overall response of a system, as well as potential outcomes under given conditions. It can be used to explore behaviours within an enterprise, as well as between an enterprise and the wider world. Because of this, 'Systems Thinking' is used within this book, in particular to understand some of the relationships between enterprises and their surroundings. More background on both 'Lean Thinking' and 'Systems Thinking' are therefore provided.

Lean Thinking

The word 'Lean' was actually first used to describe the set
of principles and practices that originated from companies like
Toyota in Japan in the 1990's. The term was coined by Jim
Womack, Dan Jones and Daniel Roos, who were part of the
combined US and European task-force studying companies
like Toyota, to understand how they were able to produce
cars customers wanted, twice as quickly, with twice the quality
and half the cost of the Western manufacturers. Their findings,
charted in their landmark publications 'The Machine that
Changed the World' [4] and 'Lean Thinking' [5], focused upon
the principles and practices (e.g. the Toyota Production System)
that have become increasingly widespread across manufacturing,
transforming the whole industry. A number of principles were
proposed to guide any manufacturing firm, including:

- Provide the value actually desired by customers,
- Identify the value stream for each product,
- Create continuous flow of value and eliminating waste,
- Let customers pull value from the enterprise, and
- Continuously drive for perfection, perfect value with zero
  waste.

These guiding principles naturally lead to additional principles,
policies and practices, such as;

- All processes driven by customer expectations,
- Interaction and co-operation between people maximised,
  and
- Decisions being made by those closest to the work.

The Toyota Production System (TPS) is the structure with which
Toyota manages its enterprise, based on applying their founding
Principles (or Philosophies). Today, this has become synony-
mous with many ideas, such as 'Just in Time', 'In-station Quality'

and 'Continuous Improvement'. Such practices are often referred to as 'Lean Production' methods, as they were predominantly applied to the manufacture of 'Products' and the management of the supply value chain. Other manufacturers have sought to introduce them, but often without fully understanding their origins. This has left many wondering why it has not worked as well for them as it has for companies like Toyota. This is because many of them have missed the key point. The true innovation and transformation was not the Toyota Production System itself, but the creation and adoption of the founding principles for their enterprise, which in itself created the right structures and practices for them. Many of the principles underpinning Toyota's success have been well documented [6], including:

- Making decisions based on a long term philosophy,
- Levelling the work-load and minimising any overburden,
- Creating end to end process flow,
- Using flow to expose problems and eliminate waste,
- Using 'pull' methods to minimise over-production,
- Using innovation and continuous improvement to become a learning organisation,
- Developing leaders, empowering employees and involving everyone, and
- Respecting customers, suppliers and communities served.

These types of principles provide a glimpse of the 'DNA of Success' in Toyota. Whilst Toyota's main competitors have continued to slip back and shed staff, Toyota's pioneering approach has continued to see them successfully grow and flourish. It has been the most profitable automobile manufacturer for some time, and it became the biggest in the world in 2007. The learning from this is critical – Lean is not about copying tools or practices; it is about implementing the principles that allow an enterprise to continuously improve the value it provides to its customers, employees, individuals, society and the environment.

Lean Thinking is also now being applied in the service sector, pioneered by companies such as Tesco, Fujitsu Services and

General Electric [7]. The foundations of Lean Thinking turn out to be just as applicable to service industries, albeit with slightly different emergent characteristics in certain key areas. In the case of a service company, customers get more involved in the process as they consume the services the company provides. For instance, a customer going into hospital is personally diagnosed and treated by doctors, a customer entering a restaurant chooses and eats the meal they wish to have. However, in all cases the customer wants:

*   What they want,
*   When they want it,
*   Where they want it, and
*   How they want it.

They also require it:

*   To satisfy their needs completely and exactly,
*   To be provided with minimum additional demand being placed upon them, and
*   To not waste their time.

The level of personalisation and choice required by individual customers is wide-ranging. Expectations are also growing by the day. The impact on the volume, variety and variation of products or services a company has to offer is immense. Indeed, the same customer may themselves have completely different needs at different times of the day, or under different circumstances. It can also become increasingly difficult to smooth out any variation in the volume of customer demand. This is because the customer, in the process of consuming the service, is often an integral part of the process. For instance, in an Accident and Emergency department, there is invariably a wide variety of conditions that patients arrive with, and a patient cannot simply be told 'Sorry, we did not expect so many people to break their leg today, so you'll have to come back tomorrow!' Likewise, they do not want to wait in a queue. Enterprises are increasingly recognising that they cannot view a customer's time as 'Free', particularly in service industries and highly competitive environments.

Supply management in a service industry can often be more complex than in a manufacturing industry. They have to consider a wider variety of options to ensure a smooth flow of work with minimum delay to the customer. Often, additional strategies need to be considered which are capable of providing additional resource flexibility to cope with different demand levels and types. For instance, this could include the call-up of additional staff in situations of high demand. A good example of this can be seen in supermarkets, where staff stacking shelves may be temporarily called upon to attend check-outs during periods of peak demand.

In traditional companies, delays, errors and waste, along with customer and employee frustration, all occur when departments are managed in isolation and given individual internal performance targets to meet. The problem with this is that customers only see and judge a company as a whole. Moreover, customers want companies to understand and satisfy their needs; they do not want to have to spend their time understanding how companies work in order to get what they want.

Leading service companies pay special attention to making sure the organisation is managed as a whole (a System) and with a common purpose. Powered by Deming's insights [2,3], they have begun to use alternative strategies and approaches, including focusing upon:

- Customer purpose (rather than selling products),
- Delivering what matters to customers (rather than satisfying internal measures and goals), and
- Continually improving the end to end capability (i.e. the means) to create value for customers (rather than improving internal functional outputs).

Findings, from early adopters following this path, have already begun to demonstrate how service enterprises can truly re-align their business more closely around their customers, reduce waste, differentiate themselves from their competitors and improve employee satisfaction – all at the same time! They highlight how traditional service companies, by their very design, can systematically spend most of their time and resources (between 40–90%) delivering no value to customers at all, frustrating their customers and employees alike. By removing the causes of this and aligning around new structures and goals, companies are starting to re-orientate themselves, add more value for their customers, grow revenues and increase profitability. It also enables them to properly support and develop their work-force, support their local community and increasingly help the environment – value for everyone.

As an example, let us briefly consider traditional companies operating a call centre which delivers goods or services. Call centres have become increasingly prevalent over the last decade or so and yet are also the source of a great deal of frustration from a customer's perspective [8]. Traditionally, call centres have been managed as separate entities, as functions in their own right. They also often use functional measures such as call handling time (CHT) and abandoned call rates (ACR). As a result, customers making a call can often find their needs are not properly captured or taken into account. Errors and misunder-standings occur, resulting in further calls, unnecessary additional work and possible complaints. For example, this could be due to customers not explicitly realising that they have to be present at the time of a delivery/visit, or because the product/service delivered is not what the customer requested. It could also occur if the product/service the customer actually requires turns out to be rather different to that requested, leaving field operatives without the necessary items or skills to provide them. Such failures are only made worse when the delivery agent or service engineer has their own independent (and inappropriate) set of targets to meet too (e.g. visits/person/day). All of these can result in more calls being made to the call centre, either to chase the company, re-arrange another delivery/visit or to complain ... and these additional calls are often handled in the same way again!

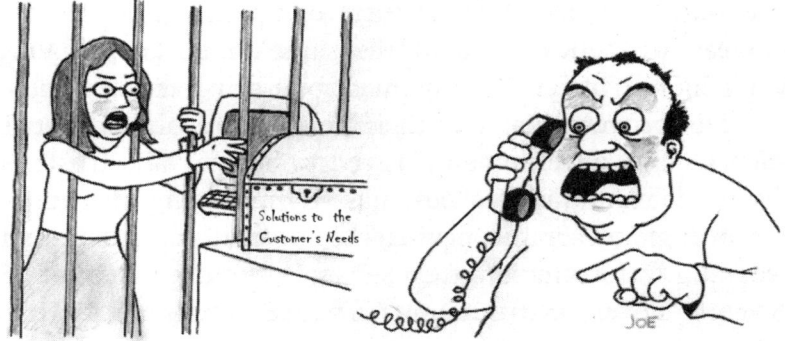

Figure 1.2 Customer and employee frustration in call centres.

This creates huge frustration and stress for customers and employees alike. Without more of an understanding of the nature of demand (e.g. new orders versus order chasing), this can create further pressure to handle calls even quicker to avoid additional abandoned calls. The whole operation begins a systematic and downward spiral, with overburdened staff becoming increasingly less able to provide value to their customers. Companies may consider further automation (e.g. through increased use of Interactive Voice Response) or moving their call centre to lower labour rate economies, to cope with the continual growth in call volumes. However, what's often missed is the fact that up to 90% of received calls result from failure; failure created by the operation itself which generates additional customer demand ('failure demand'). By changing the organisation to be able to more fully understand the nature of demand and to diagnose the true root cause of the problems, such demands are systematically eliminated rather than processed, automated or outsourced. The freed up time and resources can then be used to more fully understand and respond to individual customer's needs, with employees increasingly able to ask, listen and provide real value to individual customers.

A call centre which is part of a mail order company may start to reduce its focus on handling calls quickly to handling calls effectively, reducing its emphasis on scripts, to take the time to listen to and understand their customers' individual needs. They can then begin to use this knowledge to make sure the customer gets exactly what they want, how they want and when they want. The additional insight acquired can also be used, either to instigate improvements or highlight opportunities for further product/service development. Any problems, such as faulty goods or delivery failures, are picked up quickly by the call centre, the source of the problem identified and subsequently eliminated. For example, one mail order company found that the special delivery instructions, requested by customers (e.g. to avoid a certain time or to deliver it to a neighbour), were being recorded, but not subsequently provided to the person responsible for delivering the items (they were actually being placed inside the packages instead!). As a result, delivery personnel placed more calling cards through letter boxes, asking customers to ring in to the call centre in order to arrange another visit. By changing the process end to end, such problems disappear and the overall operation starts to become more effective.

Extending this, a number of leading service organisations are starting to broaden their horizons and alter their focus still further. They are beginning to align their purpose more closely with those of their customers; moving away from putting 'service wraps' around products and moving towards 'productising' services (or solutions) customers actually want. For instance, a growing number of enterprises, previously known for selling telecommunications and IT (e.g. telephones, networks and IT), are beginning to engage their customers in very different ways in order to provide more value for them. Such enterprises (e.g. Fujitsu Services) are increasingly productising services; creating more meaningful relationships with their customers and providing solutions that satisfy their needs more effectively. Those that are not doing this, risk being left behind and being subject to a negative downward spiral; as more traditional products and service wraps either become obsolete or a commodity. In the telecommunications and IT sector in particular, this situation is being compounded by growing levels of technology convergence, the increasing availability of bandwidth and growing levels of intelligence. For instance, traditional telecommunications companies are under more and more pressure from the development and deployment of a range of new technologies, such as WiFi, fixed-mobile convergence and Peer-to-Peer (P2P) technology. These are not just being set up by other companies either; they are being set up by communities and consumers too – in a growing trend of 'user created infrastructure'. This partly explains the rapid and successful emergence of new service companies such as Skype – an enterprise created with a bare minimum amount of capital investment and sold to eBay for $2.6 billion in 2005.

Figure 1.3 From selling communications products (Servicing Products) to developing relationships and providing solutions (Productising Service).

By focusing on potential solutions to customers real needs, a vast array of new opportunities can be opened up. However, new strategies and approaches are needed to expose and exploit them. For instance, by adopting Lean principles Fujitsu Services successfully developed its 'Sense and Respond' approach and became one of the first IT Service businesses to break away from more traditional IT business models [7,9]. It successfully re-focused itself around the real needs of its customers and transformed its market propositions. In the future, enterprises will need highly collaborative and flexible partnerships, involving both customers and suppliers, in order to optimise the value chain and to create an effective whole. By focusing on customer value and flow, Lean Thinking provides an unrivalled ability to optimise value chains. By extending this to customer demand and purpose, value chains become even more responsive to customers' needs. Given Lean Thinking is also heavily influenced by the work of Deming, the development and support of staff, as well as the wider community, also remain core purposes too. As a result of all these things, it is not surprising that Lean Thinking has stood the test of time and proven its ability to create more holistic, adaptive and sustainable enterprises – enterprises of the future.

Lean Thinking, in its widest context, provides both a set of principles and a framework for creating a more holistic customer driven enterprise, one which is highly adaptable to its environment and ever changing customer needs. It has the ability to:

- Lock onto and deliver what matters to customers,
- Systematically eliminating combined causes of waste and cost,
- Free up resources to increase the capability of the enterprise, and
- Continually create and improve the products and services provided.

This involves top down and bottom up change, creating an enterprise increasingly driven by customers, continuously improving and differentiating itself from its competitors.

Growing numbers of service companies are attempting to apply Lean Thinking to their enterprise, but many of these remain frustrated in their struggle to create successful and sustainable change. This is often because, just like their manufacturing counterparts before them, many are still trying to use 'tools' to improve their processes, or their staff, without any understanding or change to the overall 'system' driving them.

Without this level of attention, such companies are unfortunately resigning themselves to continual frustration and eventual failure. As an example, if a process is made more efficient, then some staff are naturally freed up from their current work. If a decision is taken to simply lay-off freed up staff (i.e. to 'cash the cheque'), then it should be of little surprise that the motivation and willingness of remaining staff to support such initiatives reduces. If this happens it becomes more difficult to implement continuous improvement.

In studying this whole area, it has becoming increasingly apparent that there are two general paths companies are taking – a 'Traditional Way' and a 'Lean Way'. These paths are shown in Figure 1.4. The path taken is determined upfront by the strategy adopted for freed up resources. The 'Traditional Way' highlights the route taken by those companies who primarily see the opportunity to be one of laying off freed up staff. When this path is taken, the work-force loses motivation and trust and becomes highly defensive. It offers little additional help to improve capability or to implement improvement. This is particularly catastrophic, given that many of the good ideas come from front-line staff and any desired changes ultimately need their support if they are to be implemented effectively. Managers and specialist teams, often remote from the actual work, are increasingly required to identify what to improve and to then implement it (i.e. 'drive it in'). More improvement failures naturally occur as a result. Functional silos and specialisations persist and more and more change projects are introduced by an expanding 'management factory'. To counter-balance and spread the additional overhead costs associated with this, greater targets are often set for front line staff to increase the number of parts/service they provide per hour – namely 'Productivity Drives'. This whole approach creates a negative and downward spiral of reduced customer outcomes, loyalty and revenues. This will continue to occur until a company either embraces an alternative way and changes course, or disappears completely due to a process of natural selection. A Lean Way provides an alternative course. Its primary intention is one of utilising freed

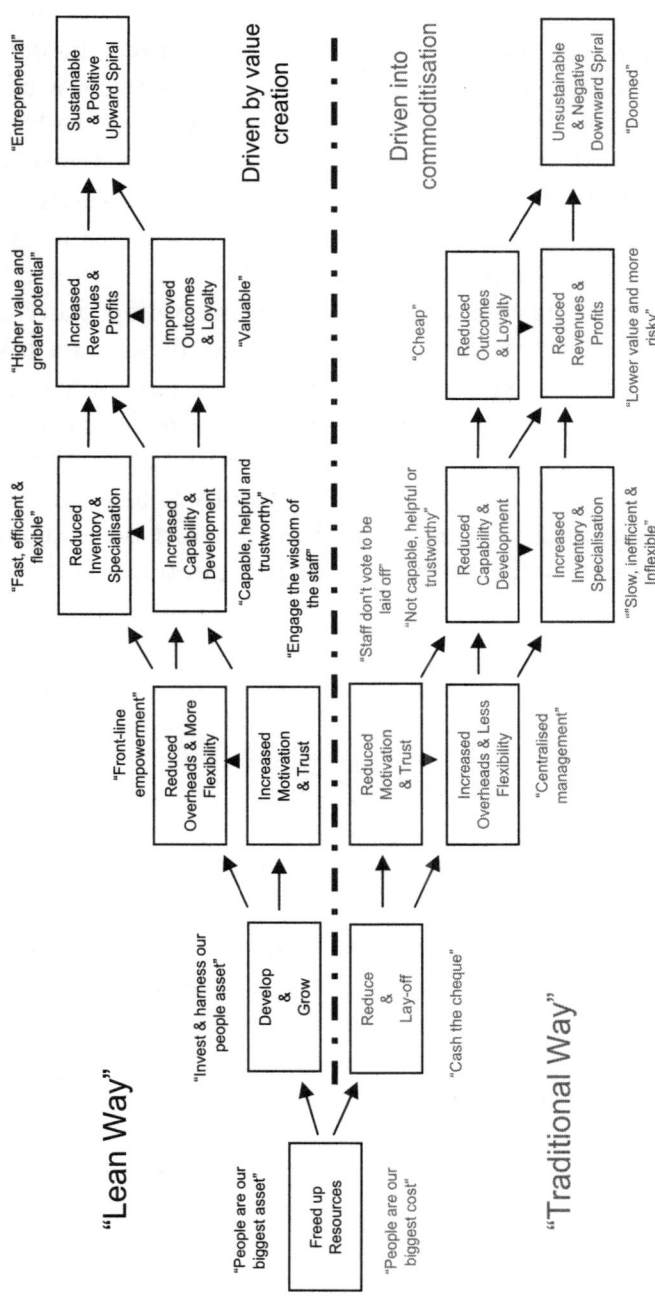

Figure 1.4 The 'Traditional Way' and 'Lean Way'.

up resources, developing their people and create more ways their company can add value for their customers. This approach creates a positive spiral of development and growth, involving customers and front-line staff alike. It increases levels of motivation and trust, breaks down functional barriers and reduces overheads. Staff work closely together with customers to identify new and better ways of providing value; a characteristic sometimes referred to as 'field innovation'.

On considering what has happened in the automobile industry, history to date has shown that competitors (e.g. GM, Ford) find it extremely difficult to catch up with those who take the lead (i.e. Toyota). By freeing up resources and utilising those resources to identify new ways to provide value, a chain reaction occurs which allows a company, which starts to lead the way, to catch up and continue to accelerate away from any competitors. The challenge today to traditional enterprises is a stark one – move to the alternative path soon, or risk extinction!

Systems Thinking

Systems Thinking is a powerful approach that can be used to understand and communicate the dynamic nature of the world around us. It explores and explains the relationships between connected entities that together form a system [10]. It provides the context in which to view a complete system, which reduces the risk of decisions being made in isolation and in the absence of a full understanding of additional consequences that could potentially occur.

It can be used to model virtually any system, from simple problem solving to more complex relationships such as stress, enterprises, economies, populations and the environment. Virtually any model is a simplification of reality, but by using systematic approaches to create them they are able to provide a great deal of invaluable insight. Systems Thinking models are particularly useful to capture interdependent entities in a system, understand the ways they connect together and the dynamic relationships between them. Whilst some models built are highly complex in their nature and level of detail (e.g. detailed economic computer models), models do not always have to take a lot of time or be highly detailed in order to provide valuable insight or start to predict behaviour.

In Systems Thinking, simple causal loop diagrams can be used to describe relatively complex systems, in terms of cause and effect relationships. They are able to provide both context and insight as to what is important and the general behaviour of a system. They represent a system clearly and succinctly, allowing complex systems to be communicated and explored in a simple way. They help enterprises to avoid poor decisions and to make sure that changes are successful.

A commonly used example of a simple causal loop diagram is shown in Figure 1.5 and demonstrates a number of key features. The model demonstrates the process of taking action to achieve a particular desired state. The diagram shows how a current state will steadily move towards the desired state, as a result of

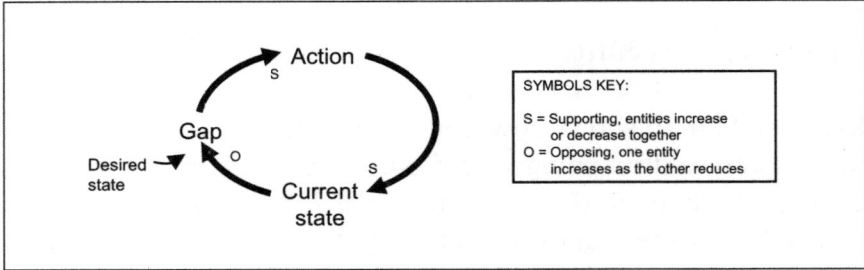

Figure 1.5 Simple Causal Loop diagram for reaching a desired state by taking action.

continued action to reduce the gap. It is like a central heating (or air conditioning) system responding to the temperature setting of a thermostat. Interrelationships between entities either show a subsequent entity being 'Supported' by the growth of the previous one (labelled 'S'), or 'Opposed' by its growth and therefore reduced (labelled 'O'). If there are an odd number of 'O's', then it is known as a 'balancing loop'. Balancing loops tends toward the desired target or goal, as in this example.

This could for instance represent a functional team striving to meet their target (e.g. a productivity or sales target), or an improvement team trying to reach their goal (e.g. reducing costs by a certain amount). Such a team will identify and implement actions to reduce the gap between the current and desired state, until the desired state is met. Once it is met, the team will tend to either relax or, more likely, be given a new/different target and goal. This explains why setting a target and paying attention to it often creates improvement. However, it also explains why many of these improvements are regularly short lived; disappearing once either the attention or target is removed.

Setting a desired state (e.g. a target) can generate other unwanted characteristics too. As with any complex system, any action taken can also create unintended consequences as well. For instance, when a central heating system is controlled by a single thermostat, an individual starting to feel hot may open a window/door next to them (an unintended consequence). This allows cooler air to enter and more heat to escape, which forces the central heating system to work harder to reach/maintain the desired temperature. To take unintended consequences into account, the model has to be developed further. An additional loop is added to show other consequences that could occur as a result of the action being taken (see Figure 1.6). In the example shown, the additional consequences are negatively impacting on the current state (denoted by the 'O'), opposing the otherwise positive effects of the actions taken. In this case the outside loop is actually a 're-enforcing loop' (i.e. the opposite of a 'balancing loop'), derived from the fact that there are an even number of 'O's' around it in totality. In this case, if the impact of unintended consequences is worse than the otherwise positive outcomes from the actions, then the gap will start to get progressively wider, not reduce! This situation is not as uncommon as one might think, particularly over the medium/long term, as there can sometimes be a significant time lag between a particular action being taken and the impact of unintended consequences becoming apparent. When this is the case, early positive results can be mistakenly used to indicate success and result in attention being diverted elsewhere.

This type of model can be used to explain why, by giving a target to a particular function, it is often achieved (e.g. jobs/person/day in a field team). But it can also show why such targets are regularly achieved at the expense of others (e.g. customers, call centre operations, suppliers) or the value chain as a whole

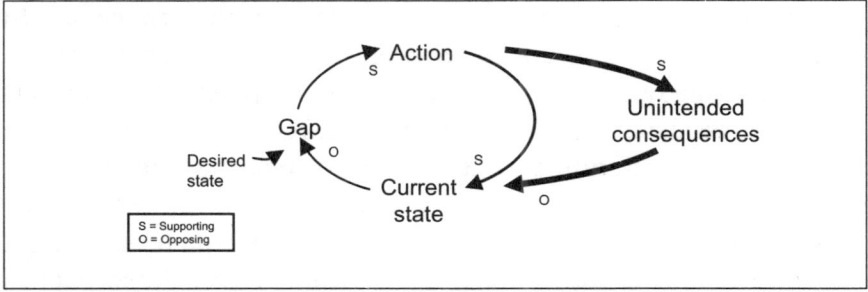

Figure 1.6 Simple Causal Loop diagram showing unintended consequences, highlighting how a potential fix can fail or make things even worse.

(e.g. increased errors, re-work and inventory). Changes made by other functions can also negatively impact on their own. Measures and goals therefore need to relate to value, from the end users perspective and to the value chain as a whole (e.g. % customer requests perfectly met). Only by doing this can any sub-optimisation be avoided and the complete value chain aligned to the needs of the customer.

Setting targets, without a proper understanding of how they are able to be achieved, can also result in cheating. Setting increased functional productivity targets are particularly renowned for this. For instance, a stretching productivity target (i.e. jobs/man/day) given to a field team can result in them working faster, but with reduced quality of workmanship. This can create more faults and problems down the line for their customers; problems almost invariably more costly to fix at a later stage. This can create a negative impact on the customer's experience, increase overall costs and stop customers from getting what they want. It also often results in additional measures and targets being added, in an attempt to stop all the potential cheating strategies. In reality this serves only to increase complexity and management cost. The best way to stop cheating is to stop setting arbitrary targets! The best process for setting a future performance target involves obtaining a thorough under-standing of the operation, the key barriers to performance, as well as their relative impact. Once all of these are known, changes can be identified, prioritised and planned, and expected levels of performance improvement understood. Hence, the proper way to determine a target in effect removes the need to set a target! Perceived management wisdom of adding more and more targets therefore needs to be replaced by a philosophy of ensuring a thorough understanding of their operation and progressively eliminating targets!

Additional unintended consequences also include reduced staff morale and increased customer frustration. Whilst the impact of unintended consequences can often be delayed they can also be very great (e.g. no repeat orders). They are often the things that result in an enterprise going out of business (e.g. no customers)!

Hence, unintended consequences should never be overlooked and companies should stop any activity that's destined to fail or likely to make things worse. Instead they need to focus their energy and resources on identifying those things that really matter to customers and systematically removing the barriers stopping them from providing even more value to them. By doing this, they will start their journey along a different way – a Lean Way.

Part Two

Lean Enterprise Management

Enterprises around the world are increasingly applying 'Lean Thinking' within their organisations. However, whilst most companies are applying tools, leading enterprises are successfully applying Lean as their philosophy, transforming their organisations forever. They are embarked on very different strategies, using continuous improvement to create transformation and to generate successful outcomes for everyone – customers, employees, investors, communities and the environment.

Lean is a journey of discovery and offers a new path to a different world – a Lean World. The destination and routes individual enterprises take will rarely be the same, but the principles they apply will. Such philosophies and principles start to provide a blueprint for success (i.e. the DNA of Success™). However, more is needed (i.e. the complete DNA). To date, the somewhat limited application of 'Lean Thinking' (i.e. applying tools rather than philosophies) has been, at least in part, due to leaders not being able to clearly visualise what 'Lean Thinking' actually looks like or what it could mean for them. Few executives are brave or bold enough to take a radically different path, without a better understanding of both of these things. Those that do are often referred to as leaders who are prepared to take a 'leap of faith' or possess a unique entrepreneurial flair. Neither of these has to be true, although they may sometimes help! Enterprises embarking on a Lean Way gather data in order to learn, make decisions carefully and act decisively. Many understand Lean principles and often point out they are mostly common sense. Companies applying Lean Thinking often create a future state vision and roadmap for a particular process. However, the elements that have, until now, been missing are a clear visual understanding of what a Lean Enterprise looks like as a whole and how any enterprise can become one.

By observing leading enterprises and by going 'back to basics', the 'DNA of Success' has been uncovered further. A unique and generic management system – called the Lean World Management System – has been successfully identified. It can be applied to any enterprise and it is capable of creating sustained success.

The Lean World Management System provides a model for how companies, governments and agencies, can successfully co-operate together with common purposes and in doing so provide more value for everyone. This includes individuals (customers and employees), communities (families, friends, nations) and the overall environment they rely upon. However, enterprises do not always have to exist. Around the world, groups of individuals can be found organising themselves on a daily basis. They support each other and carry out all the tasks they collectively need to do, without the need for money or enterprise structures. Some build shelters, some farm or hunt and others provide clean water. In more developed communities, communication, resources and knowledge have led to mankind creating enterprises capable of sharing out day to day tasks even more effectively. They have also allowed more specialist skills to develop and for additional activities to be carried out. Some educate the young, others help the sick or injured, whilst others research additional ways to enhance people's lives and improve the environment in which they live.

All enterprise systems interact with individuals, communities, as well as the overall environment. One should never consider an enterprise in isolation from its surroundings. They exist within an overall system containing many symbiotic relationships (see part III, The Lean World). If this is not done, enterprises risk taking on a purpose all of their own, striving for goals that do not positively support others or the environment. For instance, they could create more stress and anxiety for individuals, divide communities, destroy habitats or even eliminate the planet! A Lean World Management System is one that helps enterprises create positive outcomes; to reduce stress and anxiety, connect and develop communities and also support the environment.

The Lean World Management System is a management system for governing a Lean Enterprise. It is used by employees, within an enterprise, to serve individual customers and communities, whilst seeking to positively support the environment. At its very highest level, it is represented as a house (see Figure 2.1). It includes the foundations ('direction setting') used to underpin the pillars ('processes' – often called 'value streams') that support the roof ('outcomes'). This simple house analogy offers a unique and meaningful way to visualise a complete management system.

It classifies and describes the key activities required within any successful enterprise, from strategy and direction setting, through to the various processes required and the outcomes that result. This chapter describes in more detail the individual components of the management system, and in doing so it allows everyone (e.g. executives, management and front line staff) to visualize a Lean Enterprise in a more meaningful way.

To implement a Lean World Management System in an enterprise today involves a significant amount of change. Companies

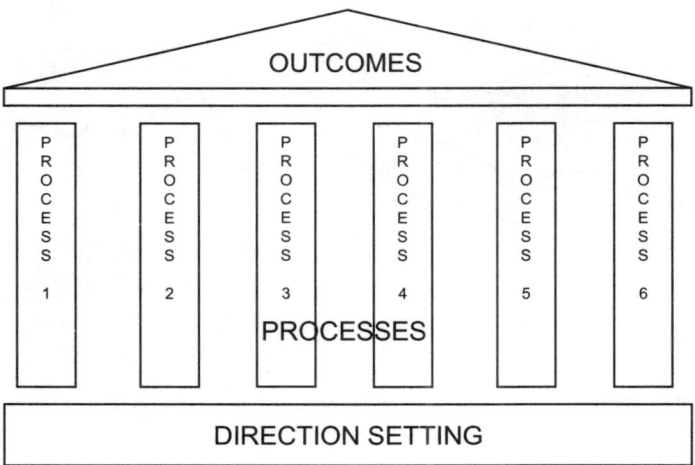

Figure 2.1 High Level Lean World Management System.

need to leave behind traditional ways and strike out along a new way, a Lean Way (see Figure 2.2). The destination is a much better place (i.e. 'paradise' instead of 'desert') and each company has to find the best path for them. As time progresses, pot holes increasingly appear along the Traditional Way whilst the Lean Way becomes further hidden (e.g. by mountains). Changing course is possible as opportunities exist for all those wishing to change direction (e.g. shown pictorially in the form of bridges, tunnels, boats and ladders). However, the gap between the two paths gets wider as time progresses and the initial change in direction becomes more difficult. Hence, embarking on a Lean journey and implementing a Lean World Management System should be started as soon as possible.

Implementing such a system is not easy and doesn't happen overnight. It takes time and energy. However, by going down this path, it increasingly frees up resources and creates huge amounts of motivation and energy. When an enterprise embarks on a Lean Way, it is like a snow-ball rolling down a hill; once it starts,

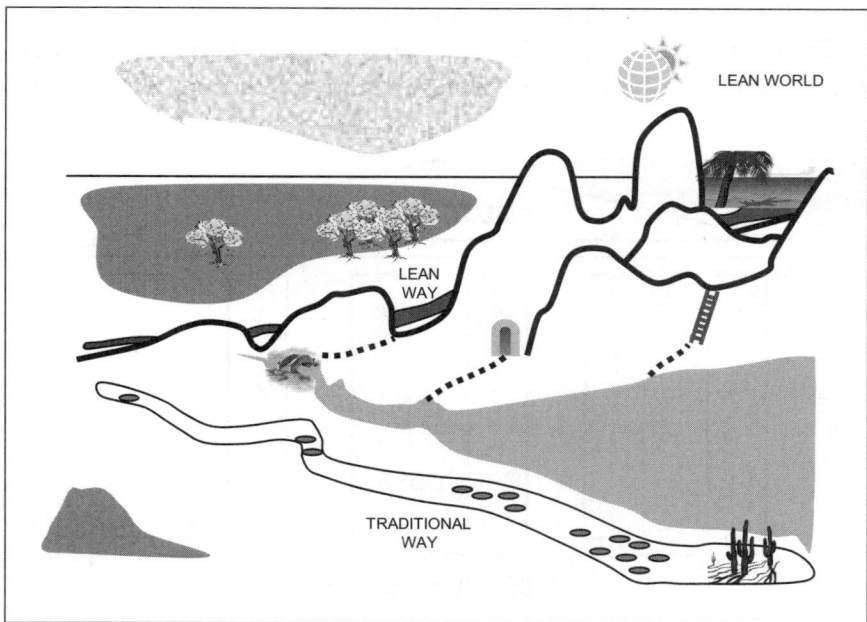

Figure 2.2 A Lean Way to a Lean World.

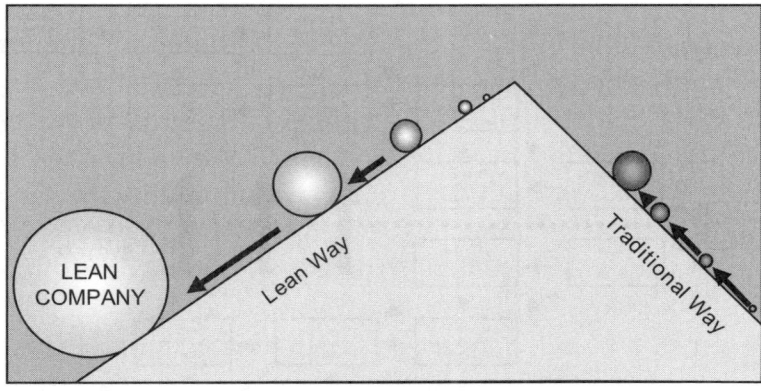

Figure 2.3 Lean companies gathering momentum.

it picks up momentum and pace, and quickly reaches a point where it is hard to stop and difficult to catch (see Figure 2.3). The gulf only gets wider and the obstacles faced by traditional companies get ever larger (see Figure 2.2). Those blissfully unaware, or choosing to blinker themselves from the task in hand, need only ask one question; 'How much longer will their business survive when competitors are transforming their businesses in this way?'

Care and guidance are needed along a lean journey; particularly at the point the enterprise steps off their current journey and starts to significantly alter its course (Figure 2.4). However, enterprises must not only change course, they need to stay on course. For this reason, any change system must become an integral part of the management system. It should therefore be of little surprise that the change system, known as the 'Lean Navigation System', is comprised of components that are already contained within the Lean World Management System itself.

Traditional companies tend to create change using bottom up approaches (by front line teams) or top down approaches (by central change teams). For instance, front line staff may be involved in local improvement initiatives, or submit improvement ideas to management. Whilst this increases the level of support and involvement of staff, these approaches by themselves tend to create a wealth of ideas but suffer from a lack of clear and

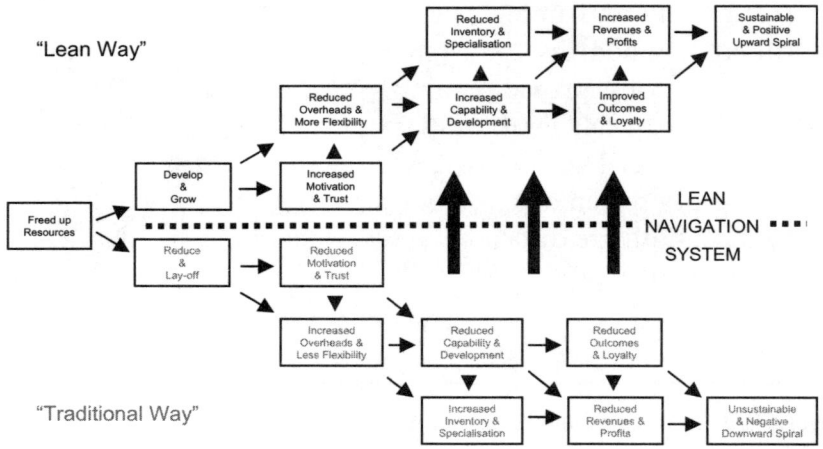

Figure 2.4 Changing to a 'Lean Way' using a 'Lean Navigation System'.

consistent direction. Managers also often become concerned about a potential loss of control. Top down approaches, such as some six sigma programmes, tend to provide more control and prescription. However, more often than not, centralised change teams are deployed and moved from project to project in an attempt to understand and resolve specific performance problems. Whilst this provides an increased level of control, they rarely involve everyone or focus on what really matters to customers. They rarely change the enterprise management system in any significant way (e.g. performance management systems) and often only result in 'sticking plasters' being placed on broken processes in order to create 'Quick Wins'. Without focus, commitment and involvement of everyone to radically change end to end processes, most change programmes are destined to fail to create any real or sustainable improvement.

The 'Lean Navigation System' uniquely joins together policy deployment with continuous improvement. By doing this, it is able to surpass more traditional 'Lean' approaches, which tend to be characterised by a slow and gradual implementation across an enterprise. The enthusiasm and involvement of everyone is combined with clear direction and prioritisation from executive teams. By doing this, enterprises are able to harness innovation, reflect carefully and implement quickly. They are also able to co-ordinate, standardise and pull through the changes needed. 'Lean Navigators' provide support to enterprises who are installing a 'Lean Navigation System'. They stop them from stalling or falling. They help them to create the means to improve and the ability to remove any barriers, quickly. Because of their importance, both are discussed in more detail in Chapter 4.

Chapter 3

Lean World Management System

The 'Lean World Management System' is a management system for governing a 'Lean' enterprise. It consists of a simple one page model to describe a whole enterprise. It can be applied to any enterprise, manufacturer or service provider, public or private, big or small, local or global ... and provides a new approach to management.

The 'Lean World Management System' is visually represented by the model shown in Figure 2.5. The model breaks down into three key areas, strategic direction setting ('foundations'), processes ('pillars' & 'cross-beams') and outcomes ('roof'). Strategic direction setting is responsible for providing the overall direction of the company. The processes are the means by which the company moves forward and delivers the products and services that provide value to others (often referred to as value streams). The outcomes define the value resulting from the products and services provided.

The Lean World Management System provides the individual components required to implement and run a successful enterprise. Strategic direction setting creates the 'foundation', from a company's values through to the policies it deploys. The 'pillars' are made up of the processes needed within a Lean enterprise, including:

1. Relationships Development – establishing relationships with customers and understanding their needs,
2. Provision – creating value for customers from the

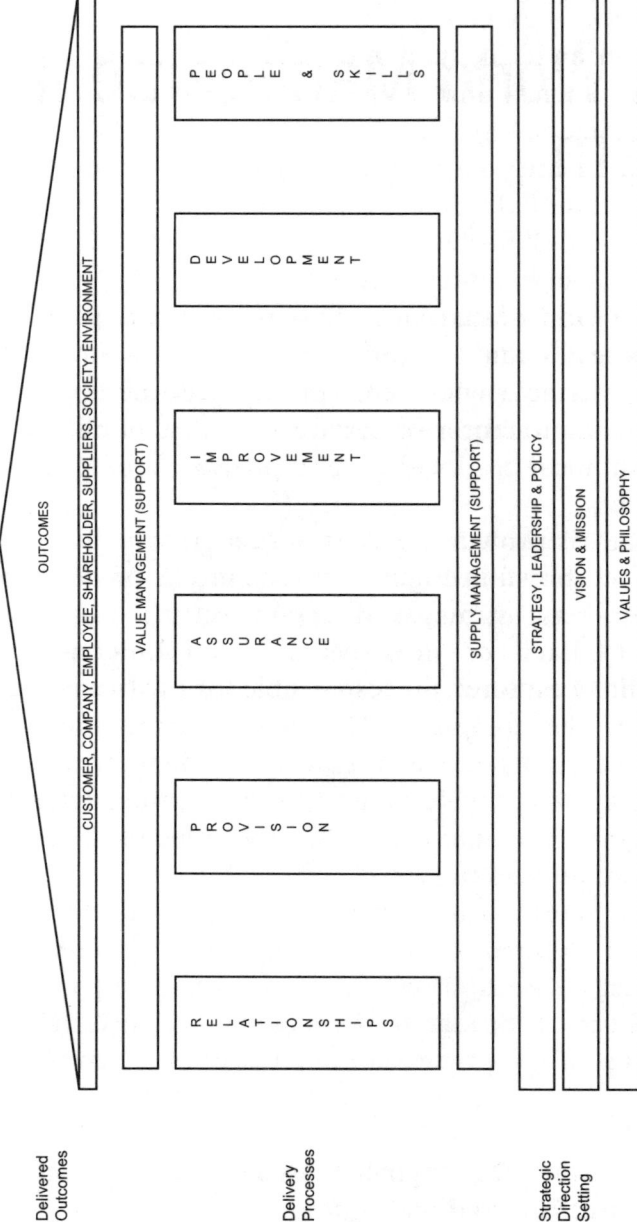

Figure 2.5 The Lean World Management System™.

product/services the enterprise is currently capable of providing,

3. Assurance – avoiding and recovering from problems that occur when trying to satisfy a customer's needs,
4. Improvement – improving the capability to provide value to customers,
5. Development – developing new products/services which offer additional value to customers,
6. People and Skills Development – developing the capability and skills of individuals and teams,
7. Supply Management – supplying material and resources to all processes, and
8. Value Management – determining the capability and accounting for the level of value provided to all stakeholders.

These processes provide the overall delivery capability to create outcomes for all stakeholders, including customer value, total shareholder returns, as well as individual and community development. Each component of the 'Lean World Management System' will be explored in more detail in the following sections.

Strategic Direction Setting

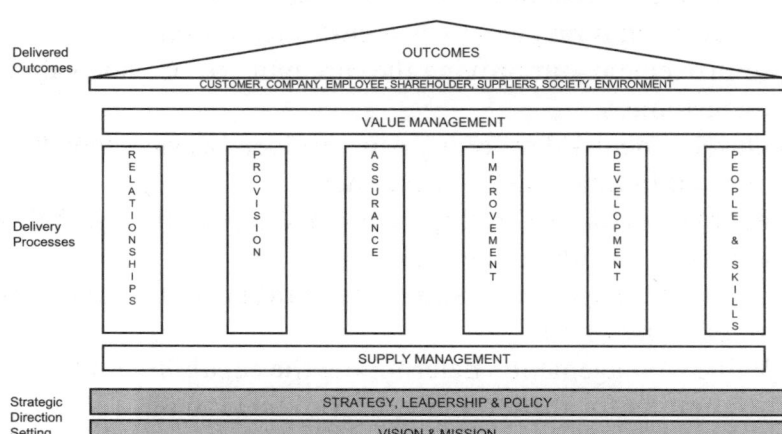

Figure 2.6 Strategic Direction Setting in the Lean World Management System.

Strategic direction setting is crucial to the overall success of a Lean enterprise (see Figure 2.6). It defines the 'what' and the 'how', which themselves determine how effective the enterprise will be. To understand this more, we need to define what effectiveness is. Effectiveness means 'being capable of producing a desired effect'. Effectiveness and efficiency are often thought to mean similar things, but they do not. Efficient means having a high ratio of output to input. Therefore, people can be efficient but not necessarily effective, for instance by producing lots of work output that has little value or effect. Likewise, people can be effective by focusing upon desired outcomes, without necessarily being ultra efficient or carrying out excessive amounts of work.

This can be seen in everyday life. For instance, a rowing team can have the most efficient and strong athletes, but they will not be effective or win the race if they are not co-ordinated together. A call centre can be efficient at answering all calls as quickly as possible, but they will not be effective if most of the calls answered are simply 'chase up' calls due to mistakes or errors previously made. Different combinations of efficiency and effectiveness are visually represented in Figure 2.7. It shows why being effective is often much better than one that is only efficient. It also shows why being effective and efficient is best of all.

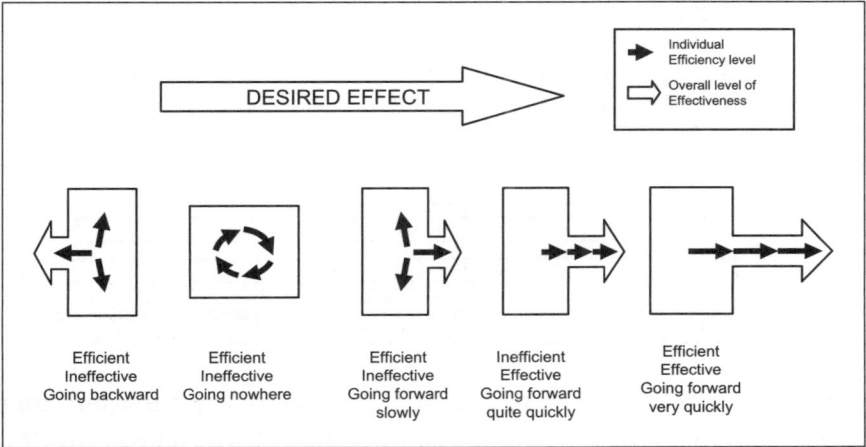

Figure 2.7 Lean direction setting – Effective and Efficient.

Strategy and direction setting forms the foundations on which everything is built. The foundations consist of three layers, namely:

1. Values and Philosophy,
2. Vision and Mission, and
3. Leadership, Strategy and Policy.

These layers create a robust and solid foundation. However, the strength of the foundation does not result from its constituent parts but how they build upon each other and interconnect together.

Values & Philosophy

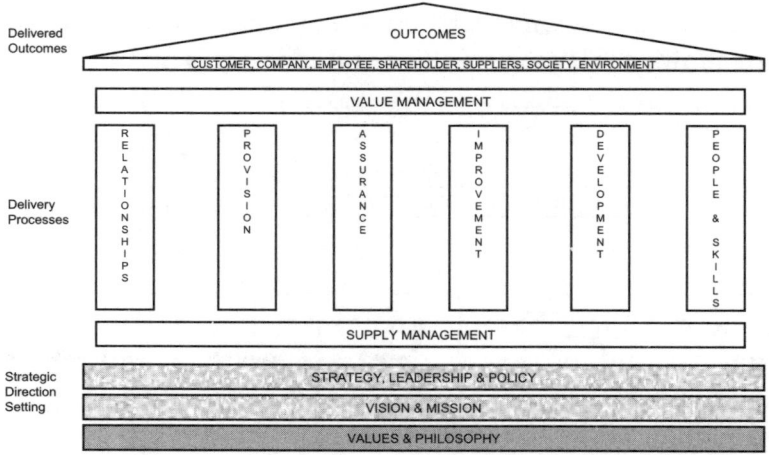

The values and philosophy of an enterprise are the basic building blocks on which everything else is built. They define, at the highest level, how the enterprise carries out its business. They provide the foundations of 'How we do things' and it's therefore imperative they are right. Virtually every enterprise today has developed a set of stated values. In many companies, staff are given 'cards' containing the company's values to carry around with them, to remind them of the values they are meant to demonstrate to customers and colleagues. Typical values include statements such as:

1. Honour,
2. Honesty,
3. Trustworthiness,
4. Respect for each other,
5. Work as a team,
6. Put the Customer first,
7. Develop our people,
8. Contribute to society,
9. Create a sustainable environment, and
10. Continuous Improvement.

However, values are not something simply to be carried around on cards, or to be recited if asked by a manager or an auditor. The whole strategic direction setting process, from values through to policy, must build the values into everything a company does. They must become the actual way we do things, not the way we would ideally like to do things. It is important to note that these values shape the culture. Culture is formed over a period of time by both individuals and groups, developed from a set of basic beliefs and re-enforced by individual experiences. If a company wishes to change its culture, it almost invariably can and quickly. But to do this, a company sometimes has to admit to itself first that its current set of values, whilst perhaps being right and proper, are not always followed. Top level commitment to properly establish and demonstrate the values are essential. Executives must lead by example, put the right policies in place and ensure that appropriate action is taken. By doing this, it is possible to quickly turn around a company, properly embed the values and create an infectious and positive culture change. Honesty, communication and involvement are all essential [11]. Customer focus is paramount.

The philosophy of an organisation is often less well known, but it should state the key philosophy, or organising principle, of the enterprise. This should not simply be a repeat of the values, but the one, single principle in the company that has meaning to everyone, including customers, front line staff, leaders, managers, suppliers and shareholders alike.

In today's climate of increasing competition, enterprises might choose an organising philosophy of putting the customer first. However, whilst this is obviously a key value for a Lean company, it does not encompass everything. The organising principle for Toyota is more accurately represented by continuous improvement, which sits at the very heart of the Toyota Production System (see Figure 2.8). It builds upon a foundation of level production and it allows Toyota to continually improve its production processes through progressive application of Just-in-Time principles and Quality approaches.

In the 'Lean World Management System', the generic

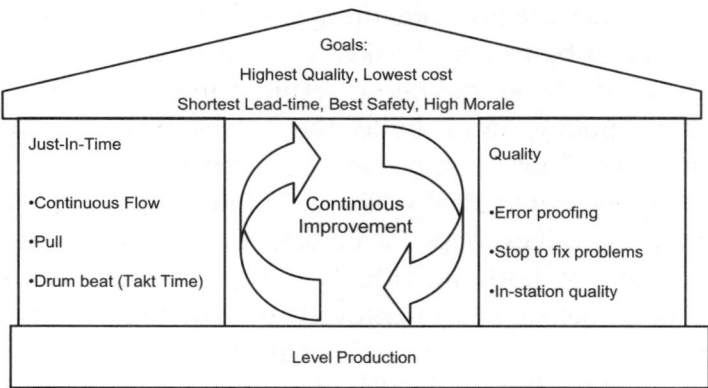

Figure 2.8 Continuous Improvement at the heart of the Toyota Production System.

philosophy used is one of 'Continuous Improvement – Complete Success'. **Continuous Improvement** involves everyone delivering more value. **Complete** means for everyone, namely the customer, employee, enterprise, community, shareholder & the environment. **Success** is defined by the level of value being created. This is also a philosophy which involves taking decisions for the long term, even if they are at the expense of short term financial goals. It is very noticeable that companies which already employ this type of philosophy stand out from the crowd, for instance Toyota and Tesco ('Every Little Helps'). They are generating growth, developing their staff and continuously improving the level of value they are able to create.

Vision & Mission

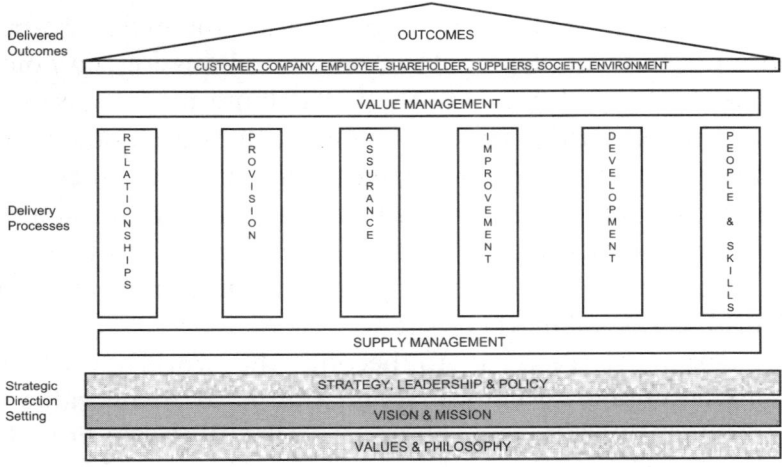

The vision and mission of the company defines the purpose of the enterprise, what it's in business to do and what it's looking to achieve [12]. Whilst the values and philosophy provide the foundations on 'How', the vision and mission provide the foundations for 'What'. They articulate the direction of the company.

'Vision' means 'to see' and its purpose is to provide a meaningful and imaginative future view of the enterprise and of the world around. A vision should be something everyone in the enterprise can understand, connect with and desire to bring about. It should be ambitious, distant and rational. It should stretch the imagination, engage and motivate. It needs to be able to unite the enterprise into achieving more than anyone could believe possible, creating an aspiration and focus on a much bigger and meaningful goal.

'Mission' means 'to send' and its purpose is to communicate a 'statement' of intent to everyone about the particular direction being taken towards the vision. Whilst the vision provides an end goal, the mission statement is there to send out clear messages on the practical steps the company is looking to take to make the vision a reality.

The vision of Toyota is to enrich society through car making, to earn customer loyalty and to be respected all around the world. Its mission is to create lifetime customers, by adopting a customer-first strategy and by implementing the most advanced environmental technologies. Their vision and mission, combined with their values, also ensure they contribute to the success of the communities they serve, as well as the development and well being of their staff. By implementing innovative new technologies they have also created the first hybrid production vehicles; ones which are more fuel efficient and much better for the environment. Respect for Toyota continues to grow around the world, across all market sectors.

The vision of Tesco is to become the world's economic household supplier of choice. Its mission is to create value for customers and to earn their lifetime loyalty. With one of its key values being 'Choice', they have become highly profitable and grown rapidly, progressively diversifying from superstores into such areas as non-food sales, home shopping, convenience stores, insurance and communication services. Their vision and mission are also driving their growth internationally.

Care has to be taken, when formulating the vision and mission, not to limit the scope of the enterprise or to simply extend what they do now. A telecommunications company should not constrain its mission to becoming the top telecommunications company, nor should a school or hospital see its mission as always being in the top quartile of published league tables. Enterprises need to consider their vision, mission and purpose from the customer's perspective. They also need to consider the wider environment and the communities they serve. Without doing this, companies risk falling into a trap which will severely limit their ability to develop and prosper in the future. For instance, take a national car recovery business with a vision of helping people to get from A to B, but with a mission only to become the best car recovery business in the world. This company is unlikely to remain successful as cars become ever more reliable and breaking down less and less. Instead, if the company were to broaden its vision to one where 'transportation and movement are effortless', with a mission to 'allow everyone (and everything) to move effortlessly from A to B', then their potential market effectively increases, exponentially! They begin to explore more widely the real value of travel and key needs during travel; for instance opportunities to provide communication, entertainment, navigation and tracking services, as well as additional and alternative forms of travel, such as taxis and other forms of shared transportation. If they do not, others invariably will.

Customer focused organisations, wishing to focus on customer loyalty, have to think about how they become loyal to their customers. Loyal customers are not created – their loyalty has to be earned. To do this, enterprises are increasingly aligning themselves with the vision and mission of their customers. For instance, leading outsourcing and IT firms (e.g. Fujitsu Services) are increasingly adopting their customer's mission, goals and desired outcomes (e.g. effortless passenger flights for an airline) in the services that they offer. This whole area will be covered in more depth in the 'Relationships' pillar of the 'Lean World Management System'.

Strategy, Leadership and Policy

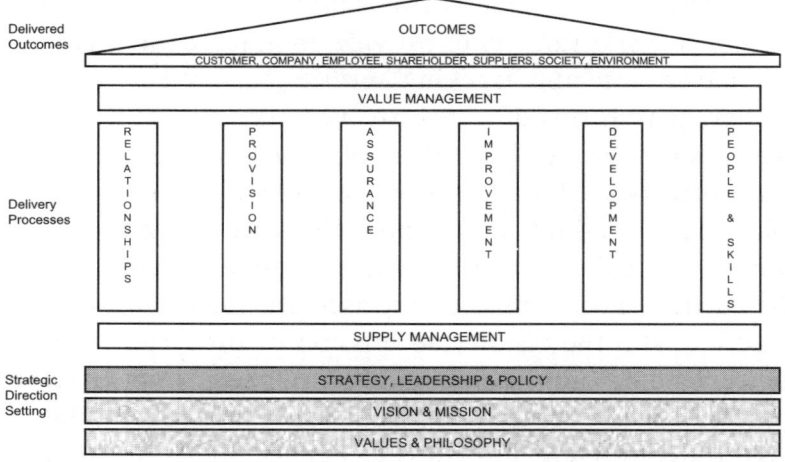

The strategy, leadership and policy are responsible for turning a vision and mission into reality. They provide the structure, plans and frameworks necessary for effective decision making and actions to take place.

'Strategy' means 'plan'. It involves creating an elaborate, systematic, bold and challenging (but achievable) plan of action. It provides the details of 'How' the company is to achieve its mission, articulating the steps to be taken towards the vision. It is not something that is created in isolation, but formed through partnership & involvement, innovation & reflection, as well as understanding & consensus. It needs to consider all options, with proper consideration of alternatives. It needs to be formed slowly and thoroughly and it needs to be implemented cautiously and effectively. It is not something that cannot or should not change, it is a living plan and will undoubtedly need to adapt along the way. It will change as the company implements its strategy and learns more about what needs to be done. It is very similar to a game of chess (see Figure 2.9). The enterprise has to become a learning organisation, one that constantly reflects, continuously improves and learns by doing.

A strategy can be broken down into distinct phases, or steps. These are often set out into yearly stages, as by doing so, it is easy to communicate the focus of attention for everyone, its overall fit into the bigger plan, as well as the progress being made. It also breaks the journey down into bite size chunks, ones that in their own right are challenging but achievable. If everyone is only given the end goal, with few clear steps to achieve it, they are likely to be interested, but sceptical. By breaking down the plan into simple steps, it becomes clear, challenging and motivating. It focuses on the vital few. For example, a Lean implementation strategy needs to involve creating the capability to change – i.e. a Lean Navigation System. This includes putting the continuous improvement, policy deployment and personal development capabilities in place. One fundamental strategy of Toyota has been to continually focus on improving the flow of value and in doing so eliminating any waste uncovered. This is a fundamentally different strategy to that used by the vast majority of industry, who still tend to focus more upon improving efficiency than the flow of value. This unique and different approach is a critical part of Toyota's strategy and it has successfully allowed them to pull away from their competitors.

A strategy can also be broken down into distinct themes. For instance, Tesco has broken down its strategy into Core UK,

Figure 2.9 The strategy consists of the steps to achieving the mission.

International, Non-food and Retail services [13]. This break down into themes, then allows the creation of separate and distinct plans for each area. This is particularly helpful when an enterprise has areas of business which differ greatly in their levels of maturity or the products and services they offer.

When breaking down a strategy into themes, steps or both, it is important to split them into components that are relatively independent. For instance, one mistake that is commonly made is to create a strategy (i.e. plan) for growth and a separate one for efficiency. The first is given to sales, marketing and product development to implement and the other is made the responsibility of operations. This is the equivalent to the marathon runner building up muscle by exercising with weights (i.e. sales teams) and removing body fat by going on a diet (i.e. operational teams). It is not the way to become fit, build strength and stamina, or to win. Companies, therefore, have to be very careful not to fall into this trap when carrying out strategy formulation. Another common mistake is to break down a strategy based on technology or products/services it currently sells, rather than the actual value provided to customers. For instance, a telecommunications company may create a strategy based around technology or product themes, such as broadband, mobile, IT, voice, data or entertainment, instead of focusing on the overall value individual customers need from a combination of these.

As the strategy is formulated, it requires strong leadership throughout the company to implement it. Leadership is about taking responsibility and being able to inspire others. Executive leaders help to set direction, but this is a collective and inclusive process, not an individual one. Leaders often demonstrate great foresight and imagination, but the one thing great leaders always show is their ability to inspire others.

Leaders are highly motivated, able to engage people and share their knowledge. They constantly challenge and support, rather than dictate. They get others to think and to take the initiative. They gain more satisfaction from helping others to ask the right questions and generate solutions, rather than simply giving everyone the answers. They teach people 'how to fish and find food', rather than continually 'providing fish and food'. They are role models of their company values, they take responsibility, are not afraid to ask, to make mistakes or to say, 'I don't know'. They go to see for themselves, learn by doing, continually seek improvement and challenge & support all those around them. John F Kennedy once said 'Leadership and learning are indispensable to each other'; something Lean leaders never forget.

By definition, leadership is the responsibility of everyone and should not be delegated to a few. Unfortunately, in traditional companies, leadership has often been left to a few top executives, with managers and front line staff doing what they are told rather than taking responsibility and inspiring others around them. In this situation, without a clear strategy of making it the responsibility of everyone, even the strongest and most charismatic of executive leaders can struggle to create effective leadership. Hence, executive teams have to be clear upfront about the type of leadership they want in the future, top down leadership or leadership that involves everyone. This decision is vital to the long term success of an enterprise. Top down approaches, more often than not, result in more 'command and control' type structures rather than inclusive or supportive ones, thereby creating management rather than leadership.

Lean leadership is about self reliance, listening, taking responsibility and creating a learning environment, where everyone is encouraged to be open, innovative and to learn from any mistakes.

Strategic direction setting creates focus, a game plan and the leadership necessary for action to take place. The processes the company operates are where action actually takes place. The interface between direction setting and daily decision making/actions (i.e. processes) are the policies an enterprise uses to govern its processes. Policies, together with the process of policy deployment, are crucial in an enterprise. They translate the strategic direction of the business into the decisions it makes on a daily basis.

Policies are needed to provide overall governance. They include the roles, responsibilities and rules adopted across the company, based upon its overall philosophy, mission and strategy. As an example, they define the roles and responsibilities of front line staff, managers and executives. Roles and responsibilities are no longer built around an organisation or set of departments, as any structure needs to be adaptable to the changing needs of customers. Policies have to be linked directly to the company values, philosophy, vision, mission and strategy. They are mostly generic in nature and apply to the processes the company operates.

Unfortunately, in many traditional companies, processes are often poorly understood. They are also rarely managed from 'end to end' or governed by effective policies. Instead, policies are used in different ways and for many different things. For instance, policies, more often than not, are introduced to improve efficiency, functionalise work and assign decision making to particular groups, such as a product teams, purchasing, finance or human resource departments. The origins of these types of policies are often difficult to trace and are tenuously linked to the overall direction desired by the company (e.g. based on its values, mission or strategy). These kinds of policies often become a source of great frustration, particularly for front line staff. They hinder them from providing the value customers are demanding from them, and they create unnecessary delays, in-effectiveness and stress. In this situation, customers also become frustrated trying to obtain products and services from the company. This creates a negative downward spiral, as customers stop buying from them and the company tries hard to find new potential customers to replace them.

Policies of a company like Toyota, link accurately to their vision, mission and strategy, and include:

1. Ensuring any decisions are based on the long term, as well as the short term,
2. Focusing on the value provided to customers and creating flow,
3. Levelling the workload and use 'pull' systems to avoid overproduction,

4. Using continuous improvement to expose problems and eliminate waste,
5. Getting quality right first time,
6. Involving everyone and creating a culture of learning by doing, and
7. Respecting, challenging and supporting both staff and suppliers.

These provide the foundations for the Toyota Production System and are documented in more detail in books such as 'The Toyota Way' [6]. These types of policy clearly underpin their strategy of implementing excellent processes. They focus on getting brilliant results by allowing everyday people to operate excellent processes. In contrast, traditional manufacturers tend to obtain average (or worse) results from trying to use otherwise brilliant people to manage broken processes.

All processes need governance, or rules, under which they can operate on a daily basis. The process of policy deployment is responsible for creating policy and implementing it across the organisation. Creating or changing policy results from the overall direction setting process and from improvements identified by the enterprise as a whole. Policy deployment therefore links directly into the key change processes within the organisation, namely continuous improvement, product/ service development and staff development. This whole area will be explored in more detail in the chapter on the Lean Navigator.

Lean policies, once implemented, create simplicity, control and very little management. Enterprises often get tied up trying to decide what the best organisational structure needs to be and policies to determine the rules of engagement within the structure. Traditional structures (e.g. See Figure 2.10) include:

1. Functional groups; such as marketing, sales, customer service, operations, finance and human resources,
2. Products or service groups; such as telephony, broadband, mobility and IT, and

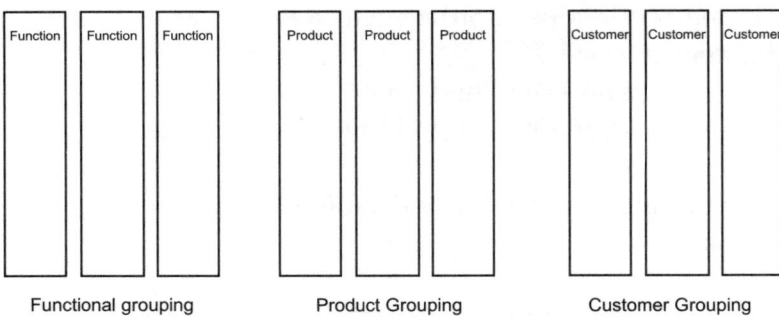

Figure 2.10 Traditional organisational structures.

3. Customer groups; such as corporate, small business and consumer.

Each has its pros and cons. The choice of structure tends to depend on the volume, variety and complexity of the market-place, as well as the individual preferences of the executive team. However, it is not always critical which one is chosen and it can always be changed. They all offer a potentially convenient way to group individuals, but in a Lean Enterprise they all focus on one overriding objective –supporting and improving the end to end processes that deliver value to customers (Figure 2.11). In effect, whatever grouping method is chosen, a Lean enterprise manages its value streams.

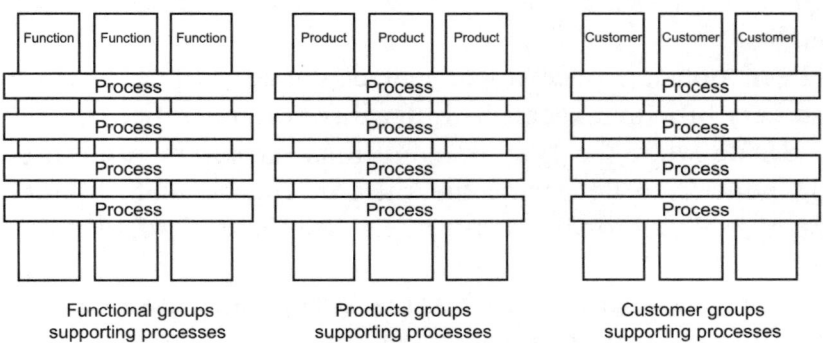

Figure 2.11 Organisational structures governed by processes.

Lean Enterprises primarily govern end to end processes, not functions or products, and they do so via the policies they put in place and through the abilities of all their staff. The following sections will explore these processes in more detail.

Processes

The processes used by a company to deliver value to customers consist of those that directly deliver value to stakeholders and those that support them in doing so (as shown in Figure 2.12). Support processes, whilst necessary, are always kept to a minimum, to ensure the maximum amount of time and resources are dedicated to the processes that directly add value. This section explores each of these processes in more detail; first the delivery processes, then the support processes.

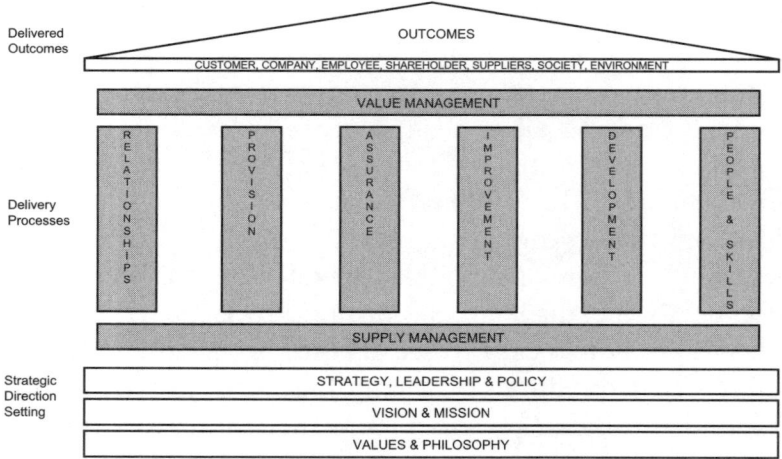

Figure 2.12 Processes in the Lean World Management System.

The delivery processes in the 'Lean World Management System' are the means by which an enterprise delivers value to its customers, and other stakeholders. Lean enterprises manage the capability to create outcomes (i.e. the means), rather than output [14].

Focus on separately managing departments and functions (groups carrying out individual tasks) has diverted the attention of many traditional companies away from their end to end delivery processes, much to the frustration of their customers and employees. Enterprises often do not know what their key processes are and almost no-one knows how they really work. When embarking on a Lean journey, it is often a revelation, to everyone involved, to find out what actually happens in the process of providing a product or service to a customer. What they find almost invariably bears little resemblance to any documented processes/procedures and leaves many to wonder how they ever worked! The reality is that many companies are struggling to survive, despite the heroic efforts made by their staff to negotiate their way around all the barriers placed in front of them to deliver value to customers. This consumes huge amounts of mental energy and physical effort. It also involves large amounts of non-value add 'glue' being administered to hold everything together (e.g. reviews, plan changes, reactive fixes).

Companies often take a sharp intake of breath when they consider managing all of their processes. This is often because it is difficult to 'see' them or they believe there are too many of them to manage. In a manufacturing plant, one can normally quickly see the key process in operation, including the physical layout and the flow of work all the way from the receipt of raw materials to the dispatch of finished goods. However, office processes are not so easy to see, as they are generally less visual and are often spread across many locations. Service industries often find it difficult to understand their processes as a result. Many companies also believe they have hundreds of processes, described in many thousands of documents. In reality, when one considers value from the customers' perspective, they can be broken down into a few key processes (called value streams). In the Lean World Management System there are six key value adding delivery processes:

1. Relationships development,
2. Provision,
3. Assurance,
4. Improvement,
5. Development, and
6. People and skills development.

These processes are responsible for creating effective relation-ships with customers and developing the capability of the staff. They also deliver value directly to customers, by responding to their different types of demand, including:

1. Provide – requests to provide customers existing products and services.
2. Develop – requests for new products and services capable of creating further value, but which are not currently provided.
3. Restore – requests to assure, recover, fix or replace a product/service provided incorrectly or which has subsequently gone wrong (this is also often referred to as 'Failure demand').
4. Improve – requests to improve the value and remove wasted time / resources associated with current products or services.

The dynamic inter-relationships between these processes (or value streams) are shown in Figure 2.13. This is sometimes referred to as the high level value stream map. Relationship development involves getting to know the customer and to truly understand their individual needs. It uses this knowledge to help determine how the company can offer the customer what they need (e.g. provision, assurance) and also used to focus the enterprise on creating new products or services capable of offering even more value to the customer (development and improvement). It also involves creating more formal relation-ships, such as through commercial bids and contracts. Provision involves giving customers the products and services the company can currently offer. Assurance involves ensuring any products or services provided do not go wrong and are either quickly fixed or replaced if they do. Improvement is responsible for identifying and fixing problems and improving the value provided to customers. Development involves creating and implementing new products and services which are capable of providing even more value to customers, creating success and growth in value

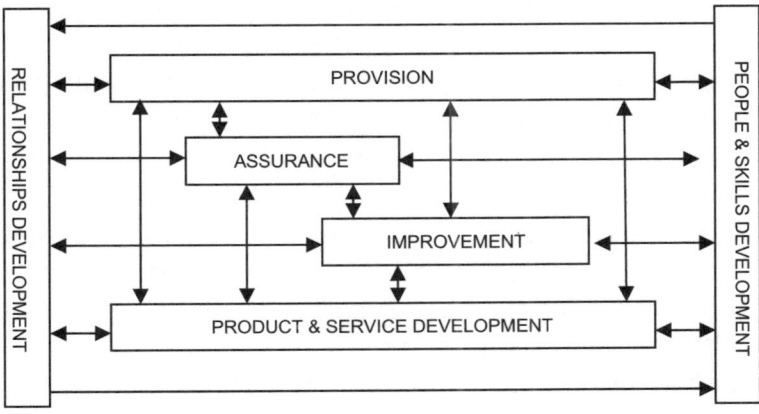

Figure 2.13 Lean World Management System – High level process map.

for everyone. It also involves identifying the people development needs of the organisation, which are implemented through the people and skills development process. People and skills development is uniquely classed as a delivery value stream. Lean Enterprises class the nurture and development of staff as a core purpose, not a by-product of doing business or an optional support activity. In the Lean World, the support and development of individuals, groups and communities becomes just as important as satisfying the needs of customers themselves.

The delivery processes are supported by two support processes. Support processes are non-value adding in their own right, but are necessary to ensure value continues to be delivered to customers. These include:

1. Supply Management
2. Value Management.

Supply Management involves managing the supply of resources. This includes 'transformed' resources such as raw materials, consumables, energy and waste materials. It also controls the supply of 'transforming' resources, such as staff, equipment (e.g. IT/robots), tools (e.g. software/manual) and infrastructure (e.g. building, catering). The supply process involves making sure there is a smooth flow of material and resources across the enterprise in response to customer demand.

Value Management is about accounting for the value provided (to customers and all other stakeholders) by the enterprise as a whole (including staff and suppliers). It is responsible for providing reports to individual customers at one level, whilst presenting the corporate annual report/accounts to shareholders at another. It is also responsible for accounting, both individually and collectively, for the overall performance of the enterprise, from the customer's perspective. It focuses on value, not just revenue and cost. Value Management obtains the information necessary to steer change and to measure its success. It is also responsible for paying staff, suppliers and obtaining payments from customers.

Lean enterprises simplify everything, minimise unnecessary complexity and increase the level of standardisation within their processes. Standardisation is the bedrock for continuous improvement, particularly for manufacturing companies. However, in service industries, whilst standardisation is also important, it is not at the expense of delivering value to individual customers. The variety in customer demand, their values and their needs, makes completely standardised procedures wasteful. By over-standardising, more waste can be created, from both the customer and enterprise perspective. Lean service companies, therefore, understand that there is no such thing as a standard customer. Even individual customers can have completely different needs at different times of the day or week. For example, a person in a hurry to buy milk on the way to work is likely to have completely different needs to later in the week when they want to browse around and gather their weekly shopping.

Processes have to focus on value from the customer's perspective and must be flexible and effective at serving their needs.

Relationships development

The process of relationship development is about getting to know your customers and understanding their needs. The needs of customers are not generic or collective, they are individual. Value from a customer's perspective can be similar to that perceived by others in many ways, but value is rarely exactly the same. On approaching customers, one must also avoid treating customers how you would like to be treated . . . it's about treating each customer how they want to be treated! Increasing attention is therefore required to understanding customers as individuals, not 'pigeon-holing' customers into particular segments or treating them in standard ways. Indeed, many markets now need to be represented as millions of relatively small groups of individuals, and not as a few small groups (or segments) each consisting of millions of individuals. Moreover, the needs of one individual often varies minute by minute, hour by hour, day by day and hence enterprises have to be agile and flexible if they are to meet an individual customer's complete set of needs all of the time.

In traditional companies, the role of a marketing function and an account management / sales function are completely different. The role of the marketing function is predominantly to build brand value for the company. Marketing departments traditionally use a number of strategies to build brand value, such as company slogans, distinctive labelling and advertising. A brand can often become a highly valuable asset, worth many billions of pounds. Companies recognised for their high brand value include companies such as Coca-Cola and Virgin. A lot of money can be spent on marketing to create brand value and add to the equity of a business. Marketing generally focuses on promoting the value the business offers as a whole, rather than focusing on the value offered to individual customers. In contrast, account management or sales teams are focused on building customer equity, understanding the needs of individual customers and trying to tailor the company's product and service offerings to them.

In a Lean company, the role of marketing and sales effectively merge. Understanding customer needs, as well as marketing the value the company offers them, becomes more individual and integrated. Brand equity and customer equity are built together, in a process very similar to 'integrated marketing'. Marketing, in terms of advertising, also changes dramatically. Lean companies still spend time and money on advertising, but they tend to use it more to create awareness and to present the company's overall purpose/philosophy, rather than to continually advertise individual products, services or offers. For instance, Toyota often use their strap line 'In pursuit of perfection' and Tesco use 'Every little helps'. Lean companies may use advertising to initially inform people about new products or services, but they increasingly rely on their customers to market their products and services for them. If customers experience the value on offer and find it to be either as good as or better than they thought, they tend to tell others. A Lean company does not have to repeatedly advertise a product/service, or have to have a massive sales force, for it to become successful. A good product/service creating value for its customers will be sold to others by their present customers, once they have been made aware of it and have started to use it. This is sometimes called 'viral marketing'. However, the product/service must be of high quality, provide the customer real value and be provided effortlessly if they are to recommend it. For some traditional businesses, embracing this can prove a little difficult initially, particularly if they have a history of providing poor products or services, or if their products/services offer limited real value to customers. However, the power of viral marketing is enormous; it costs nothing and is something that all companies need to embrace.

As an example, Tesco adverts made customers aware of a new internet telephone service by explicitly referring to a viral marketing approach. It involved customers informing family and other friends about the service too, so they could all benefit from free calls to one another. It also showed how, by starting the ball rolling, more and more people could quickly join in and spread it around the globe. Moreover, Skype did not heavily advertise its initial peer to peer communication service and left it for customers to do instead. The phenomenal growth achieved by Skype was not due to their brand or advertising prowess, but from customers realising the huge value their particular product and service offered and its simplicity of use. By focusing on getting the product and service right, from the customer's perspective, the costs of marketing can be minimised.

Lean enterprises use viral marketing in a positive way. Communication technology, such as the internet, search engines, chat rooms, community groups, consumer sites, consumer rating systems, mobile phone, voice messaging, text and now mobile video, all add to the power of this approach. Harnessed well, it has a power beyond any other form of marketing. However, it is a mechanism where opinions can also change quickly through adverse events or publicity. Therefore Lean enterprises have to be consistent . . . consistently good!

In relationship development, one cannot simply adopt a viral marketing approach. You have to offer the right product/service. The amount of marketing a particular product requires is often inversely proportional to the level of value it actually provides. Viral marketing only works properly when customers perceive and receive real value from the product or service, consistently. For customers to perceive value, the enterprise has to use every opportunity to ask questions, listen and understand every individual customer need. The value customers perceive and receive from a product is rarely the same and often turns out to be different to what an enterprise first imagined it to be. For instance, enterprises once thought a wrist watch was purely for telling the time and a mobile phone for making and receiving calls. Now enterprises increasingly realise the additional value such products provide; not just as communications tools but as fashion accessories capable of offering a multiplicity of services.

Understanding the needs and aspirations of customers is not the responsibility of a single department, but becomes the responsibility of everyone. Once the company has started to understand their needs and goals, they are able to use this insight to:

1. Determine how the company can offer each individual customer what they need,
2. Generate sales for existing products and services,
3. Harness the innovation and ideas of their customers as well as the enterprise, and
4. Focus the enterprise to develop future products or services capable of providing their customers even greater value.

Relationships are developed through the overall process shown in Figure 2.14, known as the ABC of Lean Relationship Development. The first step is one where customers begin to gain an Awareness of the enterprise and likewise the enterprise becomes increasingly aware of the customer. It involves making customers aware that the company exists, its purpose and the value it offers. This is where advertising, through the various means available, does create value to the customer, as without it, they do not know you are there! The second stage is where individual customers develop an Affinity with the enterprise; beginning to connect with the values of the company and what it has to offer. The third stage is when a customer begins to do an Assessment of the company and the products and services it offers. This includes seeking information from the company, friends, colleagues and previous buyers; all activities which

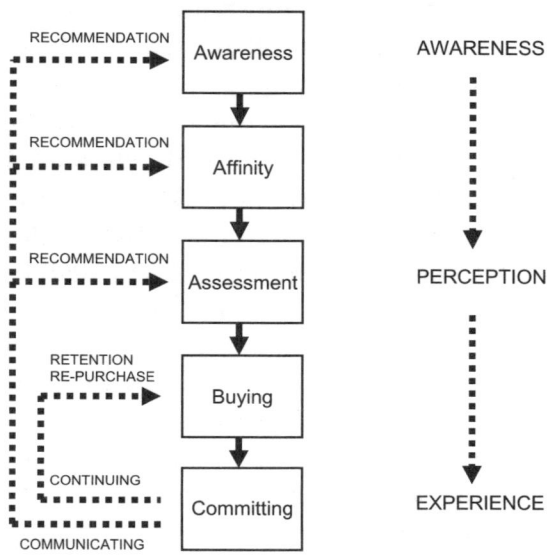

Figure 2.14 The ABC of Lean Relationships Development.

increasingly involve the internet. The fourth step is when customers choose to engage with the company and begin Buying products or services from them. Once products are bought by the customer, they are also able to feedback their view of the enterprise to others (good or bad). On consistently receiving good products and services, which add real value to them, they will tend to commit to, and continue to buy from, that enterprise, whilst also communicating to other family members, friends, communities and work colleagues. This creates a viral boomerang effect, where customers continue to return again and again (i.e. 'retention and repurchase'), whilst bringing new customers to the company too (i.e. through 'recommendations').

Whilst this process may, at first, seem long winded or difficult to realise, it is not. Information and communication technology are increasingly providing solutions capable of helping at each and every stage. With the advent of the internet, a vast amount of information is now readily available. However, users need additional help if they are to become aware of it and at the same time avoid drowning in a sea of it! Being able to quickly and successfully find relevant information is crucial and search companies (e.g. Google) have started to become successful because of this. They tend to provide a structured list and description of the information most likely to be of relevance to the user, based on any key words entered, their personal profiles/preferences and the popularity of the information with other users. By providing an effective portal to the world of information, they have naturally captured a great deal of advertising revenue too. At the same, internet companies such as eBay and Amazon have also been very successful; providing a heightened awareness of the vast array of products available alongside a portal for people to buy and sell them. Crucially, these enterprises also allow buyers and sellers to rate a product (and each other) and recommend them (or not) to others. By doing this, they are starting to develop leaner relationships; with customer feedback helping to heighten awareness, create affinity, offer assessments and indirectly generate more orders for the same product (as long as the product is good and the provider is reliable/trustworthy!). Clearly there is much more that can and will be done, but its success in creating sufficient trust to allow private individuals and complete strangers to remotely transact with one another (sometimes from opposite sides of the globe) is something that would only probably have been dreamt of a few years ago.

Providing a company's current products/services well is a good start, but it is only the beginning of Lean relationships. It does not guarantee future loyalty or purchases. Companies must also continuously improve their products/services and at the same time develop the new ones customers want moving forward. They also need to ensure that they build an affinity with potential customers; connecting with their wider set of values and needs (e.g. the environment). Most customers are not likely to be loyal until these additional elements are in place, or until the company demonstrates that they are loyal to their customers first. The growing power of communication and the internet ensure this is so. On the other hand, as a company introduces Lean relationships development, customers begin to market the company by themselves, as well as its products and services. They also help to create the new products and services they will require from the company in the future . . . and all of this **for free**! When this occurs, Lean relationships have truly been created.

The examination of value from the customer's perspective can completely change what an enterprise offers to its customers. It is like viewing the world in a new light and through a different set of lenses, 'Lean Lenses'. Lean Relationship development makes use of Lean Lenses and this opens up a whole new world of opportunity. It can change a road-side recovery business to one focused on transporting customers (and products) effortlessly from A to B, or a telecommunications company into a relationship development company. It can also change a wrist watch manufacturer from a company creating products to tell the time to a service provider providing fashionable items and a multiplicity of consumer services (e.g. communications). The change, on applying Lean relationship development, can be very profound and should not be ignored or underestimated. It is only by doing this that the huge amount of new potential products and services can become visible to everyone, creating motivation for change and removing the fear of change becoming a simple cost reduction exercise. It puts customers at the heart of the business, allowing them to increasingly shape what the enterprise provides and stopping it from just selling more of what it currently makes.

As an example, Toyota found, through the conversations they were having with other companies, that most corporate executives were not buying Toyota cars [6]. Toyota were recognised for their exceptional levels of engineering and quality, but many corporate executives bought cars from different manufacturers because they lacked a certain level of affinity with Toyota. This was due, at least in part, to the fact that they were also interested in the status and prestige they offered, as well as their quality and performance. With this insight, Toyota launched a new brand, called Lexus, which offered premium luxury and style, as well as performance and quality. This proved to be highly successful in the executive market-place and many, very satisfied, owners then began to market their cars to others.

In the case of Tesco, through the introduction of their loyalty card, they sought to develop a deeper understanding of their customers and began to foster brand loyalty. By uniquely understanding the local buying patterns in their individual superstores, they have been able to successfully change what each superstore needs to stock and when. It has also allowed them to introduce a unique form of convenience store, known as Tesco Express, which allows quick, convenient shopping which is highly tailored to local customer needs. Likewise, by creating awareness through initial advertising, they are using viral approaches to market new services such as their internet phone service. Once awareness of this new service is raised to a sufficient level, it has the potential to continue to grow by itself, as long as the product adds value to customers, is of sufficient quality and can be used effortlessly.

Provision

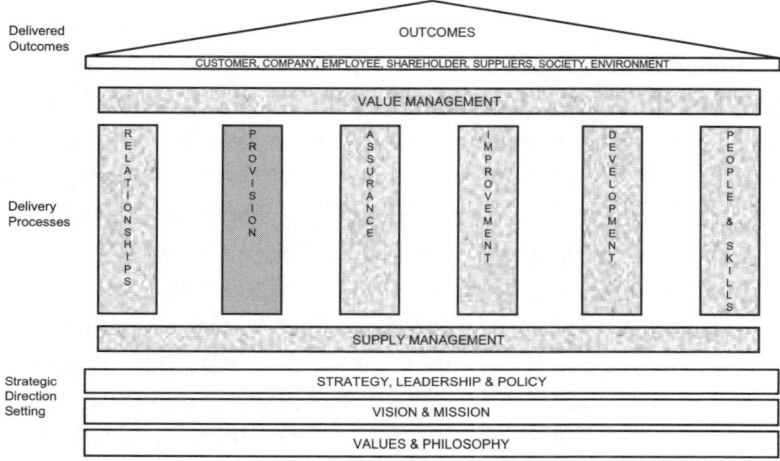

Once a customer is aware that the company exists and has reviewed the type and quality of products/services it has to offer, they may seek to buy from it. This is where provision comes in; providing customer's with products, services or both.

Provision processes need to be slick and customer friendly. They also need to be flexible and capable of personalising the product/service to the needs of each individual customer. Provision processes, be they production or service processes, have to take into account the following:

1. Value of the product/service, as perceived by individual customers,
2. Volume of products/services required,
3. Variety in the products/services required,
4. Variation in volume of products/services required.

These are often referred to as the '4 V's' and they are used to design and optimise processes. The Value of the product/service is defined as the value perceived by the individual customer. Differences in the Value required by customers create a need for Variety in the products and services offered. Provision is not about making a single product that is capable of doing everything any customer may want to do; it is about providing each and every customer with precisely what they want. This avoids customers who only want a basic product/service being over-charged for what, to them, is something that has been over-engineered and over-processed. Provision is about treating customers as individuals, customising products to meet their individual needs and personalising any service they receive. It gives them what they want, where they want, when they want, how they want. It is about serving customers how they want to be served, not about serving all customers the same or how you we would like to be served. Some individuals prefer to order a product online simply by clicking on it, others like to go to see the product for themselves or to talk to someone about it. This can very much depend on the type of product required, as well as many other factors such as its value, availability or the time of day. By providing choice, customers can choose the best product/service for them, as well as the way they would like to receive it. By not providing this, customers and loyalty will be lost.

In addition to the traditional '4 V's', there is a fifth 'V' that needs to be taken into account – Vicinity. The location of raw materials, suppliers, processing facilities and customers are all critical to the effectiveness of any 'end to end' provision process. For instance, if suppliers or factory production facilities are situated half way around the world, it invariably increases delay, transport and inventory costs. It also reduces the capability of the enterprise to respond quickly and effectively to changes in customer demand, which increases the risk of being out of stock of popular items and having to sell unwanted products by offering huge discounts.

The primary purpose of provision is to create Value from the customer's perspective. For instance, a maintenance business fixing cars may be assuring value (e.g. servicing) and restoring value when they go wrong (e.g. breakdown recovery), but it is not creating value (e.g. transporting someone or something from A to B). Provision is only about creating value, not assuring or recovering lost value (i.e. assurance responds to 'failure' demand). Provision in a service centre is therefore about providing customers with products or services that create value and success, not managing or putting right those things that should not have gone wrong in the first place. Provision also includes managing changes or upgrades to products/services in response to customer needs and also ceasing/re-using materials when a customer is no longer in need of them.

The secondary purpose is to create the flexibility necessary to support individual customer's needs. The variety in value that customers seek to obtain creates a multiplicity of business opportunities. Enterprises can choose to focus on providing niche products/services which are highly valued by a few, providing a multiplicity of products/services valued by many, or providing both. The diversity in customer needs creates a wealth of opportunity, but it is also the source of major challenges. Enterprises have to become far more flexible in order to satisfy the needs of individuals, not generic groups or segments. To create loyal customers, they also have to be able to respond to the varying needs of the same customer, depending on the time of day, day of the week, or month of the year. For instance, on entering a supermarket, the needs of a customer requiring a single item on the way to work are very different to the needs of the same customer who, later on in the week, wishes to carry out their weekly family shop. Likewise, the needs of a customer urgently requiring to top up their car with petrol on their way to work is very different to the same customer who on another day may want to pick up food, beverages and magazines for all their family before starting off on a long journey. Provision processes need to be able to customise the products and personalise the service provided to customers. The value, volume, variety, variation and vicinity are all used to optimise the provision processes a company operates.

The third focus becomes one of optimising the flow of value, as perceived by the customer, minimising any delays and maximising the capability of the enterprise to create value. The time taken within a process is classified into four different types:

1. Operation – activities directly adding value to the product or service,
2. Transportation – movement of goods or services between one activity and another,
3. Inspection – checking goods or services for availability, time, cost or quality,
4. Delay – including waiting in storage or waiting in a queue between activities or for resources to become available.

The first one is classed as value adding, the latter three are not. One of the simplest ways to visualise this can be found at petrol stations. As a customer, one can quickly identify the activities needed to obtain petrol and note the time it takes to carry them out. By way of example, a visit to a Pay at the Shop (PATS) petrol station is shown in Figure 2.15.

From a customer's perspective, the only steps which Operationally add any value in the process, involve putting the petrol in the tank and paying for it. All of the other activities carried out do not add any value and either involve Transportation, Inspection or Delay. Analysis of the amount of time spent

Activity	Elapsed time	Activity time	Value Type
Enter petrol station	0:00:00	0:00:00	Transport
Choose pump and join queue	0:00:02	0:00:02	Transport
Wait for current car to leave	0:01:45	0:01:43	Delay
Drive closer to petrol pump	0:01:50	0:00:05	Transport
Wait for current car to leave	0:06:56	0:05:06	Delay
Drive up to petrol pump	0:07:00	0:00:04	Transport
Leave car and arrive at petrol pump	0:07:05	0:00:05	Transport
Open petrol cap	0:07:09	0:00:04	Operation
Choose petrol type and place nozzle in tank	0:07:12	0:00:03	Operation
Wait for petrol pump to be enabled	0:07:18	0:00:06	Delay
Fill car with petrol	0:08:24	0:01:06	Operation
Place nozzle back and put petrol cap back on	0:08:37	0:00:13	Operation
Walk and join queue to pay	0:09:09	0:00:32	Transport
Reach pay point	0:12:25	0:03:16	Delay
Agree payment	0:12:36	0:00:11	Inspection
Provide payment	0:12:40	0:00:04	Operation
Receive payment confirmation and leave pay point	0:12:46	0:00:06	Inspection
Reach car	0:13:14	0:00:28	Transport
Get into car and leave petrol station	0:13:23	0:00:09	Transport

Figure 2.15 Example breakdown of activities when filling a car at Pay at the Shop (PATS) petrol station.

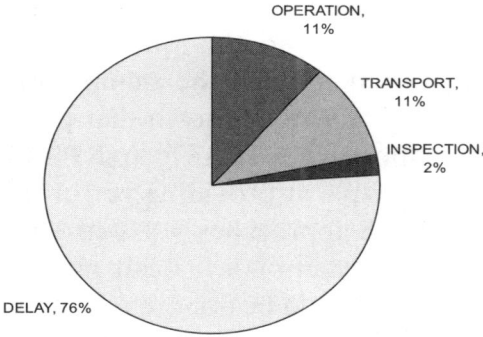

OPERATION,
11%

TRANSPORT,
11%

INSPECTION,
2%

DELAY, 76%

Figure 2.16 An example breakdown of activity types when filling up a car at a Pay at the Shop (PATS) petrol station.

in each category (See figure 2.16), quickly reveals that only around 11% of the time actually taken was spent adding any value, the rest of the time was wasted (76% in queues). In addition, the percentage of time the petrol pump (i.e. delivery system) was actually providing value (i.e. petrol) to a customer was only around 17%. This is wasted capital and losing potential revenue too. These types of figures may sound particularly poor, but in fact they are not unusual for a traditional provision process. Some provision processes have less than 1–2% of their time being spent adding value to the customer before Lean Thinking has been applied.

On applying Lean Thinking, provision starts to be revised to enable the customer to flow quickly and smoothly through the process; obtaining the value they want and eliminating any steps that waste the customer's time. For instance, Pay at the Kiosk (PATK) approaches have been introduced, to make sure customers drive their cars away from the petrol pump as soon as they are full and provide payment at a separate kiosk. This reduces the need for cars to queue behind other cars before obtaining petrol and also removes the need for the customer to walk to/from the till in order to pay. However, it still involves joining another queue at the till. A further development has been to introduce Pay at the Pump (PATP) approaches, which remove the need to go to a separate kiosk or to join a queue in the shop.

The only potential queue now is one to gain access to the petrol pump in the first place, and this queue is minimised due to the removal of wasted time at the pumps. In fact, using the figures in Figure 2.17, it can be shown that petrol stations using these alternative approaches (PATP and PATK) are between 200–400% more effective at providing petrol to customers than more traditional PATS approaches (e.g. petrol pump utilisation). This provides a good example of 'Lean provision' in practice. There is still more that could be done, as the need to queue at the beginning, to get out the car at all, or to enter a card into a machine to pay, are all areas for potential further development.

So why aren't these approaches commonplace at every petrol station around the world? Well, the answer partly lies in the fact that customers often do not want to buy petrol alone and that petrol stations make little profit from petrol at the prices they sell it for. Customers often buy many different items from a petrol station, such as snacks, beverages, food, papers, magazines or cigarettes. Some customers buy items from petrol

	Value Type	Pay at the Shop (PATS)	Pay at the Kiosk (PATK)	Pay at the Pump (PATP)
Drive up to petrol pump	Transport	0:00:04	0:00:04	0:00:04
Leave car and arrive at petrol pump	Transport	0:00:05	0:00:05	0:00:05
Open petrol cap	Operation	0:00:04	0:00:04	0:00:04
Choose petrol type and place nozzle in tank	Operation	0:00:03	0:00:03	0:00:03
Wait for petrol pump to be enabled	Delay	0:00:06	0:00:06	0:00:06
Fill car with petrol	Operation	0:01:06	0:01:06	0:01:06
Place nozzle back and put petrol cap back on	Operation	0:00:13	0:00:13	0:00:13
Walk and join queue to pay	Transport	0:00:32	-	-
Reach pay point	Delay	-	-	-
Agree payment	Inspection	0:00:11	0:00:11	-
Provide payment	Operation	0:00:04	0:00:04	0:00:04
Receive payment confirmation and leave pay point	Inspection	0:00:06	0:00:06	0:00:06
Reach car	Transport	0:00:28	-	-
Get into car and leave petrol station	Transport	0:00:09	0:00:09	0:00:09
Total elapsed time		0:03:11	0:02:11	0:02:00
Operation (%)	Operation	47%	69%	75%
Transportation (%)	Transport	41%	14%	15%
Inspection (%)	Inspection	9%	13%	5%
Delay (%)	Delay	3%	5%	5%
Petrol pump utilisation (%)		35%	60%	55%

Figure 2.17 An example breakdown of activities and types when filling up a car at different types of petrol station when no queues are present.

stations, without buying petrol or even owning a car. However, traditional petrol stations tend to lower the price of petrol in order to entice potential customers to stop and shop. Long queues, passing by the many goods for sale, increase the likelihood of additional purchases, from which they profit.

To gain customer loyalty, a Lean provision process needs to cater for individual customer needs and offer customers a range of options which satisfies all their needs (e.g. pay at the pump, pay at the shop). This is likely to encourage a move away from 'pay at the kiosk' approaches, as the alternatives offer more customer choice. By focusing on flow, customer value and profitability also grow together. Petrol stations continuing to offer no choice to customers, other than to pay in the shop, may have to use further loss leading petrol prices (or other promotional incentives) to attract otherwise non-loyal customers away from other, more effective approaches.

Whilst creating flow is a key goal, many traditional provision processes are set up to provide individual products/services in discrete batches. This involves creating a given quantity (i.e. batch) of a particular type all together. From bread making to automobile manufacturing, batch processing is regularly used to make certain numbers of a certain type, with processes then altered (or 'changed-over') to make a given quantity of a different type. This approach has developed over generations, and for some considerable time it has been used to maximise efficiency and exploit 'economies of scale' (i.e. cost reductions resulting from making more of them). However, from a flow perspective, such an approach creates inherent delays, queues and storage. It also increases the risk of overproduction and capacity shortfalls across its various products/services. The use of large batches reduces the ability to respond to variations in customer demand, and as a result it can increase cost (e.g. inventory, storage, space) instead of reduce cost! A move towards single piece, continuous flow, starts to minimise these problems. By focusing on single piece flow and ensuring that orders flow continuously from one activity to another (e.g. workstations), delivery of value is maximised and any delays are minimised. It also reduces the need to hold significant levels of finished goods inventory in advance of firm orders. For example, bakers shops and bread factories are increasingly utilising more smaller sized ovens to make smaller batches of numerous different types of bread in response to the customers demand for choice and freshness (e.g. white loaves, brown loaves, bloomers, baguettes and rolls).

Actual customer demand can be more closely met when a company is capable of creating value quickly and effectively. This is particularly critical for products which have high levels of customisation (e.g. computers), limited shelf life (e.g. food) or goods with high levels of capital value and depreciation (e.g. cars). Whilst many producers have sought to adopt these principles within their supply chains, this whole area is just as important for service companies, who often find it hard to predict the precise value, volume, variety and timing of customer demand.

Service companies often suffer from not being able to stockpile the value they provide to customers. Customers regularly consume the service at the same time as a company provides it and their time must not be classed as 'free' (e.g. a restaurant, an emergency service). Hence, service companies have to be particularly effective at responding to the needs of their customers. By way of example, an Accident & Emergency (A&E) department cannot use batch processing approaches to treat patients, for instance by choosing to treat all burns victims on one day and all car accident victims on another, or by treating burns or accident victims only when they have the 'right' number of them to process! This may be obvious, but it does highlight the particular pressures on service providers to minimise delay and maximise the rate at which value can be provided to individual customers. A Lean A&E service would seek to treat patients one at a time and as soon as they arrive, minimising any non-value added activities, hand-offs or referrals. For instance, patients would like to see a healthcare practitioner immediately on entering and receive all the treatment they need, without having to visit a reception desk and getting transferred to many different specialists or departments.

Variation in the volume of demand can also make it difficult to avoid queues and inventory, even when single piece flow is operated. Queues and inventory can build up anywhere where supply does not exactly match demand, including queues of customers, work-in-progress inventory and finished goods. A critical skill needed in any Lean Enterprise is the ability to level demand/production in order to create smooth flow. If customer demand is naturally stable and level then this is obviously ideal. However, this is rarely the case and levelling production (i.e. provision) to meet average customer demand is often used to create smooth flow, particularly by manufacturers. This then allows techniques such as Just-in-Time to be utilised. Levels of inventory and delays increase slightly, but are a lot less than those of traditional companies once Just-in-Time has been successfully introduced. It is important to note that Lean enterprises also introduce additional flexibility in order to be able to more closely match supply with demand. These include the use of more flexible resources, for instance in the type/size of tools, machinery and infrastructure used. It also includes the flexibility created from increasing the range of activities their staff are able to carry out. For service companies with highly unpredictable demand and who cannot level their provision processes easily, the latter of these is absolutely essential and strategies such as flexible working and multi-skilling become common-place.

Customer demand is often difficult to predict and rarely the same. It varies hour by hour, day by day, week by week, and year by year. As a result, Lean enterprises use actual customer demand (including patterns/trends) to plan the supply of products and services. They also often find that much of the instability in traditional production processes is not caused by variations in customer demand. It is actually a result of using batch processing techniques (e.g. Economic Order Quantities) within the supply chain. These remove the ability of all suppliers in the value chain to see the real underlying end customer demand and only allow them to respond to purchase requests. This creates instability in supply chains (known as the 'bullwhip' effect), leading to over-production, stock shortages and continual 'fire-fighting'. Lean enterprises, therefore, focus on actual customer demand across the complete value chain, sharing this information with suppliers and focusing on levelling demand over a given cycle. For instance, this could mean an automobile manufacturer making a certain number of cars per week, matched to known customer demand. It could also be achieved by companies choosing to use quieter times to create small amounts of finished goods for certain types of products (e.g. ones with low capital, depreciation and storage costs, combined with high levels of demand certainty).

In a service company, they may not easily be able to level demand, as they cannot easily store the value they create or delay providing value to customers (e.g. Emergency Services). Customers are often tied up in the queues themselves, suffering delays and unable to carry out other activities whilst they are waiting. To deal with this, service companies can implement a number of approaches to create a smooth flow of value and minimise any delays. These include adopting innovative ways of supplying resources and providing customer information. For instance, this could include increasing the level of flexibility of staff to carry out a wider range of duties when required (e.g. supermarket staff being able to divert from stacking shelves to operating check-outs and vice versa). It could also mean providing customers more information on how to obtain services, for instance by making them aware of quiet times and possibly offering incentives (e.g. some DIY superstores and cinemas).

Once demand has been levelled, principles such as 'Takt Time' and 'Just-In-Time' (JIT) can be implemented. Takt time is the heart-beat, or rhythm, by which provision is co-ordinated. It is similar to the cox of a rowing team, providing the rate at which each person/station needs to work to ensure a smooth and steady flow of value throughout the process. In addition, work is no longer pushed onto the next activity in the line, independent of whether they need it or not, as this generates excess inventory and overproduction. Work is now only done, 'Just-in-Time', when a signal (known as a 'Kanban') is received from the next activity within the process (i.e. a request for more value to be created). Just-in-Time is sometimes thought to mean no finished goods, no inventory and no activity, until a customer order is received. It does not. Whilst minimising inventory is a valid Lean goal, Just-in-Time refers to the signalling system (i.e. 'Kanbans') used to 'pull' value (including resources and inventory) based on customer demand, which could be real customer demand or levelled customer demand over a given cycle. Levelling demand and Just-in-Time are explored in more depth in Supply Management; as provision processes naturally extend beyond the enterprise and connect everyone involved in the supply chain (known as the 'value chain').

Just-in-Time minimises levels of raw material inventory, work-in-progress (i.e. inventory in the process of being trans-formed) and finished goods inventory held. By delivering to a level schedule based on actual customer demand, overproduction is minimised. However, by doing this, it starts to expose all the problems within a process because there are no longer large buffers of inventory to make up for any short-falls in quality or delivery. Hence for such a system to work, it is essential that any problems are exposed and eliminated. Quality assurance must become part of each and every station/activity, not left to a Quality Control team at the end of the process. When any operator detects a problem, they must have the ability to stop work and to resolve the problem. However, stopping work at one station can quickly stop the whole provision process. Whilst this may seem a disastrous thing to do, it is this that creates unprecedented focus on finding the root causes of problems and eliminating them, rather than expecting operators to continually seek ways of working around problems. In practice, the biggest mistake in the long run is to continue to work around poor components and broken processes.

Continuous improvement is therefore essential for effective provision. Large batch sizes and high levels of work in progress hide problems and waste within a process. This includes wasted time, resources, space and materials (e.g. due to defects). Improv-ing the flow of value involves minimising delays, removing unnecessary activities and hand-offs, reducing batch sizes and the levels of inventory held. Focusing on flow continually exposes problems and waste within a process which continuous improvement must eliminate. When these problems have been resolved, the 'goal posts' are effectively re-set once again; batch sizes and inventory levels are reduced further and continuous improvement is once again used to help strike a path towards the goal of single piece, continuous flow. This approach to removing waste is unique to a Lean Enterprise and helps it to stay ahead of any competitors.

Key to improving flow is minimising any hand-offs between teams and departments. Every time a request is passed from one department to another, there is almost invariably a queue of orders/customers, or a buffer of work-in-progress. Traditional enterprises (focused on maximising efficiency) are generally split into functional departments. In such an enterprise, large queues/buffers not only exist; they are viewed as critical to ensuring each department's kept 'busy'! Activities are also constrained to stay within these departments, in the mistaken belief that it provides economies of scale and maximum efficiency. Dismantling traditional ideas is often required to move away from simple efficiency and towards effectiveness.

In a Lean Enterprise the work-force becomes more highly skilled and they are able to carry out more activities within a process. This reduces hand-offs and delays. Staff also gain more value, motivation and meaning from their work, as they start to carry out more of the tasks within a process, rather than only being able to focus on a single task with an uncertain purpose. Activities are grouped into small cells, which combine activities together and create a team responsible for carrying out all the work within the cell. Team members can easily and flexibly adjust how they carry out the work within a cell. For instance, a single person may take a request through the cell from start to finish. When there are more team members present requests may pass between individuals instead, with each person carrying out a sub-set of cell activities. This flexibility allows cells to increase and decrease their capability, which allows them to respond to customer demand more accurately. Cells simply replicate when they need still more capacity. Cells take on additional responsibilities beyond provision and over time become self-managing. They take responsibility for quality and continuous improvement. They take more responsibility for staff development/ training and support the creation of additional products/services far more effectively. All of these things improve motivation and staff morale. As small groups they welcome the opportunity to take responsibility, to improve what they do and to develop themselves, both as individuals and as teams. Cell working creates the ability to add more value and minimise delays, but it offers a lot more besides.

Many traditional companies are heavily embarked on strategies to provide customers more and more information; offering self-service and self-help to customers in the belief it will improve customer service. In reality, these are almost always introduced to reduce cost and in the majority of cases serve only to increase the time, cost and frustration felt by customers. This is demonstrated by the growth in automated Interactive Voice Response (IVR) and queuing systems. It is also evident from the growing number of online ordering and self help systems provided over the internet; many without a telephone number to call for customers needing to talk to someone. Whilst some customers prefer such methods to understand/order simple products/services, it is often incorrectly assumed that customers are willing and able to work out what is best for them and that their time is 'free'! Most customers are seeking to obtain value from enterprises, not to be given the job of creating all the value for themselves. Customers do not want to be forced into an automated call centre or a web site with little/no option of talking to someone – they want choice. Customers want an enterprise they can trust and converse with. Fully automating a provision process can radically reduce the number of conversations a company has with their customers. These include potential conversations which could have helped to ascertain why people are looking to buy it, what value they are looking to gain from it and what needs to be done to improve it. It also reduces the opportunity to understand their needs, what's important to them and what could help them a lot more in the future. Conversations such as these need to grow in number, not reduce, if a company is to continue to be successful in the future.

Companies need to optimise their provision of value to customers and take care not to commoditise what they provide. A provision process must offer both value and choice, helping to create 'customer loyalty'. Care must be taken, when standardising or automating parts of a provision process, not to destroy the very ability to customise products or to personalise the service provided to customers. This is not saying that technology developments, such as voice recognition or the internet, cannot provide value to customers – because this couldn't be further from the truth. However, it is saying that any technology must holistically improve the value adding process, from the customer's perspective. Using technology to make a process appear cheaper (from an internal perspective), but at the expense of the customer, is 'fools gold'.

Whilst customers are demanding more value from companies, a growing number also want the opportunity to provide value to others themselves. This is a phenomenon which has become particularly apparent since the arrival of the internet. Many individuals and communities around the world are now able to buy things, make things and sell things for themselves, without having to rely on traditional retailers, second hand stores or complex supply chains. New technology is continually allowing more products and services to be offered (e.g. the digital revolution in the entertainment industry). Growing numbers of individuals are creating value for others and obtaining something in return. In some cases the return is a financial one (e.g. for goods sold, using Amazon or eBay) and in others it is not (e.g. providing free content to develop relationships with others, using YouTube or MySpace).

The gap between relationships development and provision reduces in a Lean World (as shown previously in Figure 2.14). The choice available to customers becomes endless; the range of customer demand almost infinite [15]. Provision processes have to be sufficiently flexible to respond to this natural variety. With unlimited variety in customer demand there is ample opportunity for enterprise and choice. Individuals, communities and enterprises all provide value to one another within this demand continuum and in a combined way, satisfy each others needs.

Assurance

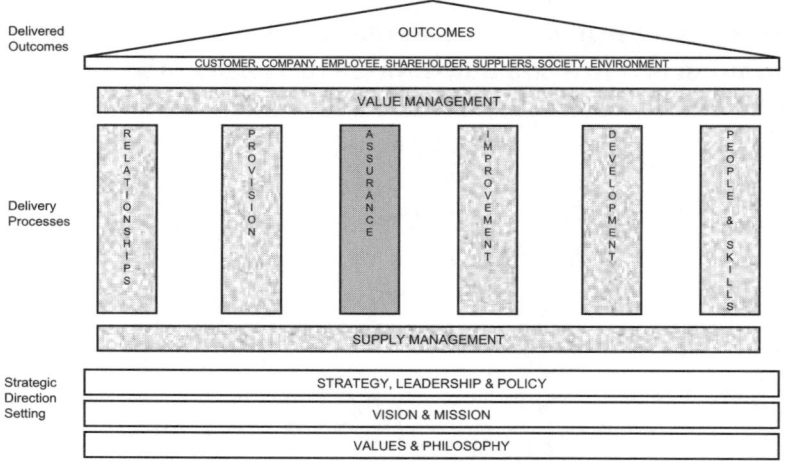

Once a company has sold a product or service to a customer, they generally have an additional responsibility to ensure nothing associated with it goes wrong in the future. This is particularly true for products, with most manufacturers offering warranties for their products for given periods of time. This includes cars, computers, washing machines, food and virtually all products people buy today. Retailers and product providers tend to offer customers either an exchange for another item, or their money back. However, it equally applies to many service providers, such as restaurants where the food is found to be spoiled, or communication companies whose broadband services no longer work properly. The purpose of assurance is to make sure nothing goes wrong in the first place, but to also put things right if they do.

Customers do not expect a product to go wrong or a service to be unacceptable. Hence, during the provision process, quality assurance becomes an integral activity. It is no longer left to a 'Quality Control' team at the end of a process or an after-sales 'Customer Service' team once the provision process has finished. When any operator detects a potential problem, they must have the authority to stop work, seek support, resolve it and eliminate it. By improving the quality of provision, the value, flow, speed, dependability and flexibility all improve. These reduce the need to update, manage or manipulate work on behalf of customers. By improving quality, companies save time and resources, which they then re-divert into activities which provide additional value to customers. This creates a positive feedback cycle of continuous improvement and increased value-adding capability. It also starts to reduce the levels of stress and frustration, for both customers and employees. As a result, more meaningful relationships develop and levels of loyalty, motivation and morale improve.

From the customer's perspective, time spent putting faulty goods or services right does not add value, it only restores lost value. They lose time from doing other activities, as well as the value gained from the use of a product or service for the period until it is restored. The time and resources spent by the company putting things right also adds to cost, but not to value. This demand is often called 'Failure demand'. In many traditional companies, most of their resources and costs can become consumed responding to this type of demand. Some companies even become trapped into thinking that this is what their business is mainly about, with the ability of their customer service department to respond to problems being one of their main differentiators! In reality, on considering their activities from a Lean perspective, these companies are effectively spending most of their time giving investors' money away; replacing faulty goods or giving customers their money back (e.g. through warranties and service guarantee payments).

Assurance has an additional and just as critical purpose; to ensure improvement is subsequently carried out to identify the root cause of why things are going wrong and to eliminate them. It is not enough just to become more proactive, for instance by fixing more problems before the customer sees them and responding quickly when they do (e.g. proactive fault monitoring of broadband services). Likewise, it is not about retailers and insurance companies selling customers expensive insurance policies and profiting from customers having to cover themselves against potential problems. It is about removing the causes of problems so the company and the customer spend a minimal amount of time and resources on assurance. The goal of assurance is therefore to minimise and eliminate itself.

Unfortunately, in many companies, assurance has grown into an industry, with companies mistakenly believing assurance to be a key differentiator and something they can profit from. For some, it has proved to be highly profitable up until now, but with communications technology such as the internet and pressure from the media and lobby groups, consumers are becoming more aware and less tolerant of it. Companies are also starting to adopt alternative, value creating strategies which will completely transform the market-place and undermine companies trying to profit from assurance. For instance, Fujitsu Services have moved away from offering services based on standard repair Service Level Agreements, to ones focused on minimising lost value and maximising the value they are able to create. Companies, such as PC World, are also starting to focus more upon understanding their individual customer's needs and providing products and services which will support them, rather than trying to sell the most profitable products and after-sales warranties. This alternative approach builds long term relationships with customers, creates loyalty and ensures they will not only purchase again, but will also tell others about it. It creates long term revenues and profits, not short term profits at the expense of customers.

This provides significant challenges, particularly for those companies with business models based primarily around assurance. This includes companies like motor repair shops, car recovery services, washing machine repairers and insurance companies. Already we are seeing cars that rarely go wrong. In the UK, they only require an inspection after three years and service intervals are increasing. Vehicle breakdowns have also reduced dramatically and when they do break down, the ability to fix them on the spot is reducing due to the increased variety and complexity of automobiles (e.g. intelligent engine management systems). As production improves, for some products it can be just as costly to fix them as it does to buy a new one. Disposing of faulty goods (rather than fixing them) creates more demand for the company making that product, but only if customers maintain their level of trust in them and choose to buy another product from them again. Customers expect continuous improvement and sometimes play a part in it. Building in reliability, using properly tested technology, becomes essential to developing successful relationships with customers and the long term prosperity of a company. More people expect enterprises they purchase from to act responsibly; by minimising the amount of products people dispose of and maximising the amount they are able to recycle. Concern is growing over unnecessary negative effects on the planet and the need to conserve the world's limited natural resources.

On starting a Lean journey, many service companies find that more traditional management approaches have created huge departments for dealing with the resolution of problems or progress chasing. In fact, much of the growth in call centres around the world has been due, in part, to the explosion of time and resources devoted to fixing problems under the banner of 'customer service'.

In a typical traditional business, restoration (i.e. failure) demand can consume anywhere between 40–90% of their time and resources [16]. All of this is waste from the customer's perspective as well as an unnecessary cost for the business. Such companies tend to find they have, by their very design, been set up to process problems efficiently, rather than eliminate problems altogether. Worst still, they find that the operating environment is actually designed to increase levels of failure demand by itself, sometimes referred to as 'self-generated failure demand' (see Figure 2.18). Excess variability and errors in any of the work carried out generate additional customer demand ('failure demand'), which is then managed by intervention and efficiency teams. These groups intervene even more and introduce more stretching output targets (i.e. in order to process increasing demand). These result in even more variability and errors and a growing cycle of self generated failure demand! For instance, a company may drive their call centre staff to handle calls as quickly as possible, as well as their field staff to fix

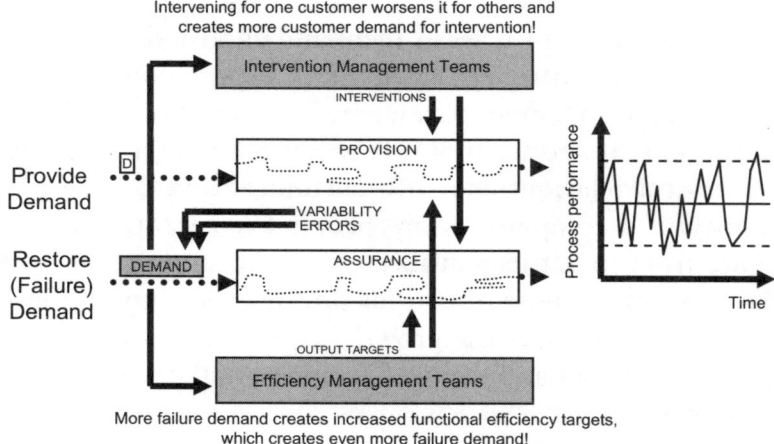

Figure 2.18 Self generated failure demand in a traditional enterprise.

problems as quickly as possible too. In this case, the call centre staff may seek to close calls too quickly, to not properly understand all the customer's needs or explain the whole process to them. As a result, errors and misunderstandings invariably occur and result in aborted deliveries or visits. Similarly, field staff may seek to rush their work, creating further problems and faults which subsequently need to be fixed. All of this creates product/service failures and the need for additional work. These problems are compounded further by the fact that these companies also often suffer from large queues of work and high levels of re-work in their processes. These delay completion of activities and remove the ability to respond quickly and precisely to customer demand. This also creates significant additional activity, taking calls from customers who are chasing, checking, rescheduling, cancelling or complaining about deliveries. Subsequent interventions serve only to create further unpredictability and to amplify failure demand even more. Whole departments (e.g. after-sales, customer service management and customer complaints) are often set up because of this self-generated failure demand. These departments can take on a life of their own, effectively driving extra work which they then have to manage. They sometimes congratulate themselves on how well they are able to handle/process problems too, in the mistaken belief that they are adding value to customers by doing so. Instead of creating and managing problems, they need to eliminate them.

Minimising the need for assurance, stops companies from heading into what would otherwise be a negative downward spiral of increasing failure demand and customer dissatisfaction. Figure 2.19 shows a causal loop diagram demonstrating how increased variability and errors creates more restoration demand (i.e. denoted by 'S's'), but it also highlights how this demand reduces delivery performance as well as customer loyalty (i.e. denoted by the 'O's'). Traditional enterprises often state they are too busy to free up front line resources to help improve the situation. The reality is they cannot afford not to free them up!

Traditional companies, faced with increasing work volumes, tend to focus on driving everyone in the company to work harder and to process work more efficiently. This increases the risk of the business becoming further disconnected from its customers. It can also result in a company seeking to outsource activities to lower labour rate economies so work is processed more cheaply. Companies embarking on a Lean journey, quickly realise that

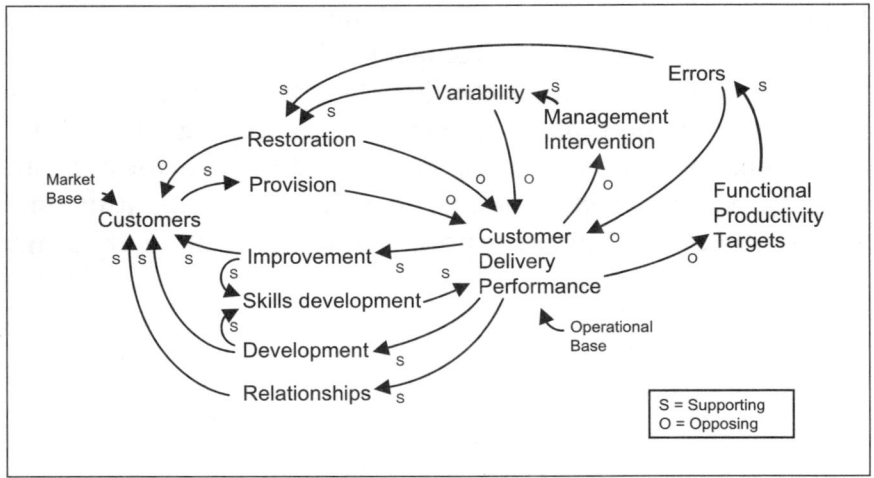

Figure 2.19 Causal loop diagram showing the impact of traditional management intervention and targets on customers and processes.

they need to start to intelligently manage demand, eliminating all the self-generated demand and using freed up resource to identify further opportunities to add value for customers. Call centres stop themselves from becoming an industry in their own right and become an integral part of a company's value creation processes. Lean companies avoid automating or outsourcing failure. They focus on eliminating it instead.

Take Accident and Emergency, or hospital wards. They should not be viewed simply as departments, or processes, for resolving accidents or treating particular health problems. Both of these would serve only to focus attention on processing and restoring value (i.e. people's health). Indeed, in many cases additional health problems are obtained by actually going into hospital, such as further complications resulting from super bugs, errors or insufficient isolation from other patients. Hospitals need to help progressively eliminate health problems, not create more! One hospital starting to apply Lean practice referred to this as not only a process of making people better (permanently whenever possible), but also one of continuous improvement – learning how to improve further and to minimise the risk of killing them! Healthcare groups are increasingly focusing on how to assure people's health, supported by additional groups such as Health and Safety Executives (e.g. accidents) and Social Services (e.g. accidents or social environments). They are trying to stop problems from occurring in the first place, advertising and warning people of various dangers, such as drink-driving, drugs, HIV and smoking. The long term goal of healthcare must be to improve people's well-being and to reduce the amount of time and resources spent either restoring or assuring it – a challenge indeed.

Improvement

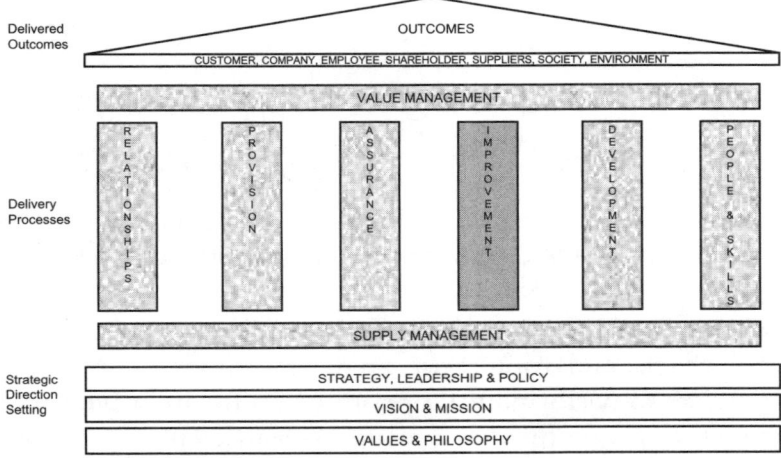

Continuous improvement is an essential part of a Lean Enterprise, providing the central tenet of the business. It is not something left to chance, or for when there is nothing better to do. Customers increasingly demand improvements to products and services. If they are asked, they are often also willing to contribute to identifying and helping to implement them. In an increasingly global market, enterprises which fail to harness the full potential of continuous improvement are destined to drop back in their overall competitiveness and lose customer loyalty.

When carried out correctly, improvement creates a huge buzz of excitement, as well as increased motivation and a multitude of improvement ideas. It can quickly generate thousands of improvement ideas to be prioritised and assessed. Continuous improvement (known in Japan as 'Kaizen') has been presented in many different guises, including Quality circles (TQM), the Deming Cycle of Plan-Do-Check-Act (PDCA) and Six Sigma's Define-Measure-Analyse-Improve-Control (DMAIC) process. Each approach can be visualised as a wheel of continuous improvement and the DMAIC process (shown in Figure 2.20) starts by defining a problem or objective. The

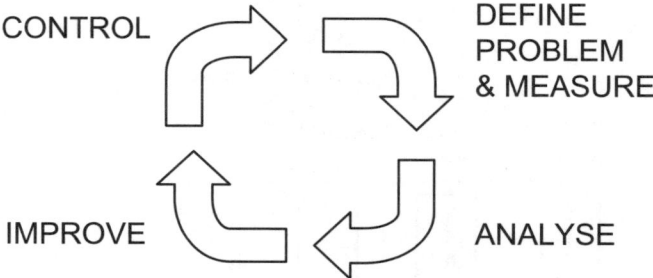

CONTROL   DEFINE
                           PROBLEM
                           & MEASURE

IMPROVE   ANALYSE

Figure 2.20 Basic DMAIC continuous improvement wheel.

current performance is then measured and analysed (e.g. using control charts and root cause analysis). Having captured the key barriers to performance, opportunities for improvement are identified and quantified (e.g. using a lean toolbox). Improvements are controlled and implemented, and project teams continue once again around the circle to analyse, identify and implement more solutions to problems.

Whilst continuous improvement wheels all look very similar in nature, their actual effectiveness depends very much on how they are implemented. Six Sigma uses the DMAIC process, a step by step process for defining, measuring and analysing a problem, then improving and controlling any changes made in order to improve the situation and to sustain any gain made. Most Six Sigma DMAIC improvement projects use the 'Define' step to 'Define the Problem'. For instance 'Productivity is too low' or 'Costs are too high'. Such problems are often hypothesised and bear little relationship to what customers want to see improved. They are sometimes identified through benchmarking, but are more frequently identified through target setting (e.g. improve individual productivity from 3 to 4 jobs / day, or cut costs by 10% per annum). From a Lean perspective, by taking this step, a trap is set for two reasons. First of all, defining the problem does not start with value, from the customer's perspective. Secondly, by setting arbitrary targets for improvement, projects risk sub-optimising the overall performance of the business in the pursuit of them [17], only to relax back once targets have been met and effort has been focused onto other problems (see Figure 1.6 in the chapter 2, highlighting the creation of unintended consequences). Combined, losing sight of the pursuit of perfection and value from the customer's perspective can result in little/no change, or worse still deterioration, from a customer's point of view.

Therefore, the process of continuous improvement in the Lean World has to be more precisely defined to ensure maximum effectiveness, as shown in Figure 2.21. By doing this, continuous improvement becomes prioritised and centred upon improving the level of value provided to the customer. The 'Define' step focuses on value, as perceived by the customer and based on their particular purpose. Measurement is focused on value, its nature and relationship to customer purpose, as well as how value flows through the organisation. Analysis involves identifying barriers as well as potential solutions, carefully considering all options. During this stage, involving everyone, learning by doing and ensuring any unintended consequences are minimised (e.g. from applying Systems Thinking), are all critical. Once this has been done, improvements can be successfully implemented across the company and in a standard way. Then, rather than simply seeking to maintain control of the problem, the process continues to search for additional ways to increase the level of value being

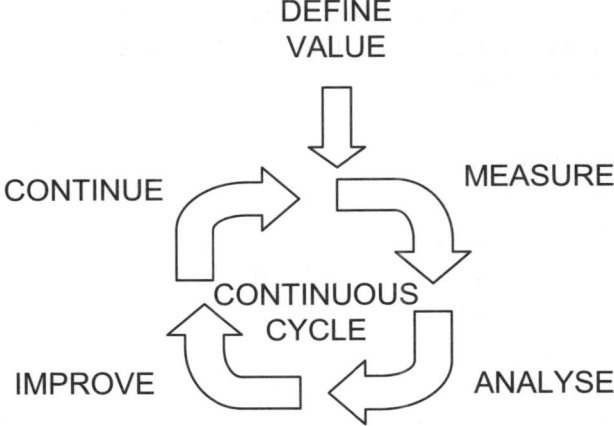

Figure 2.21 The Lean World continuous improvement wheel

added and to eliminate problems. Improvement becomes the responsibility of everyone, not separate improvement specialists. It creates increased motivation in the workplace and a continual challenge to improve the relationships and value provided to customers. It is not about pushing costs onto customers or suppliers, but co-operating and working closely with them to improve the effectiveness of how value is created as a whole. Indeed once started, customers and suppliers quickly become a key source of ideas for improvement; alongside all the companies own staff. By focusing on customer value and flow, a unique positive cycle of improvement develops, one which ensures Lean enterprises become world class in their field and continue to accelerate away from their competitors. Improvement is no longer about processing all demands quickly, but managing different types of demand intelligently (e.g. removing failure demand). It stops unnecessary outsourcing or automation of failure and instead focuses on systematically eliminating it.

In Toyota, continuous improvement lies at the heart of the Toyota Production System. Their focus on perfection, value and flow, led them to pursue a strategy of single-piece continuous flow, removing over-production and increasing flexibility to respond to customer demand. Value stream mapping helped them to identify specific barriers to flow and to eliminate waste. By mapping the complete production, provision and consumption process, an entire picture of the value and waste within a process can be identified [6]. The different types of waste (called 'Muda' in Japan) include:

1. Overproduction,
2. Waiting,
3. Unnecessary transport,
4. Over-processing or incorrect processing,
5. Excess inventory,
6. Unnecessary movement,
7. Defects, and
8. Untapped employee creativity.

These different categories of waste can be caused by many things, including the un-evenness of demand (called 'Mura') and the overburdening of staff (called 'Muri). These two are particularly critical, as by reducing both of these things, value starts to flow more effectively and other forms of waste can begin to be eliminated too. For instance, highly un-even demand can result in unnecessary queues, delays and excess inventory. Similarly, overburdening staff can result in increased defects, stress, absenteeism and reduced employee creativity.

Toyota continuously reduces batch sizes and increases levels of quality to improve the flow of value. This approach helps them to prioritise waste that needs to be removed. On removing this waste, batch sizes are reduced still further and more waste is exposed, and then eliminated, in a drive to create single piece continuous flow. This approach reduces overproduction, inventory levels, defects and all other types of waste in the process. It is also underpinned by policies of levelling flow (to minimise unevenness) and ensuring staff are not overburdened (minimising 'Muri'). All of these go a long way to explaining why Toyota has caught up with and accelerated away from its main rivals (e.g. in terms of its levels of quality, growth, profitability and revenues).

As customers take more of a central stage in improvement activities, they provide essential help/guidance to identify and prioritise areas for improvement. Indeed, without this it can be difficult to determine which of the thousands of potential improvement activities to do first. Many companies first turn to customer satisfaction surveys or benchmarking data for inspiration. These are often obtained through highly scripted surveys, which are overly complicated and carried out by third parties. They regularly involve answering numerous detailed questions, rather than exploring at high level what matters to them, how they would like things to be improved and why. As a result, most of the highly valuable feedback from customers is not captured. Customer complaints can be a good early source of information, because most customers only tend to complain if something is seriously wrong. Similarly, if a customer takes the time to complain it probably means they care! A complaint resolved quickly and effectively can transform a potential dissenter into an advocate. In good faith, some companies have set reducing customer complaints as a key company goal, only to find that rather than eliminating complaints they are hiding them, by making it more difficult for customers to complain. In many enterprises, customers with complaints face increasing difficulty talking to anyone about them, or conversing with someone who is either interested or in a position to take effective action. Customers are often told to put their complaint down in writing and to either post or email it to a complaints department. By forcing customers to spend more time doing this, valuable information is lost, as customers either give up or struggle to clearly explain in words the actual problem, their feelings or its impact upon them. Only through proper dialogue can the true impact and the cause of problems be understood, improvements identified and complaints eliminated.

When gathering customer feedback, and carrying out any survey, it is important to remember that the valuable information is not the actual scores/ratings themselves, but the information provided alongside them. A huge amount of time in many traditional companies is spent obtaining data for very specific questions, analysing trends and hypothesising what might be done to improve them. Surveys and feedback can help to improve the products/services provided, but only if they ascertain value, from a customer's perspective, as well as their priorities and ideas for improvement. This involves more listening than questioning, as well as less scripted questions and answers. However, above all, it focuses on creating more effective action.

For a long time, leading companies have realised that simply reducing customer dissatisfaction is not enough. Some have also realised that focusing on customer satisfaction is also not enough to retain customers and capture new ones; hence they are seeking to develop loyal customers. Loyal customers result from companies being loyal to their customers, and hence a change in thinking and approach is needed (see the previous section on Relationship development). To understand what needs to improve, detailed surveys are not needed but broad conversations are. By taking the time to understand the customer's purpose and value from their perspective, insight into what needs to improve becomes quickly apparent.

By asking a few simple questions, Lean companies find they are quickly able to transform the effectiveness of their improvement programmes and the loyalty of their customer base. The question 'On a scale of between 0 and 10, would you recommend us to others?' may initially be asked, which provides a simple indicative score for customer loyalty. Whilst generating high level information, it is listening and understanding the responses provided to additional questions where real insight/knowledge is gained. Additional questions include 'Why did you give this score?' and 'What would make this improve?' These questions prompt the customer to prioritise and inform the enterprise what needs to improve and why. It also often prompts the customer to offer improvement ideas of their own. By qualifying the feedback provided, showing customers they have been listened to and calling them back to tell them of action being taken, the effectiveness of improvement programmes can be quickly transformed and customer loyalty improved, without the need for complicated surveys, detailed analysis, or huge teams of marketing and change specialists.

Development

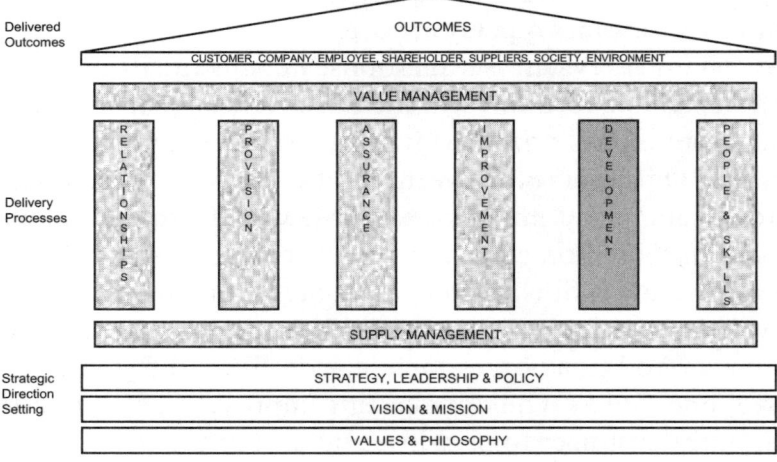

In today's increasingly demanding world, using improvement to provide business as usual, but better, will not be good enough by itself. Customers also expect companies to be constantly developing new innovative products and services that create even more value for them too. As such, product and service development is also a core process, involving customers from the outset and subject to continuous improvement in its own right.

Development is crucial to an enterprise, creating the future products and services the enterprise will provide to its customers. As such, it needs to understand value and success from a customer's perspective and respond to their unmet needs (sometimes termed opportunity demand). It involves creating new relationships, products, services, processes and technologies, as well as developing staff.

If development is not operating effectively within a company, then it's unlikely to survive for long in a Lean World. Lean enterprises are uniquely able to see the world in a completely new light, through a different set of lenses that are capable of exposing the true value customers seek, together with a plethora of new products and services they need and would be more than willing to pay for. By embracing this, continuous improvement is also made more effective, because staff become more motivated when they can see the prospect of improved job security and more development opportunities available to them.

Conversations with customers can quickly reveal new ideas for products and services, but enterprises intent on selling existing products or services fail to listen and often miss such opportunities. By intelligently managing demand, opportunities are captured and help to create the future products/services of the company. In a Lean enterprise, customers wishing to engage and explain the value they need and why they need it are nurtured, not turned away. Such customers care and they have real needs, as well as many potential ideas to share. They are also often in a very good position to identify potential gaps in a market, having failed to find any company offering the type of product or service they need. In addition, conversations with existing customers, as part of relationship development, uncover the real purpose and value customers are seeking, which help to shape future developments. Product and service development therefore becomes highly collaborative, heavily involving customers, the whole workforce and suppliers.

Ideas from these conversations can result in the potential extension of products or services (e.g. radical and new, or incremental changes to existing products and services) or their expansion (the same products or services but sold in different locations or through different channels). Both are valuable and able to provide increased revenues and profitable growth. However, the greatest opportunities are found by stepping into the shoes of the customer and finding out what really adds value for them. For instance, consider for a moment a wholesale communications company. A traditional wholesale communications company is likely to focus on reducing the cost of its current communications products, whilst trying to sell new products with slightly enhanced features. In contrast, a Lean wholesale communications company would seek to understand the real needs of their customers, including mobile service providers needing to increase their service capacity whilst also reducing costs. In the UK, mobile operators tend to gain planning permission, site and build their own masts and infrastructure, and separately request private circuits from BT as a wholesale provider to interconnect them all to their central stations (i.e. switching centres). With nearly half a dozen mobile operators in the UK, this lack of sharing has collectively resulted in an infrastructure being built which is up to 80% inefficient (in terms of cost and capacity). This partly occurred because operators initially viewed the level of network coverage as a key source of competitive advantage, rather than a short term differentiator. Unnecessary costs, coupled with the increasing level of difficulty to obtain planning permission for new sites, have limited the level of growth and prosperity within these markets. Sharing infrastructure can be a very effective strategy and it has been successfully used by a number of operators around the world (e.g. Australia). In the UK BT, the local wholesale provider, is in a potentially unique position to be able to offer a complete infrastructure solution (i.e. including the provision and maintenance of masts) in a wholesale fashion to all mobile operators. This would potentially allow mobile operators to gain extra coverage and capacity, slash their costs and allow them to focus more of their time and resources on offering real value adding services to their customers (e.g. personal communication services capable of intelligently managing a combination of personal and business communication). This would also significantly expand the scope of current wholesale services, or potentially allow other providers to enter the communications infrastructure market and offer additional services to those they currently provide (e.g. street lighting, electricity distribution).

The development cycle involves a number of generic steps, including; defining requirements (i.e. based on customer value and success), designing and developing solutions, followed by implementing them. Once this has been completed the continuous improvement cycle is applied and more products/services are developed (See Figure 2.22). Whilst the development process, at its highest level, may appear obvious, the optimum way to implement it is less so. Common implementations see the process

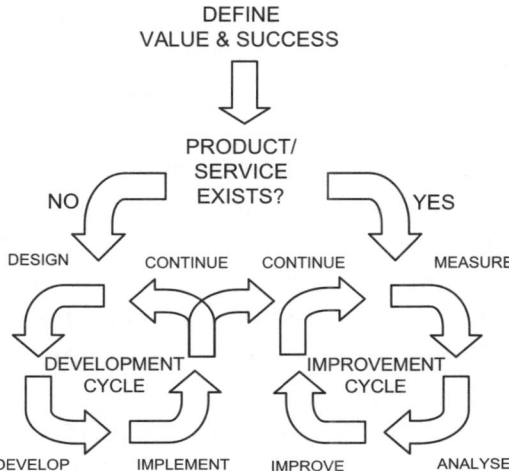

Figure 2.22 Lean development and improvement cycles.

split into discrete steps, with each one given to a different functional group. Each group completes their particular activity and then passes it on. This often results in reduced responsibility, commitment and ownership. It also creates unnecessary delays, errors and rework; all of which add to cost. Along the way, value, from the customer's perspective, gets progressively distant and in some cases completely lost. Development programmes can get easily diverted into making products or services that are easy or exciting to make, rather than what the customer actually needs. Products and services can also be over-engineered and not customised to cater for customers' individual needs. All of these create waste and lost value.

Most of the cost of any new product or service development is locked in at the design stage. This includes the costs of the final product or service, as well as the cost of developing and improving it. Hence, in a Lean development programme, time and resources are spent upfront to optimise the design and to meet customer requirements. This is a highly iterative process, carefully considering all options and one continually challenged by the principle of no compromise – i.e. not 'This or That' but 'This and That'. Design activity not only involves marketing and designers, but process engineers, operational staff, customers and suppliers. The process avoids snap decisions too early in the design process, and fosters collaboration and competition between design options instead. Customisation approaches are also utilised to allow a greater range of customers needs to be met. The design process must consult widely and continuously reflect, to ensure all strengths are optimised and any potential weaknesses minimised. By doing this, costly errors are avoided, as re-work later on in the process can cost 10–100x more to correct than during the initial design stage. By avoiding errors and re-work, designs can be implemented quickly and successfully, resulting in a rapid speed to market.

The design stage not only designs the product or service, but the processes to provide and support it too. Products and processes must be designed together. Provision processes need to take into account the 5 V's, value, volume, variety, variation and vicinity. This ensures that processes are designed to optimise the value they provide and are capable of handling the levels of volume and variation in customer demand. It also makes sure that provision processes are flexible enough to cope with the variety in individual customer needs. By adopting Lean practices, both over-engineering and under-engineering of products/ services, provided to individual customers, is avoided. Lean practices involve standardising and 'flexidising' processes, optimising flow, and applying numerous Lean techniques (e.g. design for manufacture, cell working, mistake proofing).

The design stage also identifies any staff development required to support the new product/service, including the likely number of staff, their skills and locations. This can highlight significant areas of development, offering staff numerous opportunities and challenges. This is achieved by involving staff upfront, as well as supporting them and not overburdening them. This is underpinned by continuous improvement and a 'learn by doing' culture, where all staff and employees take responsibility for the future of the company and support each other in the process. Any temptation to locate in areas with lower labour rates are always scrutinised carefully, in terms of the perception of, and actual impact on, their customers, individuals, the overall enterprise and the communities they serve. For instance, these include potential difficulties arising from differences in language or cultures, or inherent issues associated with operating supply chains over very large distances.

The design stage determines the technology required, either in the product or service, or as engineering tools/software required to create the new product or service. Technology is not introduced for technologies sake, but because of the value it offers. Latest technology will be used if it offers more value than its predecessors, but only when it's fit for purpose. Technology which fails, either intermittently or fundamentally, can cost a company dearly, not just in assurance costs but in terms of lost loyalty. Technology is brought in to support staff, not to remove the need for staff, for instance by taking on high volume repetitive tasks and ensuring things do not go wrong (e.g. Quality control). The intelligent and inherent flexibility of people is highly valued and never undermined by the deployment of technology.

The process of development is one managed by a single individual, often called a Chief Engineer, with a team responsible for the design and implementation of the product or service from start to finish. A Chief Engineer (and their team) calls in specific additional expertise at each stage of the development cycle, to ensure the best possible outcome in the shortest possible time. Temptations to fast-track or cut corners during the design stage are avoided, as they offer false economy. Lean enterprises find that the best way to speed up the development process is to design carefully and to implement rapidly. This avoids unexpected last minute changes to designs; which are the most common cause of high costs and long delays. The development team takes responsibility for prioritising requirements from the very outset, setting common goals, communicating them clearly and ensuring that value, from the customer's perspective, is the primary focus of everyone throughout the process. They are effectively responsible for creating the future of the company, harnessing innovation and at the same time motivating and challenging those around them. As such, Chief Engineers, and their teams are always highly respected and selected very carefully.

In its own right, the development process is subject to continuous improvement, focusing on improving the value created and the flow of value within the process. Products and services are designed to be as effective as possible from the outset, minimising the need for re-work and future improvement. By continually improving the process of development, the final competitive frontier is created. Companies capable of developing value, quicker, faster and more effectively than others, have the potential to create the most loyal customers. Those that stay where they are, not listening, developing or improving their means of creating additional value for customers, will not satisfy customers increasing demands and risk falling by the wayside.

As an example, consider the development by Toyota of the Lexus brand and their range of hybrid vehicles [6, 18]. These resulted from a combination of a more thorough understanding of value from the customers' perspective, a no-compromise philosophy, and a process, led by a Chief Engineer, focused on designing carefully and implementing rapidly. Such approaches to development have allowed revolutionary new products to be delivered much more rapidly to market, with their market share steadily increasing as a result. The Lexus has proved itself to be a highly successful, no-compromise, luxury brand in the executive market and demand for hybrid cars, such as the Prius, is flourishing in a world with growing fuel costs and ever increasing concern over the environment.

Similarly, Tesco have been quick to innovate and develop new services which provide more value to their customers. For instance, Tesco Express has been recently introduced, harnessing the unique knowledge and insight from their loyalty cards, to provide customised convenience stores. Learning by doing has helped in the introduction and development of Tesco.com, delivering directly to peoples' homes. Listening to customers has also resulted in the extension of their products and services range into other retail areas, such as non-food products, insurance and communication services.

People and Skills development

It is often said that the greatest asset of any enterprise is its people. How true this is and yet how rarely it is practised. Whilst enterprises regularly use such words and phrases, many in reality still view their staff as their biggest cost. Companies regularly set up improvement goals in terms of head-count reductions, and seek either to automate work carried out by staff or outsource their jobs to suppliers, possibly in lower labour rate economies. It is of little wonder that many employees become suspicious, or worse still paranoid, about the real intentions and desires of the company they work for and some of those around them.

The traditional role of management is based on meeting targets, as well as controlling and managing staff. This has sometimes migrated to one of 'empowering' employees to make sure they meet their manager's targets whilst giving them 'coaching'. A 'climate of fear' continues to exist within many enterprises. Many still believe that 'management by fear' is the most effective approach to getting the best out of employees. In reality, stress and fear hinder an individual's ability to think rationally or to act effectively, causing them to become confused and to make mistakes. Stress is created when individuals' feel they cannot cope, for instance when they have been given a huge challenge with little to no support. This is relatively common in many jobs and organisations. It is often said that 'it's just the way work is', but this could not be further from the truth.

Many traditional managers believe that their staff cannot be trusted and that, without their intervention, they would do a minimum amount of work. This is particularly the case in companies who have never entrusted their employees with any real responsibility and where levels of two way communication are poor [11]. This results in staff waiting to be told what to do and when to do it, rather than using their own initiative. The reliance on management for everything ensures that the company gets exactly what it asks for, without ever finding out what its real capabilities are. It also means, when an individual isn't pulling their weight, managers are left to try to work out what is happening and to instil discipline, often based on measures taken and any targets set. Unfortunately, if inappropriate measures are used it can result in an enterprise 'coaching' the wrong staff and disciplining its best staff (or worse still firing them)! Such interventions are rarely successful and are much less effective than ones creating a shared responsibility, combining peer pressure and support.

The human mind has a great ability to filter out anything that does not support a person's belief and amplify everything that does. This mindset (or filter) can work in two ways. First of all, if a manager believes that their staff can be trusted then they will exert minimum levels of control (as well as targets) and allow their staff to do what they think is best (See Figure 2.23). Subsequent action by staff, filtered by this same 'mindset', then supports this initial assertion. They do not wait for instructions and become motivated and creative, doing the right things with minimum risk of error. As a result more trust is established and staff are given even more control. Conversely, if the mindset is one of not naturally trusting people, a manager is likely to increase the level of control (and targets) they use, because of how their mind filters any behaviour observed. But it's the initial mindset that is driving these behaviours, not the staff themselves. The mindset (i.e. the filter) determines whether it is going to be a

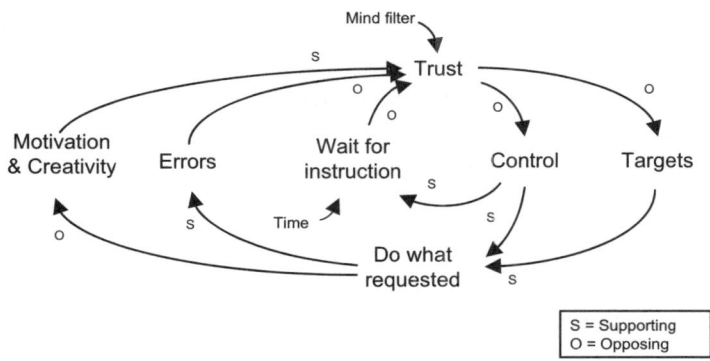

Figure 2.23 Simple causal loop diagram showing the impact of mindset on trust, as well as levels of management control/targets and staff motivation/creativity.

positive or negative spiral. It determines the amount of micromanagement introduced, as well as the levels of staff motivation and creativity that result.

Lean enterprises have a completely different approach to developing staff and the roles and responsibilities of management. This is often presented as a significant barrier to a company wishing to change from a Traditional Way to a Lean Way. Some refer to it as a culture change (i.e. of values, behaviours and beliefs) but in reality it is better described as a 'system' change. For instance, the company values might be perfectly fine, but not actually adhered to. In general, neither employees nor managers seek the demise of the business they work for, or deliberately do the wrong thing. Instead they do what the 'System' drives them to do and they are either unable to see, or apparently influence, an alternative way of doing things. This is not the case for all however. Some managers are aware of the alternatives, but are wedded to their beliefs (e.g. lack of trust) and find it difficult to change (e.g. from command and control approaches). They enjoy telling people what to do and find it extremely difficult to listen or work as a team. For these people, there are unfortunately very few roles in a Lean enterprise. As a Lean transformation begins to take off, those trying hard to undermine the change become increasingly isolated and some of them have to leave. Positive changes, which significantly improve the products and services provided to customers, are hard to argue against and rarely resisted, though some staff 'sit on the fence'. Once they see changes starting to happen however, they get behind them and add value to them too.

The core strength of an enterprise is not determined by its current products or services, but by how well its staff work together (and with customers and suppliers) to provide them and to create new ones. Staff development is therefore a core purpose in a Lean enterprise; as important as delivering value to customers. Lean enterprises nurture and develop their staff and operate a policy of 'learning by doing'. This involves not simply seeking to give people the answers, but helping them to find out the right questions to ask to obtain the answers for themselves. Similarly, Lean enterprises give increasing responsibility to front line teams to carry out more of the activities, to become multi-skilled and to work as a team to provide what customers need. They also take on responsibility for identifying how to improve the way the work works and to increase the amount of value created. Rather than setting arbitrary targets, the role of management is to support them in this process, ensuring consistency and control, whilst sufficiently challenging employees without overburdening them. The opportunities for further development need to be clearly visible to employees in order to negate potential concerns that any ideas or improvement activities will simply result in job losses. Without this, staff will naturally be reticent to get involved or be fully committed, forcing improvement initiatives to be carried out by other groups remote from the work, with reduced likelihood of success.

Staff motivation is mostly derived from the desire to make a difference and to add value for others. It also results from working as part of a team and from meeting challenges. Monetary rewards are important, as people need money to live, but they do not naturally motivate people. In traditional companies, individual bonus schemes often reduce co-operation and increase stress/frustration. Traditional companies use targets and bonus schemes to get individuals to deliver the results they want, but this can sub-optimise the operation of the overall business dramatically, as individuals are driven to find anything that helps them to achieve their target. Lean companies do not change this, they eliminate it. Rather than driving people to meet particular targets or outcomes, Lean companies focus on improving the means of achieving outcomes (i.e. their capability). Whilst company wide goals are important and sometimes linked to employee rewards, bonuses linked to individual targets and functional goals are avoided.

Pay in a Lean enterprise becomes more closely related to the actual capability of the individual to create value, for instance through increased multi-skilling or by taking on additional leadership responsibilities. For example, in a service centre, rather than providing bonuses to front line staff based on their overall call answer rate, they may choose instead to pay them based on their skills and the range of calls they are able to handle. This can dramatically reduce the complexity of the pay system and at the same time provide further incentive for individuals to develop and take on further responsibilities. For instance, an operator may progress further and take on additional roles within a group, such as a trainer/coach, improvement leader, development leader or team leader. Staff operate as small teams (called 'cells') and are responsible for carrying out a number of activities in a process. By developing their skills, individuals carry out more activities within a process and in their particular cell. This helps to reduce hand-offs and increase motivation. It also helps to improve flexibility and flow. For example, one operator may, in principle, be able to carry out all of a cell's activities in response to a customer request (i.e. from start to finish). However, more generally a number of operators co-operate and work together in order to balance the work-load. They minimise any unnecessary hand-offs and movement; attributes particularly apparent in production environments (e.g. see the multi-person / multi-activity scenario shown in Figure 2.24). Each person carries out a sub-set of activities, based on the time needed to complete particular activities (e.g. activities G and H are the most time-consuming in Figure 2.24), the range of skills they possess

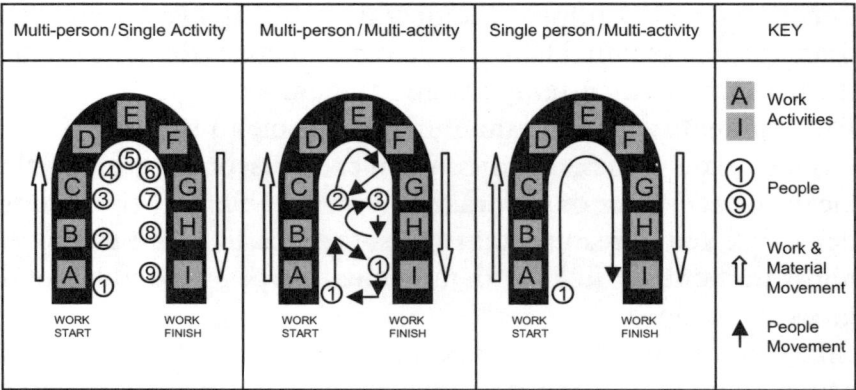

Multi-person/Single Activity	Multi-person/Multi-activity	Single person/Multi-activity	KEY

Figure 2.24 Multi-skilling and Flow within 'Cells'.

and the way that work flows through the process. Operators can pass work between them, but they avoid inventory and queues.

By extending their range of skills and taking on additional responsibility, cell workers are able to see clear and distinct career paths. They also carry out more activities within their cell, including their own training and development. This approach is often adopted to help level the work-load and reduce overburden. It also naturally reduces the distinction between managers and workers, with managers helping out in the work-place and supporting front-line staff, whilst work teams get actively involved in planning rotas and implementing improvements.

As reward schemes increasingly focus on capabilities, rather than the amount of output, reviews spend more time discussing performance in terms of current capabilities and opportunities for further development. As such, development reviews become more effective, open and holistic. The process, by its very nature, becomes less divisive and involves others; including colleagues, customers and suppliers. Care has to be taken on implementing any change to reward schemes and development however, as one housing association found out to their cost when they initially went down this path. On deciding to change from an individual bonus system (based on output) to one focused on rewarding skills, they chose initially to reward the number of courses attended. This dramatically increased the demand to attend training courses, but it did little to improve the desire of individuals to apply their newly acquired skills. They quickly moved away from this, to one rewarding applied skills only!

As an enterprise begins a Lean journey they start to see a vast array of new potential products and services they could provide. Priority grows to free up resources; resources tied up on any non-value add, mundane or repetitive activities. Through continuous improvement, freed up resources help to accelerate change and create additional capacity capable of providing new products and services. This increases the amount of 'clear blue water' between the enterprise and any competitors. Lean enterprises also take on more staff, carefully selecting, developing and nurturing them over a number of years. Just like customers, potential employees tend to build up an affinity with companies they would ideally like to work for. Lean enterprises therefore do not have to spend huge amounts of time or money to advertise jobs, as highly talented and committed individuals proactively seek out such opportunities. The pull of working for a world class company, which provides products or services they themselves have a natural affinity to (and indeed often buy themselves) cannot be underestimated. Likewise, the value of recruiting such individuals cannot be overstated. Some companies partly select new employees based on whether they own or buy any of the company's products or services themselves.

The visibility of clear career structures, personal development opportunities and their continual growth/success make Lean enterprises highly attractive prospects. Companies finding it difficult to attract staff are probably not Lean enterprises. If a company is regularly replacing their staff and executives, then they are unlikely to be a Lean Enterprise. More and more staff are leaving companies due to stress and overburden, something Lean enterprises seek to avoid. Lean enterprises 'learn by doing' and tend to nurture from within. They also achieve world class outcomes by allowing everyday people to operate excellent processes.

Lean companies recruit staff based more on attitudes than

skills. Skills can and are, often best provided and developed by the company itself. However, basic individual attitudes and beliefs are more deeply embedded and more difficult to change, often requiring a certain amount of unlearning before any learning can begin. A Lean company looks for potential employees who demonstrate drive and enthusiasm, co-operation and team-work, commitment to tasks, and a desire to be challenged. All of these attributes go towards supporting an innovative environment, where continuous improvement is the responsibility of everyone and all problems are exposed, not hidden, with the sole purpose of eliminating them. It is this collective power that traditional companies find difficult to match.

Leadership is also critical. Leaders must have the ability to inspire, motivate and take the initiative. They must also provide clear and consistent direction, as well as an exemplary demonstration of company values. They must relish a challenge and not be frightened to challenge others. They do not delegate responsibility but look to share a collective responsibility. They are happy to let others lead and ensure they support them in the process. Leaders are not afraid to make mistakes, but invariably seek to learn from any mistakes. Whilst the role of the executive team is crucial in setting direction for the enterprise, leadership is not the responsibility of this team alone. It must exist throughout the company and at all levels. In fact, when many companies start their Lean transformation, they often find that some of their previously most stubborn and resistant employees transform into some of their best leaders. Their previous resistance to change often only existed because they cared passionately about their company and customers, whilst believing there must be an alternative and better way. Once they find it, they can become some of the most committed champions of change, as well as some of the most influential.

Companies like Toyota tend to grow their leaders from within. They develop their staff and do not have to rely on continually recruiting people from outside. They support a policy of 'learning by doing', commitment and teamwork. The traditional roles of management and workers are less distinct, with leadership required at all levels and continuous improvement the responsibility of everyone. They value skills and experience, and offer development opportunities and mentoring for their staff. Attitudes, combined with skills and practical experience, tend to out-weigh academic qualifications within Lean enterprises [6].

Supply Management

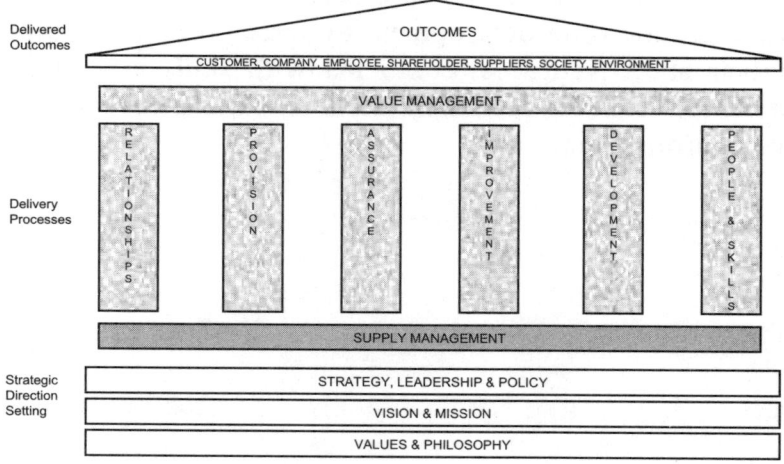

All value adding processes require resources. Some of the resources are consumed in the process of creating value, such as components, sub-assemblies or energy. Others are not consumed, such as staff carrying out tasks, equipment and tools, or the space in which activities are carried out. All of these have to be supplied to the value adding process in order for them to work effectively. This is the role of supply management. Supply management covers all activities from identifying strategic partners through to managing the complete supply process. The supply process, whilst ordering and managing the flow of goods, materials and resources, also links to the value management process to ensure payments are made.

The key purpose of the supply management process is to support the rapid and effective flow of value in its delivery processes. This involves minimising unevenness of demand and any overburdening of staff. It also involves maximising the flow of value across the supply chain and minimising any waste, such as those associated with delays, transportation and inventory. In traditional organisations, supply management is often linked to a department; one mainly focused on purchasing resources and driving down prices. This is often achieved by standardising components, negotiating volume discounts and creating economies of scale, as well as through the use of highly competitive tendering processes. Through such processes, suppliers are forced to provide their primary products or services for very little profit and even at a loss. Suppliers are then left to work out how to turn this into a profit (e.g. through a mixture of cost cutting and additional charging), often to the detriment of everyone concerned. Whilst Lean enterprises also standardise and reduce the variety of components required, they do not compromise the value provided to the customer in the process. They continually challenge suppliers to improve their products or services and to find additional ways to create value. However, rather than leaving supply decisions to market forces or aggressive tendering processes, Lean enterprises tend to rely a lot more upon strategic partnerships, co-operation and joint continuous improvement.

Supply management maximises flow and minimises waste. The first step involves minimising any un-evenness in demand. It then involves creating the necessary flexibility in each process to cope with the variety in demand and any remaining variation in volume. Combined, these minimise the risk of overburdening staff. As un-evenness is minimised and flexibility is increased, value adding processes become more stable and consistent. By becoming more consistent, they are also able to be increasingly standardised and continuously improved. The process of continuous improvement then creates a steady reduction in the levels of waste, including the amount of work-in-progress and finished goods inventory held.

Unevenness in demand can initially be reduced by introducing demand and work levelling. A great deal of variation in demand can be systematically created by traditional business models all by themselves. For instance, these could include purchase requests being stored during non-working days or as a result of batch processing. Coupled with this, operating traditional supply management practices, such as Economic Order Quantities, can remove the ability of suppliers to see the real underlying customer demand and allow them to only respond to purchase requests. All of these generate fluctuations in demand, not

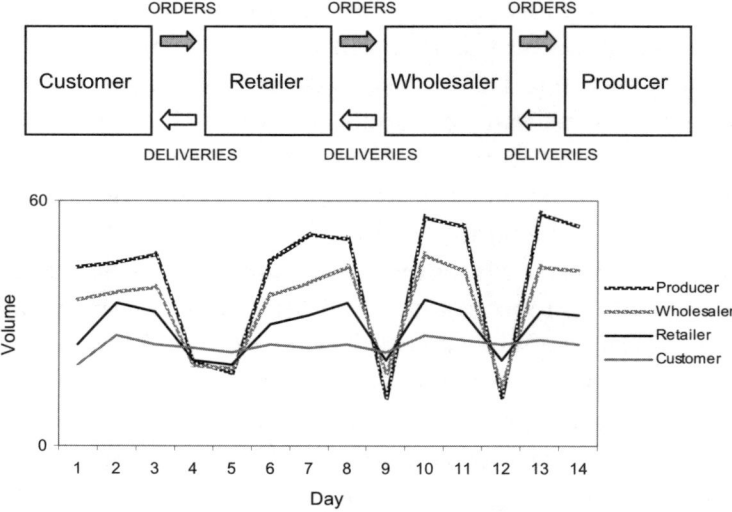

Figure 2.25 The bullwhip effect in traditional supply chains, showing the variation in order/delivery quantities across the supply chain.

related to actual end customer demand, which are then amplified through the supply chain via a process commonly referred to as the 'bullwhip effect' [19]. The fluctuations in demand grow the further away from the real source of customer demand the particular provider is. Fluctuations can also be large even when actual customer demand varies very little (see Figure 2.25).

The bullwhip effect can lead to massive fluctuations, delays and 'fire-fighting'. Lean enterprises focus on actual customer demand, share this information with suppliers and focus on

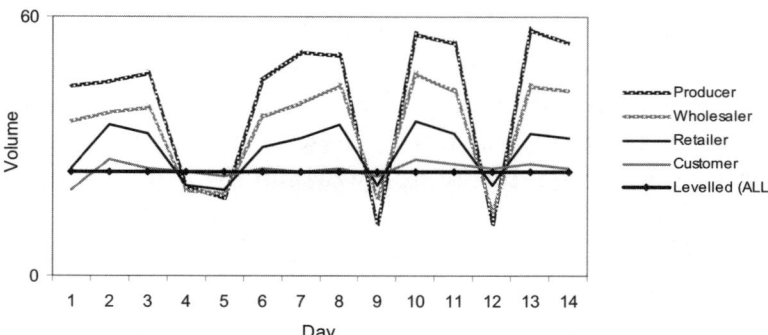

Figure 2.26 Demand levelling over a given cycle.

levelling demand over a given cycle. For instance, this could mean a manufacturer making a certain number of a product per week, matched to customer demand (as shown in Figures 2.26). All components of the supply chain operate to the same levelled demand. When a range of products are provided, levelling also involves levelling (i.e. smoothing) out the demand and production of each product type. For a given mix of demand, batch processing (i.e. which would sequence identical model types one after the other) is progressively changed to Lean processing, where different model types follow one another (see Figure 2.27). Set up times, cycle times and batch sizes are all steadily reduced, whilst the same product mix is maintained to satisfy overall demand. Levelling flow can also involve using quieter production periods to generate small amounts of finished goods inventory for certain products with specific characteristics (e.g. goods with high seasonality, low capital, depreciation and storage costs, coupled with high levels of demand certainty). This is sometimes viewed as heresy, with comments such as 'Lean is about removing inventory, not introducing inventory!' However, it must be remembered that Lean is actually a philosophy of continuous improvement, one focused on improving the flow of value. When demand for all products can effectively be levelled by slightly increasing the amount of finished inventory held

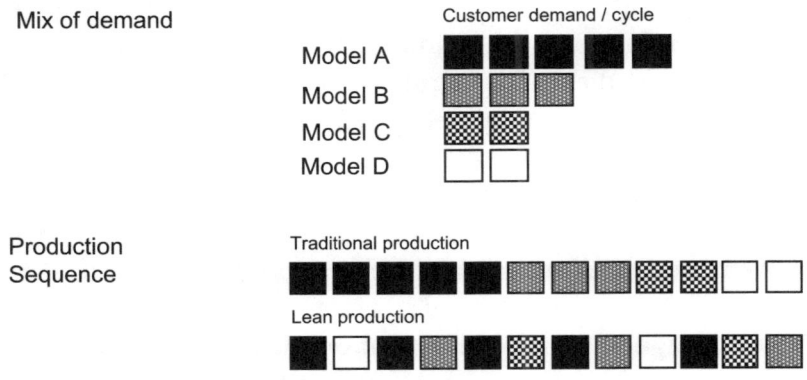

Figure 2.27 Mixed model demand and production levelling over a given cycle.

for just a few, it can be advantageous. By levelling demand, a virtuous circle of 'Just-In-Time' and continuous improvement can be applied for all products. In doing so, overburdening of staff can be reduced, all forms of waste can be eliminated and a gradual migration towards single-piece flow achieved.

Customer demand can potentially be smoothed by non-natural means too, for instance by offering discounts or incentives (e.g. DIY stores offering discounts during quieter times). However, Lean enterprises try to avoid discounting and seek more innovative ways to level demand instead.

The level of variety and remaining variation can be managed by optimising the amount of personalisation, customisation and flexible working. These are particularly important in service industries, where the level of variety and variation associated with customer demand can make smoothing flow more difficult and supply management more complex. Service companies are rarely able to 'level demand' as easily as a product company, as they are often unable to store the value they create or determine the exact timing of customer requests. A manufacturer can use simple mass customisation techniques to increasingly personalise products as they go through the process of being made. For instance, the features and upholstery in a car are only added towards the end. In a service environment however, high levels of variety can occur right from the start, with customers often requiring very different types of services and having very different needs. In this case, companies have to intelligently manage demand, clarify the value required upfront and provide only what the customer actually needs. This level of personalisation demands far more flexibility in processes, as well as more flexibility in resourcing them. For instance, flexibility within the enterprise is created by staff taking responsibility for continuous improvement as well as for the training and development within their teams. Team members use quieter periods to train and mentor colleagues, which builds in more flexibility. On the other hand, during busier times Lean enterprises are able to deploy virtually all their staff onto front line processes. Lean enterprises may also operate flexible working arrangements (e.g. cell-working, home-working, annualised hours) in co-operation with their staff. In addition, they may ensure that extra staff and resources are available from a third party during certain periods. However, if they do, such staff are always trained upfront and fully conversant with the values and standards of the company. In reality a mixture of strategies are used to provide sufficiently flexible resourcing to ensure smooth flow.

Once demand has been levelled and smooth flow created, approaches such as 'Just-In-Time' (JIT) can be implemented. 'Just-in-Time' is very different to more traditional approaches. Traditional approaches tend to maximise the efficiency of each station, by allowing them to produce as much as possible. This is often called a 'push system', as stations 'push' more material down the line whether there is actual demand for it or not. This generates excess inventory at each station and results in more finished (and unsold) goods. In contrast, with a 'Just-in-Time' approach work is only carried out when a signal (often called a 'Kanban') is received from a downstream station telling it to produce more value. This is a 'pull' process, rather than a 'push' process, as value is 'pulled' in only when it is needed (see Figure 2.28). The flow of materials is driven by demand (after it has been levelled) and takes place with a certain natural rhythm. The

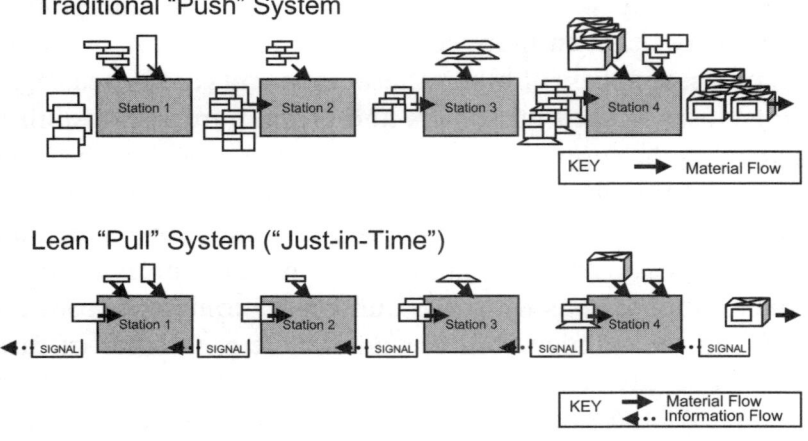

Figure 2.28 'Push' and 'Pull' (Just-in-Time) supply management systems showing material flow and information flow.

time taken for one product to be made is often referred to as the 'Takt time'. Just-in-Time, in contrast to traditional approaches, minimises the levels of raw materials, work-in-progress (i.e. inventory in the process of being transformed) and finished goods inventory held. In service industries in particular, Just-in-Time is also applied to transforming resources (e.g. staff) too. However, care is required when applying Just-in-Time, as it invariably exposes weaknesses within processes. Hence continuous improvement and a focus on quality are also necessary for 'Just-in-Time' to be introduced successfully (e.g. Toyota Production System).

Continuous improvement is used to progressively increase the flow of value and reduce levels of waste and errors. Supply management operates a process of supplying every product in every cycle. When problems have been resolved and the process improved, the 'goal posts' are reset; batch sizes and inventory levels are reduced still further and continuous improvement is once again used to strike a path towards the goal of single piece, continuous flow. Single piece flow not only reduces the levels of inventory, it also creates additional flexibility to respond to customer demand. Continuous improvement is carried out across the complete value chain. For instance, transportation and inventory levels are reduced collaboratively. A number of activities may be re-located and co-located, and component suppliers may be given more control over their supply of stock. For example, suppliers of high value components are increasingly locating closer to their customers and given more responsibility for managing the supply of their goods. At the same time, certain low value commodity component suppliers are tending to locate where labour rates are at a minimum. Purchasing, invoicing and payment processes are also simplified as manufacturers begin to pay their suppliers based on the number of complete products created and the standard bill of materials (e.g. number of cars produced and the fact that there are 5 tyres and 2 bumpers on every car). At the same time, companies, such as Tesco, have introduced systems which allow their suppliers to see actual consumer demand for their products, so they can plan production effectively and minimise any risk of shortages or overproduction. Tesco have also trained additional staff, normally responsible for stacking shelves, to operate check-outs when queues begin to build up. Customer frustration and increased employee stress often occur in more traditional companies, as large queues build up and no more staff are made available to help (e.g. freed up from other background activities). Many companies outsource background activities (e.g. staff training and development), only to find that it reduces their ability to respond to customer demand. This reduces effectiveness and increases overall costs. The potential for outsourcing (and in-sourcing!) are always there, but each situation is considered holistically and any decision is taken carefully.

Value Management

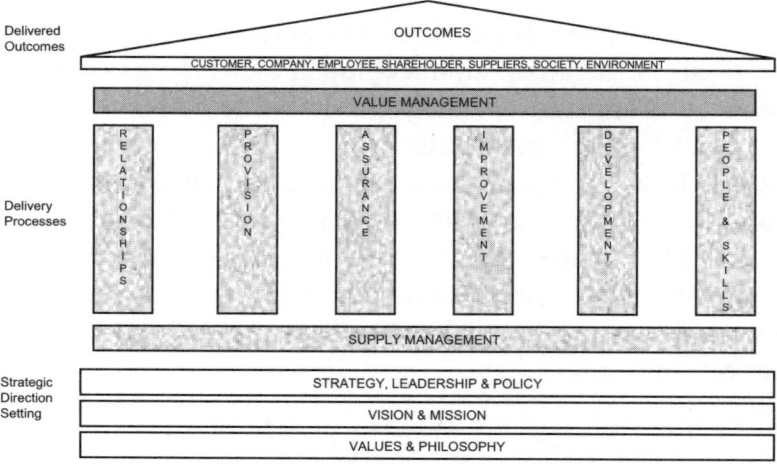

Value Management is a unique component within the Lean World Management System. It identifies business performance and accounts for both the level of value provided and the costs incurred. It also includes the processes used to obtain payment from customers and to pay suppliers (including staff). In traditional companies, performance reporting is often associated with managing output and levels of productivity. Meanwhile, whilst accounting reports on revenue and profitability, it is mainly associated with costs. Accounting also helps to set product/service costs and to report/manage costs on an ongoing basis. Value Management, as its title implies, focuses on measuring value, managing value and optimising value. This does not infer that Lean enterprises no longer understand or manage their costs. This could not be further from the truth. However, Lean enterprises do approach reporting and accounting in very different ways.

First of all, Value Management provides relevant information to all stakeholders; customers, employees, the enterprise, investors and the wider community. Relevant means meaningful, purposeful and accurate. Information is not managed or manipulated in order to present what people would like to see. Instead, the information presented is accurate, contains real meaning and can be directly used for continuous improvement. Too often, traditional companies measure virtually everything but know the meaning of very little. Lean enterprises measure very little but learn the meaning of everything. As an example, many traditional companies use approaches such as cost apportionment to allocate costs across products and services, with relatively little understanding of the real costs of providing them. Many companies also create their own internal measures and targets, which they then use to report the performance they are providing to their customers (e.g. percentage of problems resolved by next working day). More often than not, such figures have little to no relevance for individual customers. Even when measures are relevant, results are often meaningless due to the level of manipulation that arises as a result of setting targets for them.

Secondly, within Value Management the concept of having to balance everything is disregarded. The notion of compromise and constantly having to juggle levels of customer performance, financial performance and employee satisfaction are cast aside. A Lean Enterprise takes on the principle of zero compromise and the pursuit of perfection. Through continuous improvement, solutions are sought which maximise everything, all at the same time. This is not as difficult as it may first sound. Traditionally, most customer frustration, product and service failures, high operating costs and employee stress result from self-generated failure demand, systematically created by the management system itself. Hence, they can all be improved together, by moving away from a traditional system towards a Lean management system.

Thirdly, within Value Management attention is moved away from outputs and averages. Focusing on averages serves only to create an average (or worse) company. Lean enterprises focus on the capability to produce outcomes and reducing the variation in the performance of the enterprise. They create capability charts that make use of Statistical Process Control (see Figure 2.29), with the upper and lower control limits determined by statistical

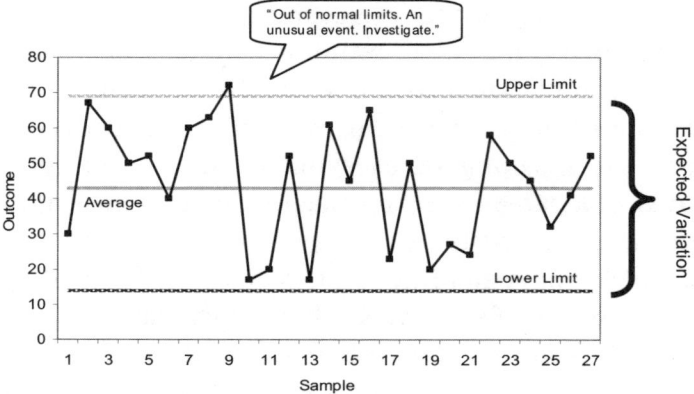

Figure 2.29 Capability chart showing the average and control limits.

methods. When outcomes are found to be within the expected level of variation, no action is taken. When they fall outside these limits, any causes are identified. In traditional companies, specific outcomes are often given to people as targets, missing the fact that over 90% of the variation is normally within the 'system' of work, and not due to the performance of their people! A Lean Enterprise focuses on changing the 'system' to reduce the level of variation in the work, and in doing so they improve the design of their enterprise.

Finally, for Value Management the highest priority measures are those related to customer value, not cost. The primary purpose of any business is to provide value to customers, to continue to do so and to create more ways of doing so. Only by doing this can businesses continue to grow their revenues, increase their profits and create further returns on investment for shareholders. Hence, Value Management puts customers centre stage. New and distinct ways of accounting for the performance provided to customers are used, both individually and collectively. First of all, value has to be defined from the customer's perspective, not from that of the enterprise. This requires a deeper understanding of the purpose of the customer and the value they seek. This is gained throughout all development and improvement processes. For instance, an airline, when buying IT services from an IT service provider, may need an IT infrastructure that will help them to make sure each customer travels effortlessly and completes the journey they need. Hence, IT services need to support the needs of customers, rather than offer the latest IT equipment/software with a better standard Service Level Agreement (SLA) for repair. First of all, this involves starting to measure, understand and eliminate IT problems impacting on the processes that deliver value to customers. Then it involves helping the airline to improve the value it adds still further, by optimising the flow of passengers throughout the process and helping the airline to create additional services. This could include offering on-line ordering, information services, ticket-less services, car-parking and local travel services, all of which allow passengers to more effortlessly get from A to B.

More sophisticated Value Management systems can be used to highlight the volume and value of different types of demand (i.e. provide, restore, improve & develop, as well as relationship & people development). They can also include the resources and overall costs (part of the overall enterprise response) associated with different types of demand as well (as shown in Figure 2.30). These are called demand profiles and they can be used at both a customer and enterprise level. In such profiles, failure demand often stands out, because it uniquely generates negative value (e.g. lost value and revenue) whilst adding to cost

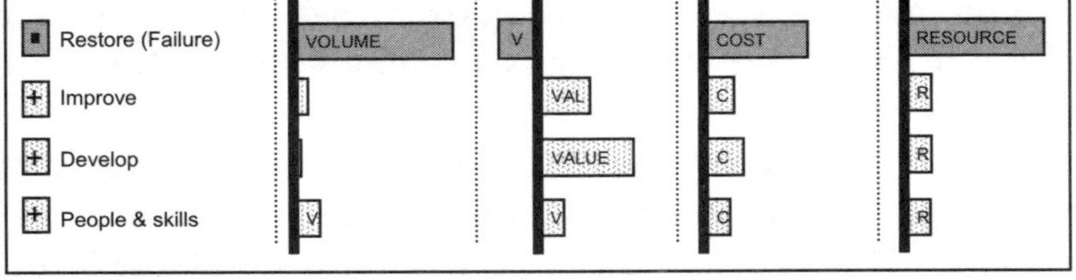

Figure 2.30 Top level enterprise demand profile.

(e.g. compensation payments and cost to resolve). In this particular example, relationships development also stands out, with low demand from customers to learn about the business, combined with high costs of marketing it (e.g. compared to a viral marketing approach). Demand data is often collected through sampling or automation, to avoid over-processing and any unnecessary cost. Such profiles are used to account for performance and to help prioritise areas for development and improvement. They allow an enterprise to visualise the true health of their business and to identify how best to deploy additional resources. Such measures are not remote from the work, but integrated into the work. The data is used to account for and, through dialogue, improve the demand profile for the whole enterprise and also for individual customers. For instance, by combining this data with a customer's own demand profile, a more holistic approach to reducing failure demand, lost customer value and non-value adding costs can be achieved.

In Lean enterprises, complex customer satisfaction measures are replaced by simple measures of customer loyalty. Simplification of the measurement process is compensated for by an increased level of dialogue and analysis into the reasons customers provide. The point of this is simple – the purpose is not to measure, but to learn and improve the product and services provided to customers based on what they actually say. It stops customers having to give detailed ratings for every part of a process and allows them to correspond with the enterprise in their own words. This removes the risk of any misunderstanding or over-simplification in the process. It also becomes increasingly personal for the customer, yet more holistic and specific for the enterprise. Enterprises are able to ascertain and deliver more precisely what customers want, instead of generating lots of data on how well their customers are 'processed'.

A simple loyalty measure can be obtained by asking one simple question; 'On a scale of 0–10, would you recommend us to others?' This provides an indicative measure of the level of loyalty a particular customer has. However, as discussed above, the value is not in the measurement itself, but in the subsequent, more detailed analysis that follows. For instance, these can be obtained by asking customers follow up questions, such as 'Why did you give this mark and what do we need to do for it to improve?' and probing to find the root cause. This dialogue and conversation, which avoids the need for detailed scripts or specific questions to answer, provides a wealth of knowledge in terms of what really matters to the customer and what needs to be improved.

Companies often develop slightly more sophisticated measurement and analysis processes; for instance, by categorising customers based on the scores they provide or the value of products/services currently provided to them. For example, one measurement system used categorises customers into promoters and detractors [20]. Promoter is the name given to a customer who has given a high score and is therefore very likely to recommend the company to others. On the other hand, a detractor is a customer who has given a low score, and is highly unlikely to recommend the company to someone else or to buy their products/services again. Detractors can also put potential customers off, as one negative comment can easily neutralise half a dozen positive ones. On identifying and implementing change, specifically focused on increasing the number of promoters and decreasing the number of detractors, more loyal customers can be created. Lean enterprises, using these types of measures and insight, are able to further harness what matters to their customers and improve/grow their business. Loyal customers tell others, viral marketing begins, Lean relationships develop, marketing costs reduce and profitable revenues grow, rapidly.

Whilst financial accounting continues to play an important part in any enterprise, statements of accounts to shareholders only ever provide a snapshot in time and are invariably out of date before they are released. They provide investors with high level financial information about the company, as well as some general trends. They ensure proper standards are employed and that profits are reported annually. However, such financial statements do not, in themselves, present the real underlying strength of a business in terms of potential future profits, revenues or future success.

Estimates of next years revenues, costs and profits are regularly used in the process of determining executive targets and pay bonuses, often driving them to meet short term targets at the expense of the long term health of the business. Yearly budgets and financial decisions are often taken at the start of the year. This creates sub-optimal decision making across the company throughout the subsequent year. Lean enterprises operate a philosophy where decisions are made for the long term, not just the short term. They also avoid using simplistic financial targets and traditional annual budget setting processes. Budget setting and decision making is moved closer to the real work, supporting and developing it rather than constraining it. Value Management holistically presents what's actually happening and helps an enterprise to plan necessary improvements and developments.

For instance, Lean enterprises seek to avoid cost apportionment as much as possible, because real costs become hidden and more difficult to remove. It can also create in inappropriate actions. For example, the cost per stock item for a particular product can be reduced if a company overproduces and builds up its level of finished goods inventory. When costs are apportioned, the cost per stock item drops as any overheads are shared across a greater number of items. However, any excess stock created may subsequently have to be sold at a loss or written off (i.e. reducing revenues and adding to costs). Any step ups in production at the end of a quarter, to reduce apparent costs, can also create increased instability in production processes and further overburden staff. All outcomes generated by the accounting system itself.

Care also needs to be taken when considering standard accounting practices. For instance, whilst the cost of finished goods inventory held is present on the balance sheet, it is not included in the cost of sales or the gross margin figures on the income statement until this inventory is actually sold. Because of this, a company beginning to reduce its level of finished goods inventory can sometimes find a one off and short-term reduction in gross margin [21]. These types of simplistic accounting outcomes can form significant barriers to progress in a Lean transformation. Hence they need to be understood and managed carefully, whilst more advanced accounting practices are developed. Financial accounting in a Lean Enterprise uses Lean accounting practices. These provide a much better understanding of the real value and costs within an enterprise. Such practices allow more accurate and intelligent decision-making processes to take place. However, the migration to such practices has to be managed very carefully and go hand in hand with the overall Lean transformation. By doing this, financial discipline can be maintained throughout.

Accounting processes, such as issuing customer invoices and obtaining payments, or paying suppliers and employees, also become the subject of improvement. In Lean enterprises, the need for high volumes of invoicing and payment become the subject of heavy scrutiny. In doing so, they invariably find new and novel ways to reduce this overhead, for instance adopting on-line billing and payment, monthly direct debit payments, automated payment systems (e.g. e-payables) and pay on use. It also includes simplifying employee reward schemes and travel claim systems. Any necessary, high volume, repetitive and mundane activities are automated or outsourced. For instance, employee payments already tend to be highly automated and subjected to potential outsourcing. As a consequence of this, banks or tax collection agencies (e.g. Inland Revenue) could take the opportunity to increase the value they offer, whilst also reducing unnecessary steps involved in other processes (e.g. tax collection).

From the employee perspective, staff commitment and morale is traditionally measured using scores given to a series of detailed questions. These scores are often linked to executive targets, as part of a balanced scorecard, and cascaded throughout the organisation. In some cases, to ensure their targets are met, some managers make a clear link between the bonus given to each member of staff in their department and the average commitment found within their department. This can increase individual scores without the need to improve anything! In Lean enterprises, the approach once again takes the form of less measuring and more listening, understanding and improvement. For instance, measuring employee satisfaction may involve asking employees the question 'On a scale of 0–10, would you recommend your job to a close friend?', then finding out the reasons for the scores they provide and what could be done to improve it. Actual skills are also measured and skill gaps identified. Development plans for the enterprise and for each individual can then created, combining the needs of the enterprise and the desires of their staff.

The company's annual review is used to present additional information on activities, plans and performance, such as the support provided to local communities and to improving the environment. These are becoming increasingly important and Lean enterprises, in particular, are devoting more time and resources to them. Companies such as Toyota support development in their local communities in many ways and were the first company to introduce hybrid cars capable of reducing the impact automobiles have on the environment. In a similar way, Tesco have increased levels of recycling and devoted large sums of money into researching renewable sources of energy and ways to reduce energy consumption and carbon emissions. One important accounting measure used by Tesco, is their percentage share of the household wallet. This has grown steadily over recent years as they have entered the convenience market and extended their portfolio with a huge range of non-food products and services. Tesco already accounts for £1 in every £8 of UK retail sales, as well as nearly £1 in every £3 of UK grocery sales.

Outcomes

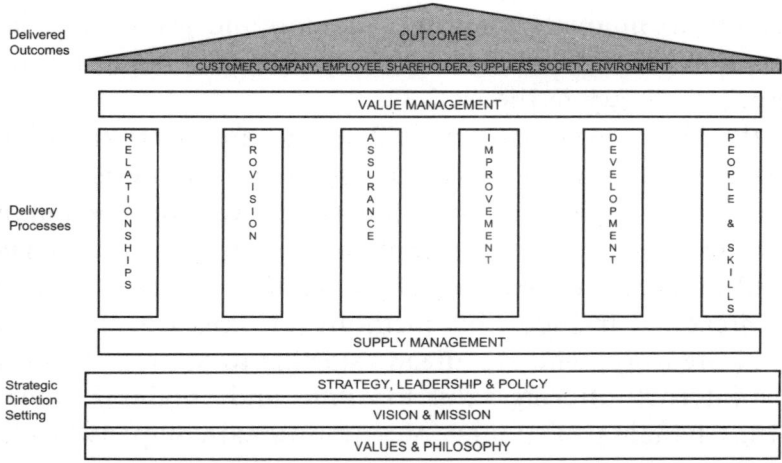

Figure 2.31 Outcomes in the Lean World Management System.

The outcomes of the business are made visible to key stakeholders via the Value Management process (See Figure 2.31). These include outcomes from the perspective of customers, employees, shareholders, governments, communities and environmental groups. Outcomes are presented in a meaningful way to each stakeholder, such as the value provided from the customer's perspective or company reports provided to shareholders.

Annual reports and quarterly briefings to shareholders provide a very public glimpse for all stakeholders into the strategy and direction of a company; its vision, mission and plans. In these reports there is growing attention given to the environmental and community activities of the company, because of the increased level of interest in these areas. If consumers are looking at these areas when they are making purchasing decisions, then investors need to be looking at them too. Investors are increasingly looking to invest in more secure, sustainable and ethical investments, as well as ones that are growing and supporting the environment. Today, potential investors look more holistically and in more depth at factors such as the vision of the company, the strategy they are adopting, the real value they offer, the loyalty of their customers and the commitment of their employees. They also need to understand the company's actual capability to innovate, improve, develop and grow. A general description of a Lean enterprise compared to a traditional enterprise is shown in Figure 2.32.

In the future, new entrants will appear and more traditional enterprises will start to change course. As this happens, a snowball effect will begin and those choosing to wait and see will find it hard to catch up. New entrants are reliant on entrepreneurs as well as investors realising the potential of Lean Thinking. Entrepreneurs include the plethora of creative individuals around the world who are already starting to harness the power of the internet; offering value to others and obtaining value in return. Changing the course of a traditional company is often harder, as it involves change and 'unlearning' current methods. Companies may also feel constrained by their past or weighed down by investors seeking short term fixes and rapid returns.

Lobby groups, unions and the media also study enterprises in an individual and generic way, providing a voice for the communities they serve and with particular interests in mind. In many cases, these studies are carried out with an open mind and with only good intentions. In other cases this is less so and information becomes heavily filtered. However, whichever is the case, they often draw upon specific exceptional events (as they are more newsworthy). The problem with this is that, by definition, exceptional events are unusual which can create a rather distorted picture of how an enterprise is actually performing. Worse still, businesses (or government departments) can become inadvertently dominated and driven by exceptions as a result. When this happens it creates a highly stressful environment; with an enterprise continually 'fire-fighting' and jumping from one issue to another. This can become a trap they find difficult to escape from. Lean enterprises employ robust strategies, strong leadership and management systems in order to stay focused. They also introduce effective two way communication. This is used to gather insight, ideas and

20th Century Traditional Enterprise	Attribute	21st Century Lean Enterprise
Assume customers time is free, getting them to do more of the work or to queue in order to maximise company productivity	Focus	Ensure adding maximum value from the customer's perspective, not expecting them to do more of the work or to waste their time
Putting "service wraps" around products in order to sell more products	Service	"Productising" services customers want and are more than willing to pay for
Seeking development and growth through cutting costs, commoditisation, standardisation, automation or outsourcing	Development	Seek development and growth by understanding customer value, personalising services and helping customers to achieve their goals
Cost driven, with management and change teams identifying and implementing top down change	Improvement	Customer driven, with customers and front line teams closest to the work continually identifying and improving the value provided
Managing separate entities (e.g. departments) using functional targets and goals, which systematically create barriers to serving customers (waste)	Structure	Managing Enterprise as a whole, systematically removing barriers to serving customers (waste)
Measuring virtually everything, but understanding the meaning and customer value of very little	Measurement	Measuring very little, but understanding the meaning and customer value of everything
Targets set to drive results, often at the expense of customers and the overall enterprise, with little real understanding of processes	Targets	Results achieved by understanding customer needs and real delivery processes, with systematic improvement of processes
Introduce technology which forces customers to add more of the value themselves (e.g. Interactive Voice Response, Self-help, Automation)	Technology	Introduce technology when it adds more value from the customer's perspective, releasing more capacity to add further value
Chaotic, ensuring everyone is stretched to the limit in a drive for efficiency, which is not necessarily effective	Culture	Calm, making sure everyone is working together with a common sense of purpose, becoming effective and not overburdened
Driven to achieve individual targets using monetary reward, often within a regime of insecurity and an environment where problems are hidden	Motivation	Driven by the intrinsic desire to develop and add value for customers, whilst ensuring any problems are exposed and eliminated
Staff rewarded heavily with bonuses, based on hitting specific individual/functional targets and goals	Reward	Staff rewarded for the level of skills they are able to apply and the overall success of the company

Figure 2.32 Comparison between a 20th Century traditional enterprise and a 21st Century Lean enterprise.

opinions. It is also used to report their actual performance for themselves and to explain to everyone what they are doing. They do not turn away individuals or groups who really care and who want to offer ideas, advice or improvement. In many cases, they get them involved in the process of improvement!

By operating the Lean World Management System, enterprises are able to grow in prosperity, reduce the stress placed upon their staff, create more contentment in the communities they serve and help to support a more sustainable environment (see Figure 2.33). They do not have to pay staff a 'stress premium' as they are able to provide a more stable and stress-free environment. They offer staff the opportunity to develop a wider range of skills and reward them on their ability to apply them. They also minimise their impact on the environment (e.g. recycling and energy consumption) and offer solutions to promote and sustain it (e.g. alternative energy sources, internet solutions). As more companies and governments implement these new approaches, positive outcomes will result for everyone and the Lean World will start to flourish.

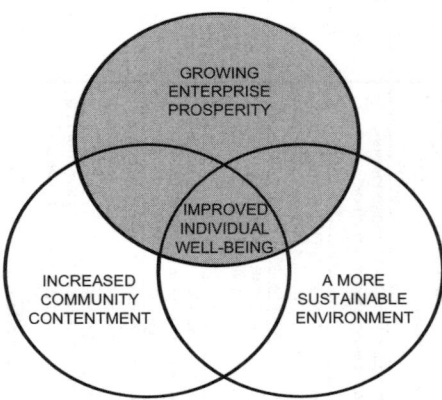

Figure 2.33 Outcomes in a Lean World.

Chapter 4

Lean Navigator

The Lean World Management System provides a framework for successfully managing a Lean enterprise. However, many enterprises also seek guidance as to the most effective way to introduce this type of system. There are a number of ways this can be achieved and many more ways it can potentially go wrong. In a competitive global market, enterprises need to make sure they are effective at navigating their way and implementing change, quickly.

Whilst the paths taken by individual enterprises are invariably different, Lean Navigation Systems can be used to help guide enterprises along a Lean Way to a Lean World. Uniquely, the Lean Navigation System makes use of the change processes embedded within the Lean World Management System itself. This allows an enterprise to not only set a new direction, but to stay on course. However, enterprises often seek the guidance and support of a Lean Navigator, particularly in the early stages, in order to implement it (see Figure 2.34). A Lean Navigator is a person who helps an enterprise to ask the right questions and to determine the best route to take. They help to expose an alternative way and to highlight traditional pot-holes. They also help enterprises to avoid long and difficult routes (i.e. crossing oceans and mountains) by exposing potential short cuts (i.e. bridges, crossings, paths and tunnels).

Once a Lean Navigation System is created, it starts to provide the necessary steer and determine the best way to implement the overall Lean World Management System. The navigation system creates a unique way of working within each individual

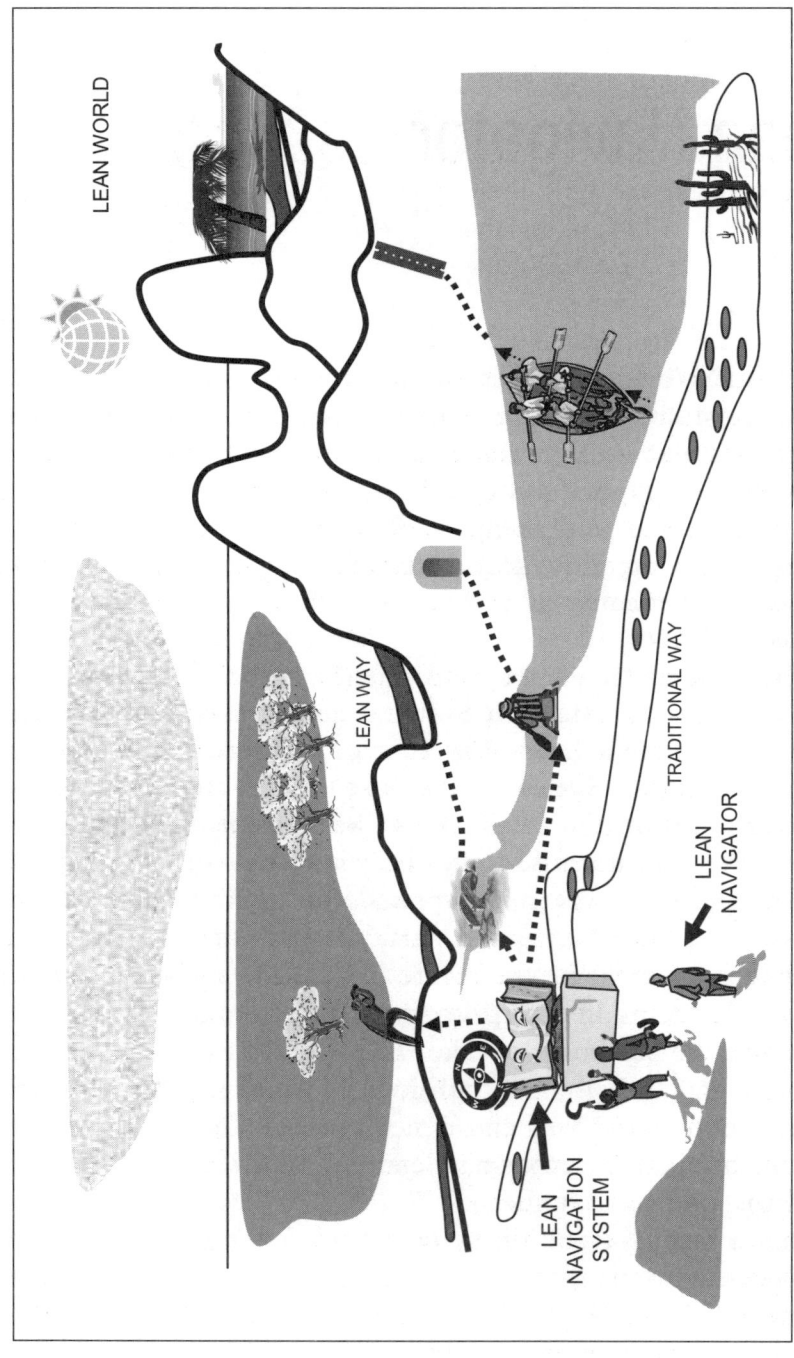

Figure 2.34 A Lean Navigator™ helping enterprises find a Lean Way to a Lean World.

enterprise (i.e. their 'Lean Way'). A Lean Navigator provides early guidance during the implementation of the system; using their flexibility and knowledge to help ensure that the transition is successful. They allow an enterprise to begin their journey, based upon their particular circumstances and needs. They help the enterprise to see a new direction, to make decisions and to learn and adapt along the way. Whilst adopting a structured and flexible approach, they also ensure a normative approach to change. Staff, managers and executives have to be involved and emotionally engaged; reflecting, taking responsibility and helping one another to implement change, decisively.

A Lean Navigator helps enterprises to see new perspectives and opportunities. They also help individual enterprises to take a new route, identify short-cuts and to stop them from stalling or falling. Just like any navigator, they help pilots to find the best course for them, providing compasses, guides and/or real-time navigational information, such as alternative routes around 'road-blocks' or 'accident black-spots'. A Lean Navigator starts by ascertaining the current purpose and starting position of the enterprise; its performance, strengths and weaknesses. They also seek to understand customer demand, potential opportunities and key threats. A Lean Navigator adapts to the individual styles of an organisation and their leaders. They are able to help successful enterprises, as well as those in dire straits. Lean Navigators maintain a highly adaptable approach, formulated from continuous augmentation of Lean Transformation best practice. For instance, the material within this book is applied and developed by Lean Navigators, to help enterprises to create their own unique Lean Navigation System. Like any navigator, they provide guidance, but they do not take overall responsibility for determining the destination or the detailed plan (these are the responsibility of the enterprise leaders and the Lean Navigation System).

Change can begin at any stage, anywhere and by anyone. It is sometimes believed that for it to succeed it has to come from the top, with high level executive buy-in from the very outset. Whilst this is obviously advantageous, it is not a pre-requisite. In fact in the case of Lean Thinking, this has historically rarely been the case. Most implementations of Lean Thinking have generally begun with small groups or localised improvement teams (i.e. a Kaizen team), starting to take more initiative themselves. They begin to apply some of the principles/tools of Lean Thinking to their area and within their sphere of control (e.g. Total Productive Maintenance). They may have even extended its application across complete processes (e.g. Value Stream Mapping), by consulting others, taking action collectively and learning in the process. Such activities start to bring out a number of key features of leadership in Lean transformations; listening, working as a team, taking responsibility, driving improvement, learning by doing and no longer waiting to be told what to do or to be given permission.

'Success breeds success' and as a result, the application of Lean Thinking has historically tended to widen only when an improved level of performance has been demonstrated. In most organisations, this process has been a rather gradual and precarious one. This is not due to a lack of commitment or hard work from all those involved. It's rarely down to a lack of positive outcomes either. Instead, it is mainly due to traditional enterprises continuing to measure and target the wrong things! Such measures, mostly internal and functional measures, are often completely unrelated to improving the real capability to provide value to customers. Customer measures are increasingly used now, but these are rarely optimal and most managers still tend to focus upon increasing functional productivity and reducing costs. Traditional management practices tend to hide true levels of value, capability and costs and in doing so, mask many of the real improvements Lean Thinking creates.

Traditional improvement programmes tend to focus on cost reduction, predominantly by driving increased productivity and head-count reductions. They also focus on selling existing products harder, so that overheads can be apportioned across more product sales. Rather than decreasing costs, these tend to generate more errors and failure demand which increase costs (i.e. the cost of processing failure demand)! These factors are rarely picked up by traditional measurement systems. They also sub-optimise, rather than improve, the capability to provide value to customers. Without a new set of 'Lean Lenses' to expose further opportunities to add value for customers, traditional companies tend to implement head-count reductions and effectively 'cash the cheque'. This can quickly halt the co-operation of staff, as few employees will 'vote' to be laid off or for their work colleagues to be made redundant. In contrast, Lean improvements increase value, reduce waste and increase operational capability. Lean implementations have to therefore overcome a number of barriers, with many a direct result of previous traditional 'improvement' programmes.

It doesn't take long to find a plethora of reasons why Lean transformations stall, or fail completely. A Lean implementation can consume a great deal of energy just to keep it going! This is often a result of 'systematic' barriers that exist in a traditional enterprise. For a Lean World Management System to be implemented, such barriers need to be identified, minimised and eliminated. Having top level 'buy-in' is obviously beneficial, but it does not guarantee success. When a CEO states that they 'support the Lean initiative' it can help a great deal, but the vast majority of CEO's know that this, by itself, is not enough. The majority of leaders, managers and front-line staff, need to become actively involved and emotionally attached for it to succeed. Executives also need to be prepared to change the way they work and to challenge some of the systematic barriers that have previously driven them! Management needs to migrate towards leadership, whilst command and control is progressively replaced by co-operation and teamwork. These types of changes are not insignificant, as they involve people and affect their lives. On the other hand, Lean implementations suffer much less from a number of barriers regularly encountered by traditional change programmes. For instance, Lean Thinking creates focus and places 'adding value for customers' central to everything the enterprise does. Done well, this is uniquely capable of motivating staff and unlocking a great deal of untapped potential, support and creativity within an enterprise. This allows more improvement to be achieved quickly and successfully, something most centrally controlled change programmes find very difficult to do (particularly cost reduction programmes!).

Lean implementations have to avoid potential pitfalls and overcome a number of barriers (mountains and rivers). A Lean Navigator can help an enterprise to succeed, by identifying key barriers and highlighting potential short-cuts (bridges and tunnels). A Lean Navigator uses their knowledge to help guide and support an enterprise to create their own Lean Navigation System. This requires a good understanding of the current situation and Lean transformation best practice. Lean Navigators make use of a range of tools and techniques. Many are well known (e.g. Statistical Process Control, Pareto Analysis, Root Cause Analysis and Value Stream Mapping) [23], others are not. For example, Lean Navigators make use of Lean Filters™. Lean Filters help to create knowledge and make decisions, when large amounts of information and choices are available. This is equivalent to a scientist using an electronic filter to extract a 'Signal', when there are large amounts of 'Noise' around it. For example, a Lean Status Filter is shown in Figure 2.35. It filters enterprises into various categories of maturity, by assessing their continuous improvement process with respect to three separate criteria; their level of customer focus, process involvement and people involvement. Those enterprises scoring highly in every criterion are most mature in their application of Lean

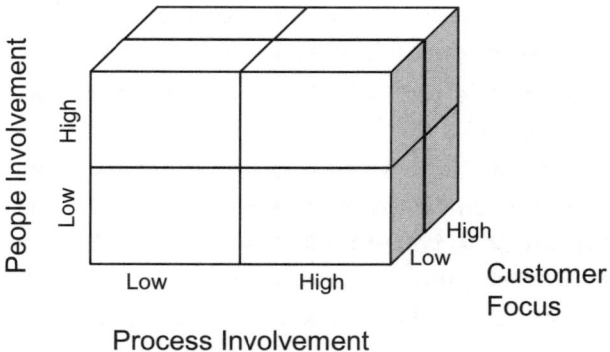

Figure 2.35 Lean Status Filter.

Thinking, whilst those scoring poorly in every criterion are least mature.

The Lean Status Filter is a three dimensional filter which shows where an enterprise sits with respect to its current application of Lean Thinking. The most basic level of maturity involves the local application of a specific Lean tool within a function (e.g. Total Productive Maintenance, 5S), with little people involvement, process involvement or customer focus. At the other extreme, enterprises are highly customer focused, with management systems focused on value streams and involving everyone (including customers, customer's customers and suppliers). A Lean Navigator uses this type of filter to not only understand the current status of an enterprise, but to help its leaders to take decisions and find the most effective path too. For instance, this may involve helping to identify how best to take functional improvement activities and develop them into value stream initiatives (i.e. increasing 'process involvement'). Alternatively, it may involve identifying the most effective way to engender executive commitment, as well as the leadership necessary to create a new strategic direction and to implement a Lean Navigation System. Once these are in place, value stream improvements can be accelerated and levels of 'people involvement' increased (e.g. as shown in Figure 2.36). As a result, a Lean World Management System can be progressively implemented in an enterprise and their unique way of working developed (their 'Lean Way').

Care is required when helping an enterprise to find the best route. For example, training more staff too early in how to apply specific tools to their particular function (in isolation of the overall value stream), may create little tangible improvement (with any potential successes short-lived). If too much training is carried out too early then it can also de-motivate staff, particularly if many of the changes they recommend are either stifled or undone as a result of action (or lack of action) by others. A Lean Navigator has to help Lean leaders and enterprises to identify the most effective path, based on their particular situation and experience. They must also continue to monitor

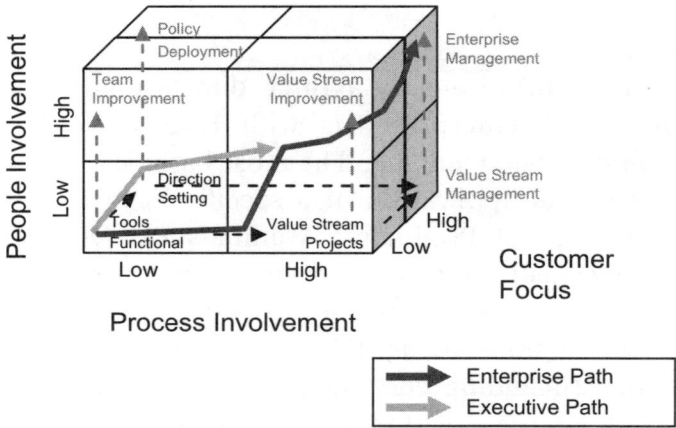

Figure 2.36 Lean Navigator identifying potential paths using the Lean Status Filter.

and adapt any support and guidance, particularly when circumstances significantly change (for better or worse). During the process of transformation, enterprise leaders progressively learn how to navigate a Lean Way for themselves. As this occurs, a Lean Navigator role migrates steadily from one of providing support and guidance, towards one that involves asking an occasional question. This progressively increases the level of enterprise self-reliance, experimentation and learning.

The Lean Navigation System is responsible for combining direction setting with value stream management. It integrates the change management processes necessary to create a fully operational enterprise management system, a Lean World Management System. Whilst recognising and acknowledging the potential of Lean Thinking, leaders sometimes express concern that Lean Thinking does not appear to show a clear, simple and visible way to manage and change a complete enterprise. This is no longer the case. The navigational processes and overall management system are not only clearer now, they can also be visualised as part of the same model (see Figure 2.37). The navigational processes include building new and improved relationships, improving and developing new products/services, as well as developing people and skills. They also include the

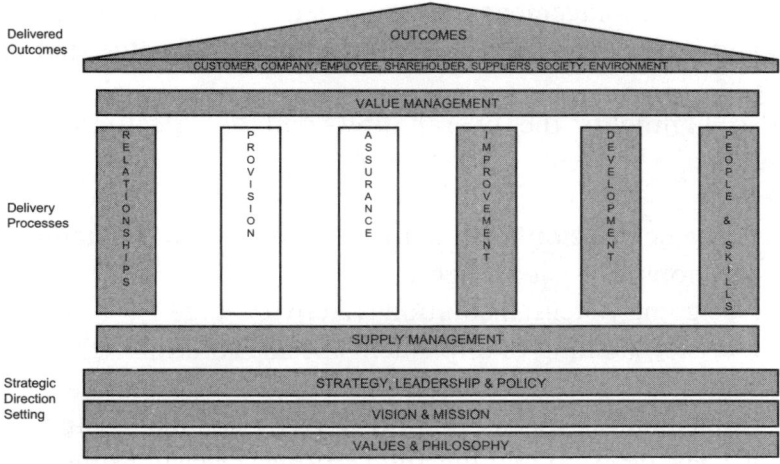

Figure 2.37 Navigational Processes within the Lean World Management System.

process of strategic direction setting, policy formulation and policy deployment.

The combination and integration of the complete set of change processes allows an enterprise to improve incrementally, as well as to radically change too. A more detailed representation of a Lean Navigation System is shown in Figure 2.38. It highlights the change value streams, including:

1. Direction Setting – determining strategies and policies required to create focus,
2. Value Management – measuring outcomes and understanding capability,
3. Relationships Development – understanding value and responding to real needs of customers,
4. Improvement – improving the value of current products and services,
5. Development – creating new products and services that increase the amount of value provided,
6. People and Skills – developing the skills and capability to lead and continuously improve the value provided, and

7. Supply Management – levelling demand, managing flow and providing necessary resources across all value streams.

It also highlights the overall flow and key decision points, including:

1. Strategic decision making to study options and potential solutions (Decision stage 1),
2. Designing potential solutions (Activity stage 1),
3. Decision making to implement specific solutions (Decision stage 2),
4. Implementing specific solutions (Activity stage 2), and
5. Review decision making and learning (Decision stage 3).

The Lean Navigation System does not provide a generic or prescriptive plan, but it does provide the integrated framework of change processes necessary to embark along a Lean Way. It provides focus and an ability to manoeuvre around obstacles in order to successfully implement change. It also highlights how changing and learning occur.

Strategy and direction setting is carried out by executive teams,

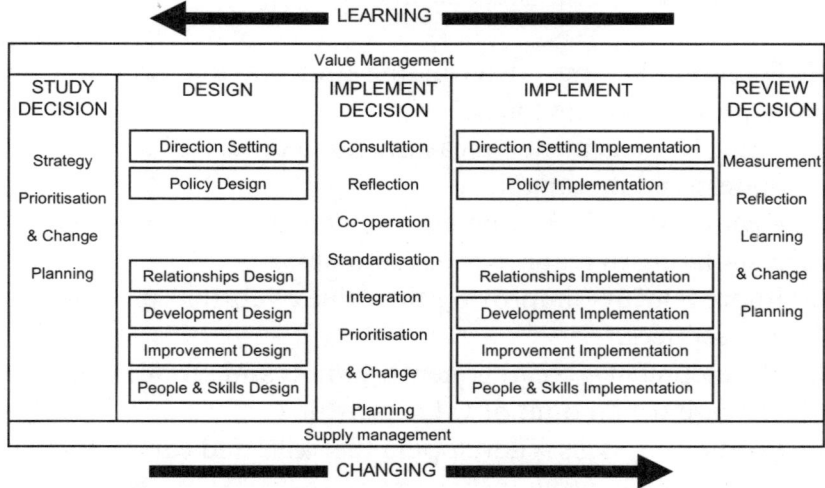

Figure 2.38 Lean Navigation System™.

from the definition of the company values all the way through to the policies it deploys. This is not carried out in isolation however. It requires a thorough understanding of the current situation, as well as the value customers need now and in the future. It is not a cold and calculated intellectual activity. It involves the engagement and involvement of staff, customers and suppliers. It is invariably a dynamic and emotional process; one that's often highly charged. This is an essential component of any successful Lean transformation. The sooner it's carried out the better, as change becomes far more effective once this has occurred. It can radically change the focus of an enterprise, for instance from reducing costs to creating value. A robustly defined strategy can enable an enterprise to move quickly away from being efficient, to one that's effective. In this way, executives are also able to co-ordinate the implementation of the entire change capability. Through phased changes in policy and revised change programmes, traditional systematic barriers are progressively eliminated and replaced by Lean policies and practices. Strategic change is carried out through consultation, careful reflection and co-operation. These are invaluable ways to learn and to improve plans. They involve everyone, without everyone having to be part of the leadership or change team. Co-operation and decision making are a central part of any Lean Navigation System implementing change effectively (as shown in Figure 2.38).

New measurement and Value Management procedures, for instance focused on customer value and loyalty, are introduced early to provide new perspectives for the business and to start the learning process. A few examples of Lean measures are highlighted in Figure 2.39. These types of measures allow management and executive teams to understand the performance of the enterprise and to prioritise resources more effectively. For instance, attention may initially focus on eliminating the causes of errors and failure demand that result from existing products or services. This frees up additional resources. Once resources are freed up, more staff can be trained in continuous improvement and help to improve value adding processes still further,

Value Stream	Potential value stream measures	Measure theme	Enterprise outcome
Strategic direction setting	Staff engagement Value created by vital few initiatives	Focus	Growth
Relationships development	Share of potential market Customer recommendations	Loyalty	Revenue
Provision	Value provided precisely Delivery lead time	Delivering	Margin
Assurance	Quality (Right first time) Safety	Ensuring	Opportunity
Improvement	Improvement ideas / employee implemented Value of improvements implemented	Improving	Morale
Development	Value of developments implemented Development lead time	Innovating	Responsibility
People & skills development	Employee recommendation Skill development	Motivating	Care
Value management (Support)	Demand type, volume and value Waste	Value adding	Partners
Supply management (Support)	Value stream flow Value stream stock turns	Co-operating	

Figure 2.39 Example of Lean Measures and Enterprise Outcomes.

generating even more spare capacity. The new measures, coupled with newly developed customer insight, also determine whether resources are best prioritised to generate further improvements to existing products/services, or to creating new additional ones customers need instead. Spare capacity is used effectively for training, development and improvement. Obsolete measures are replaced progressively, whilst maintaining overall control of the enterprise. However, any measures or targets that result in inappropriate and damaging behaviours are removed quickly.

For change to succeed and to be sustained, employees need to be able to quickly see, as well as believe, that there is a clear and sustainable growth strategy; one that is focused on the needs of customers and capable of creating new opportunities. This should be done upfront, to avoid any early temptation to make 'freed up' staff redundant. If a company cannot see a growth strategy for their business, they generally need to spend more time asking questions and listening to customers, before they embark upon a Lean journey. By doing so, the risk of their change programme failing is minimised. Lean is about continuous improvement and it involves everyone.

The involvement and leadership of the executive team can effectively allow an existing command and control infrastructure (e.g. authority) to be used to help dismantle the old operating model and phase in the new. Once this situation is reached, the infrastructure for change (i.e. the Lean Navigation System) can be implemented quickly and across the company. With this in place, the entire Lean World Management System can then be implemented. The vision becomes the 'destination', the navigation system becomes the 'steering wheel' and the people become the 'engine' (i.e. providing the driving force).

The Lean Navigation System connects management teams and front-line teams together (see Figure 2.40). They co-operate with each other and across organisational boundaries (i.e. customers and suppliers). This provides the optimum level of consultation and reflection, alignment and prioritisation, change planning and implementation. It also immerses everyone in a Lean Way and creates a 'joined up' capability across the whole value chain.

MANAGEMENT TEAMS

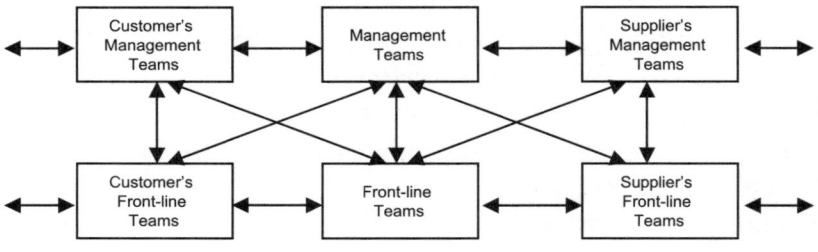

FRONT-LINE TEAMS

Figure 2.40 Collaboration and Integration within a Lean Navigation System.

The collaboration and integration occurring within change processes is also shown in Figure 2.41. It shows how the 'vital few' changes (e.g. based on improving customer 'loyalty') are integrated with the numerous 'incremental' changes identified by front line teams (e.g. based on improving customer 'value'). Management and executive teams use new and meaningful loyalty feedback and more holistic customer demand profiles (i.e. value, costs and capabilities). Front-line continuous improvement identifies potential areas where the level of value currently offered to customers can be improved. These are joined together and prioritised. Designs are created, reviewed, standardised and integrated. Resulting change plans are then reviewed, prioritised, phased and implemented. Customers and suppliers are also involved, as previously shown in Figure 2.40. By doing this, radical and incremental changes are combined together, prioritised by the customer and implemented rapidly.

Executive teams are responsible for setting direction, as well as defining and changing policy. Managers are responsible for supporting front line teams and managing changes to the enterprise. Front-line staff are responsible for carrying out delivery processes and front-line continuous improvement, supported by managers. The roles of managers and front-line staff in a Lean Enterprise become more closely linked, with managers able to carry out front-line work during particularly busy periods and

MANAGEMENT TEAMS

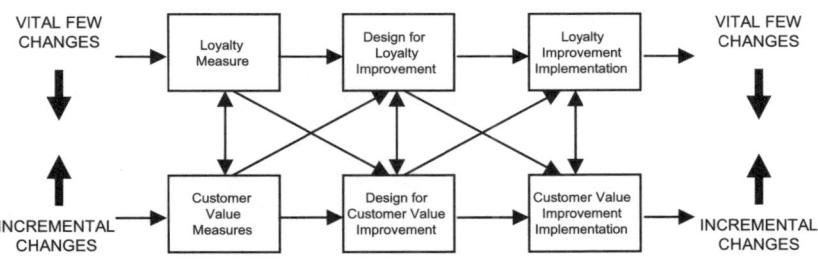

FRONT-LINE TEAMS

Figure 2.41 Integration of strategic and incremental change within a Lean Navigation System.

front-line staff taking on many responsibilities traditionally left to managers.

Vital support processes (i.e. Value Management and Supply Management) ensure an effective continuous cycle of improvement and development, by making use of Lean Filters. For instance, provision processes are developed and improved in a prioritised way, through the application of Lean Stream Filters (see Figure 2.42). Products/services and activities are filtered into categories using three criteria; their value, volume and variety. This allows similar products/services and activities to be identified, grouped together and provided in similar ways. Low volume and high variety products/services or activities tend to be managed more as 'projects' (e.g. 'one off' deliveries/ activities). On the other hand, high volume and low variety products/services and activities tend to be more highly automated and managed to maximise 'flow'. Enterprises normally start by improving the higher value and volume products/ services or activities first. They then progressively include those with lower value/volume and higher variety. Products are increasingly 'customised' at the end of processes, whilst services are 'flexidised' at the beginning.

Combining top down and bottom up approaches within the Lean Navigation System provides clarity and commitment to change; ensuring change is both successful and effective. It

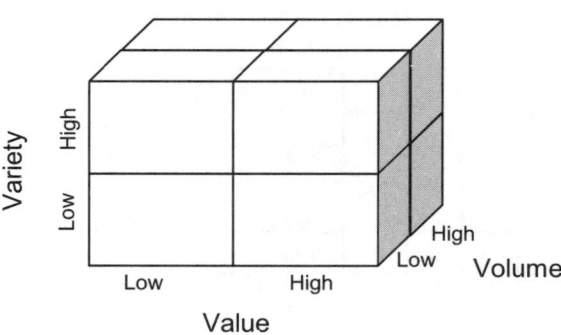

Figure 2.42 Lean Stream Filter.

minimises the time spent 'sitting on the fence', observing whether change is likely to happen and waiting for others to go first. Lean Thinking involves massive change for everyone and transforms what they spend their time and energy doing. Most people within a company seek meaning and purpose by providing value to others and from improving their own abilities. As a result, the vast majority of employees support and embrace the principles of Lean Thinking. This is particularly the case for front-line staff, who often suffer the most stress and frustration, as they attempt to provide value to customers using their company's existing capabilities. However, other employees can be much less receptive to change, particularly some of the more traditional managers. Leadership, care, guidance, nurturing and support are all needed, if everyone is to successfully make the transition to their new roles and move forward. Unfortunately, a small number will not want to change, even when they see it is the right thing for the company to do. Some will choose to leave; others will not. Lean Filters (e.g. see Figure 2.43) help to identify individuals least likely or able to adopt Lean Thinking. A Lean Filter can be used to assess staff against three criteria; whether they listen, believe or care. Some staff will need additional guidance and support (e.g. those that 'don't listen' or 'don't believe'). A few may have to be asked to leave (e.g. some of those that 'don't listen', 'don't believe' and 'don't care').

A few individuals will actively seek to 'scupper' change, given their strong belief that such a change will not be in their own best

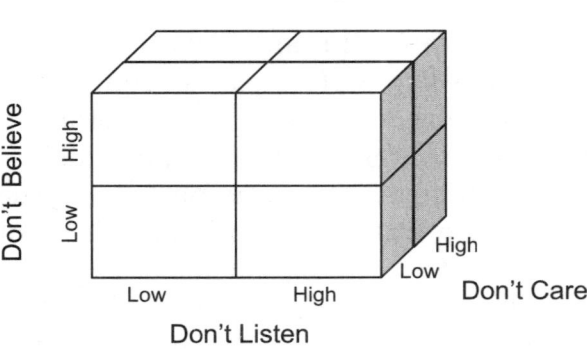

Figure 2.43 Lean Rejection Filter.

interests. Some of these may have quite considerable influence, perhaps through their position or authority. Politics and vested interests are a huge potential barrier to change. Potential block-ers are likely to use their influence and a wealth of underground 'networks' to connect and co-ordinate groups of individuals with similar objectives to their own. These groups often deploy subtle, but often highly damaging, ways to 'scuttle the ship' or to 'stop the ship from sailing'. Executives 'walking the floor' and setting up regular, direct communication with their staff, can reduce the risk of this. However, a Lean Navigator uses another Lean Filter to more precisely identify individuals of particular concern (see Figure 2.44). They include those people that 'don't care' (about customers, or the enterprise as a whole) and 'don't want' to change (or adopt Lean Thinking), but who are also highly

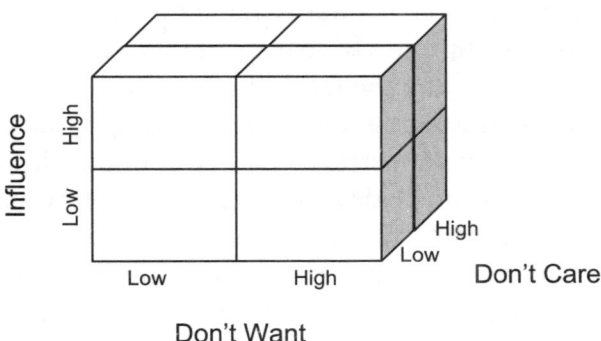

Figure 2.44 Lean Blocker Filter.

'influential' (due to their status and authority, or attachments).

Executives have a key part to play in setting the direction and implementing the strategy. Communicating the vision and strategy, demonstrating the values and 'walking the floor' are all very important. At the same time, policy deployment by executives is also critical. By implementing policies that directly support the strategy, they communicate to everyone, on a daily basis, what the company wants and how they want to achieve it. Executives, in many traditional companies, already dedicate a certain amount of time to communicating the company strategy and to 'walking the floor'. However, whilst staff may be initially enthused, they often grow in despondency as they realise the level of disconnect between the vision and company policies. Others remain apathetic, perhaps suffering from change fatigue as a result of numerous other change initiatives that have all previously failed. To counter these things, a Lean Navigation System must not only create the structures necessary to implement Lean policies, but quickly remove some of the highly damaging and inappropriate ones too.

A transformation strategy needs to include Lean Thinking, Systems Thinking and Leadership best practice. It also needs to be flexible to cope with an ever changing environment, whilst being able to create key change capabilities; including leadership, change structures, coaching and mentoring. It also needs to consistently and continuously demonstrate the progress the enterprise is making; by clearly linking performance improvements to the changes being made. Changing one highly damaging policy (or target) can quickly reduce quality failures and clearly demonstrate to everyone the level of commitment and resolve of executive teams. Resolving key, long standing, issues raised by staff can quickly demonstrate that continuous improvement works and ensures more ideas are generated. However, it must be remembered that Lean transformation involves change for each individual, in different ways and at different times. Change is not trivial, it is important and personal. Whilst everyone tends to follow a generic process, individuals naturally change at different rates and with differing levels of enthusiasm [24]. Most people (particularly front-line staff) embrace Lean Thinking very quickly and become motivated to start creating more value. Some become angry about past failures or go into denial, before they start to look ahead and take advantage of the opportunities Lean Thinking creates. Many are initially afraid of change and concerned about what it might mean for them personally. However, the majority of people come around in their own time when they start to see positive outcomes occurring around them. They become more motivated to take responsibility and to support change initiatives themselves. As they acknowledge/ discard old ways and accept/embrace the new, they learn how to add more value as individuals and create far more value as an enterprise (see Figure 2.45).

Most people don't mind changing but they don't like to be changed. Everyone has to embrace the change in their own particular way and their own time, requiring regular support and encouragement from leaders. Leadership is required at all levels, from both existing and emergent leaders. Some of the best Lean leaders are actually those that emerge from individuals who are either initially quiet, or have been highly questioning of previous change initiatives. This, more often than not, is because they care. They are reflective and have often been highly challenging

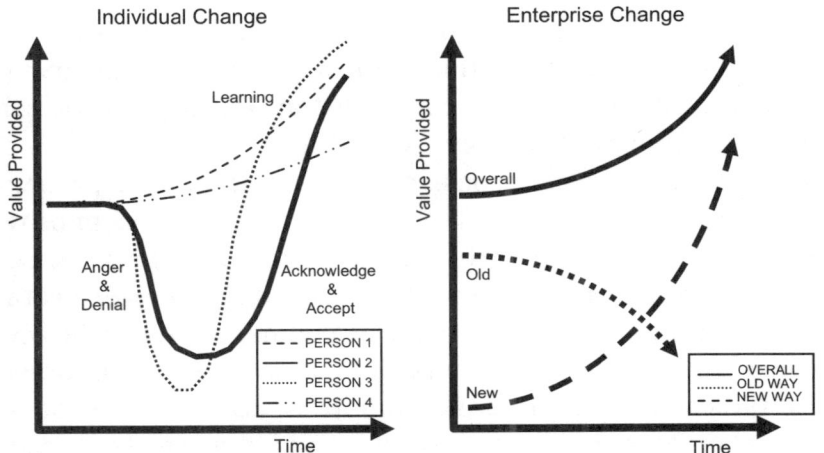

Figure 2.45 Individual Change and overall Enterprise Change.

of the way things have been done in the past. As these staff transform from challengers into promoters, they can have a quite profound effect on others around them and be far more influential than many traditional managers. Likewise, staff who naturally do not like to lead change, gain in confidence from the drive and enthusiasm from those that do. Peer pressure generates more impetus for change, whilst coaching and support structures help people during the transition phase.

The Lean Navigation System progressively makes change and continuous improvement the responsibility of everyone. By setting the right direction and harnessing the intelligence and ingenuity of all staff, Lean Thinking is applied quickly and effectively. By involving customers (as well as customer's customers) and suppliers, change is also prioritised and spread across the whole value chain and a Lean World Management System created. This often requires additional understanding of Lean Thinking in both customers and suppliers; an additional purpose of a Lean Enterprise. Long term, enterprise success is created when everyone co-operates and jointly shares in the success, not when one enterprise succeeds but only at the expense of others in the value chain. By setting a clear direction (i.e. defining success) and by implementing appropriate measures (e.g. related to success), vital strategic changes are identified, planned and implemented. At the same time, by adopting a continuous improvement philosophy and implementing additional measures (e.g. related to value), numerous incremental changes are also identified and implemented that are aligned with the overall strategic direction (See Figure 2.46).

Current Lean applications, more often than not, presently involve relatively small teams carrying out continuous improvement in a localised area or for a particular process. Improvement leaders must adopt a philosophy of learning by doing, creating momentum and increasing levels of commitment and involvement. They need to make changes and, if necessary, seek forgiveness, rather than wait to either be told what to do or to obtain permission. They are their company's first Lean leaders. A leader gathers more leaders around them, to strengthen their coalition.

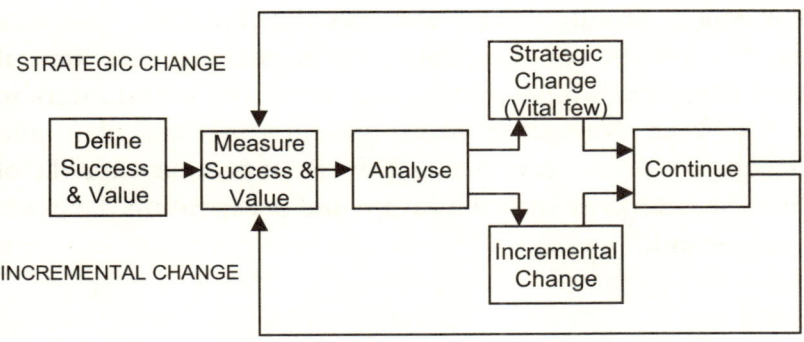

Figure 2.46 Change in a Lean Navigation System™.

Lean Filters can be used to help identify those who are most likely to lead, as well as those most likely to help (See Figure 2.47). Team commitment needs to be absolute and it must grow in strength. Barriers need to be identified and Lean tactics adopted in order to remove them or minimise their impact. An intervention strategy for engendering executive leadership is also needed at the earliest opportunity. Once executive leadership is created, they themselves focus on creating Lean leadership at all levels, implementing a Lean Navigation System and integrating top down strategic change with bottom up continuous improvement. A Lean Navigation System, by its very design, is subjected to continuous improvement. Lean Navigators are also, by their very nature, continually learning and adapting in order to help an enterprise successfully start their own Lean journey. They help to make sure that an enterprise creates stability and

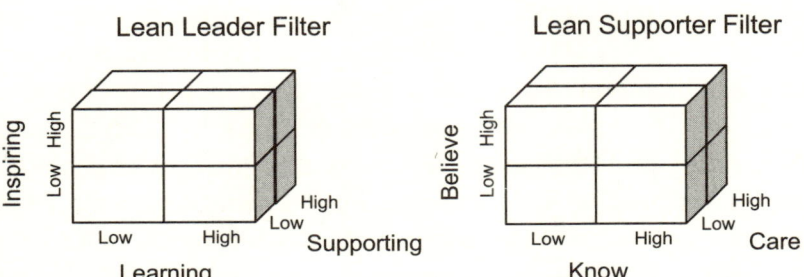

Figure 2.47 Lean Leader Filter and Lean Supporter Filter.

improvement, rapidly. They also provide essential guidance during the process of direction setting; making sure that it engages everyone whilst putting the necessary foundations in place. A Lean Navigator helps an enterprise to plan and implement its own Lean Navigation System; one capable of guiding the enterprise into the future and accelerating their rate of development.

Chapter 5

Start of a Journey

There are many potential ways an enterprise can start their Lean journey. There are no pre-requisites – it can start anywhere and at anytime. In most cases however, it originates from the drive and commitment of a few dedicated individuals, or small groups of individuals, already within the enterprise. In others, it may originate from a new member of staff, perhaps a new senior executive joining the enterprise who is already well versed and committed to Lean Thinking. Whatever its origin, the embryo of change must be nurtured for it to develop and gain in strength. This requires communication and leadership, as well as expanding levels of application and commitment. It also involves a growing level of dialogue with fellow colleagues and other stakeholders; including customers and suppliers. In the future however, Lean Thinking is also likely to become influenced by additional stakeholders too; including unions and potential investors, who each have their own reasons for making sure an enterprise is effective and successful in the future. Lean Thinking is also likely to be driven and supported by governments, keen to see the type of success it has to offer. It is also likely to arise from growing pressure from various lobby groups; such as business, consumer, community and environmental groups. These are all likely to become real drivers for an enterprise to start a Lean journey and each one is examined in more detail below, starting with the staff within the enterprise itself.

The application of Lean Thinking generally begins as a result of the curiosity, commitment, strength and leadership of a few individuals in an enterprise. It continues to develop, as these early adopters start to experiment, learn and communicate with one another. They join forces and begin to share their knowledge and successes with others. More people get involved and become emotionally engaged as a result. They start to co-operate and collaborate across the enterprise. The most effective groups include front line staff across a complete value stream, as they are often in the best position to understand the needs of customers, as well as how the company as a whole currently responds to them. They are often the most frustrated group, as they are directly responsible for responding to customer demand, whilst facing numerous barriers and constraints, created as a result of traditional management practices. Such groups need to quickly implement strategies to develop growing levels of influence and leadership, whilst avoiding potential blockers. Successful groups often seek the guidance of a Lean Navigator too, particularly during the early stages, in order to help them determine the optimum route to take, and to avoid common problems or potential wrong turns.

Individuals within such groups are the 'Lean Pioneers' of their enterprise, creating the embryo of change, spreading the message and developing more and more momentum. Lean leaders ask questions, listen and learn. They challenge traditional thinking, take the initiative and influence others. They do not wait to be given permission or to be told what to do. Some will have a great deal of knowledge about Lean Thinking. Others, may have little Lean knowledge/experience at all, but instead have a deep desire to add value and to carry out their work in a more effective way. Their passion to serve customers and their desire to make a difference are absolute. They sometimes drive changes that remove the need for the work they do. However, when they do this, it is in the belief and knowledge that such changes create far more future opportunities for their company and for themselves. Such leadership and drive is something many traditional companies struggle to engender of their own accord. It is developed through emotional engagement and by creating a real sense of purpose. As the implementation of Lean

Thinking becomes more widespread, Lean leaders are becoming invaluable assets and are already in huge demand.

Executives, managers and front-line staff all have a responsibility, individually and collectively, to initiate change. No-one should wait or rely on others. Delegating or devolving oneself of responsibility will do nothing to 'save your ship' and 'stop it from sinking'. Whilst change is not happening in your enterprise, one thing is certain; it will be in others! The publication of the Lean World Management System, the Lean Navigation System and a number of approaches used by Lean Navigators, is only likely to accelerate the depth, breadth and pace of change still further.

Executives have key parts to play in any Lean transformation. Whilst they may not have initiated it, at some stage they need to not only support it but to develop the leadership necessary to 'industrialise' it (e.g. implementing a Lean Navigation System). This involves creating a compelling vision and strategy – one that's both realistic and challenging. However, it also needs to be emotionally engaging. It cannot be created in isolation over a couple of days, but requires time and effort; with executives going to the Gemba (work-place) and understanding the real situation for themselves. It involves asking lots of questions, as well as being able to listen and learn. It requires openness, honesty, compassion and trust. It involves having effective dialogue with customers, staff and suppliers, as well as an understanding of the future potential marketplace. It needs large amounts of communication, consultation, co-operation and collaboration. It also requires strategies for identifying those who are most likely to actively support such a change, as well as those most likely and capable of blocking it.

Pressure to start a Lean journey can come from outside of the enterprise too. Customers (and potential customers) have probably the most outside influence on any enterprise. Every day customers make numerous decisions as to what to buy and who to obtain it from. There is no enterprise without customers and hence in any environment where customers have choice, customers are invariably in the driving seat (i.e. they vote with their 'feet', or more accurately, their wallet!). Even places where there has been traditionally little to no choice (e.g. certain public services) are starting to see competition introduced and more customer choice offered as a result. Customers are becoming more demanding and enterprises failing to respond are starting to find they are losing their customers, finding it harder to gain new ones and struggling to survive in a world offering choice. Most enterprises realise the importance of loyal customers, in terms of the recommendations they provide, the repeat purchases they make and the sustainable growth that occurs as a result. Loyal customers also tend to buy based on value, not on cost. Customers are in the driving seat and only by addressing the real needs of customers (and in doing so, increasing loyalty) can enterprises start to create sustainable growth and avoid an otherwise negative spiral of commoditisation and cost reduction.

Whilst an enterprise has the responsibility to serve its' customers effectively, their suppliers also have a duty to serve them effectively as well. As a supplier starts to help another enterprise (i.e. its customer) become more successful, so the likelihood of its own success improves. Conversations with their customers not only include how many products or services they require, but how they can improve them together and create new ones capable of adding more value. Such conversations not only focus on the value from the perspective of their customer, but their customer's customers too. By doing this, more collaborative and strategic partnerships are created throughout the supply chain; ones capable of holistically improving the value provided to the end consumer and removing waste. For instance, by focusing on the flow of value, stability is created and levels of inventory progressively reduced throughout the supply chain (as a result of levelling demand and introducing 'pull' strategies respectively). Lean enterprises share knowledge and best practice, whilst learning from others and improving their value chains.

Investors support companies by buying their shares, in return for potential share growth and dividends. Investors receive annual reports and statement of accounts, which provide public statements of strategy and a snapshot of their current financial position. Individuals, investment banks, pension funds and stockbrokers all study company information in order to estimate their value and potential growth. Effective investors look at companies in a great deal of depth, searching for those with clear winning strategies. These include robust plans for growing a loyal customer base. They also study a company's ability and desire to develop their staff, as well as to support local communities and improve the environment. These have all become a key part of a company's annual report. As investors begin to realise the relationship between Lean Thinking and sustained success, they will seek better ways to identify how well companies are applying it. The Lean World Management System and Lean Navigation System will help in this regard. They will help investors to identify and support winners. They will help identify a 'tanker that's successfully turning' and to spot a potential 'rising star'. As investors begin to use these methods to evaluate companies, investors will effectively drive company executives to develop and implement Lean strategies.

Governments and politicians also have a key part to play. Governments set the strategy and policies that ultimately determine the public services offered (e.g. public enterprises providing health and education), the success of nations, communities and private enterprises in their region. Population growth, resulting from increasing life-spans and people migration, is rapidly increasing the demands on governments and public services. For instance public services, such as the National Health Service in the UK, are under ever increasing pressure, due mainly to an ageing population placing growing demands upon it. This is compounded by proportionately less people being able to work and pay the tax necessary to support it. Most governments and politicians are seeking solutions which are capable of providing more and better services, whilst not having to increase taxes. Starting a Lean journey provides a unique solution to this problem. Such journeys are now beginning in a number of public services (e.g. Police and the National Health Service). These need to accelerate rapidly, supported by government initiatives and an overarching commitment to embrace the huge potential Lean

Thinking has to offer. Migrating government policies to Lean policies steadily removes many of the barriers currently faced by individuals, communities and enterprises seeking to add value and make a difference. This gradually reduces 'Red Tape' and 'frees up' more time and resources for innovation and creativity.

Unions representing staff members and communities also have a huge opportunity to help engender change. They have responsibility for the overall well-being of individual members of staff, as well as the communities they support. Lean is well known for its ability to create opportunities, safety and security, sustained growth and prosperity, as well as more jobs. It is also recognised for the development opportunities it provides and the improved levels of well-being it creates. Lean Thinking challenges traditional thinking and is able to reduce the levels of stress placed on employees within the workplace. Stress management courses offered by companies are not sufficient. More of their time and resources need to be spent on helping employees to identify and remove the causes of stress (e.g. overburden, lack of demand levelling, arbitrary target setting). The goal must become one of minimising (and even eliminating) stress, not maintaining high levels of stress and helping everyone to cope with it (i.e. 'processing stress'). Only by doing this can enterprises improve the overall well-being of their staff and the local communities they serve. Unions have much more they can do to help employees (and employers) to see different perspectives, and to embrace the changes needed to improve their lives for the better.

Groups providing a collective voice for communities can also play a big part. In the UK, they include business groups, such as the Confederation of British Industry (CBI) and the British Chamber of Commerce, as well as consumer groups, such as the Consumer Association and the National Consumer Council. They also include a variety of community and environmental groups. These groups already actively lobby governments, enterprises and a wide range of communities. They are often well versed in communications; exposing areas of weakness and lobbying for particular changes to occur. Such groups are often well known for their desire to create change, although they are sometimes focused upon a relatively small (and specific) number of objectives and a rather narrow set of interests. However, some lobby groups are becoming far more sophisticated than this; joining together with other groups to identify common goals in the pursuit of change for everyone's benefit. As a deeper understanding of Lean Thinking and a Lean World grows, with clear and common goals for communities, enterprise and the environment, it will strengthen these relationships and accelerate the pace of change – driving a more holistic environment where improvement can benefit everyone.

Chapter 6

A Lean Way to a Lean World

A number of leading enterprises have successfully begun to take a new path into a 21st Century world. They have broken away from traditional management approaches and instead adopted a Lean philosophy of management, with tremendous results. Toyota can, quite rightly, be viewed as the enterprise which originated Lean Thinking, followed by many others in the manufacturing sector. This created, what is now referred to as, the Lean movement. Equally, in the service sector, companies like Tesco have started to excel, as they have applied Lean Thinking to their supply chains and to their enterprise as a whole. Both of these companies are now classed as leaders in their fields, commanding high levels of respect. They have both succeeded in creating continuous, sustainable and profitable growth. This success has led some government agencies, offering services to society, to begin applying Lean Thinking too. In the UK, these include certain police forces, local authorities and hospitals, as well as part of the criminal justice system. This section explores how, by applying Lean Thinking, such enterprises have been able to successfully transform their organisations, increasing the value they offer and minimising waste.

Lean Production – The Success of Toyota

No book containing Lean Thinking can be written without reference to its founders, Toyota. They, have for some time, charted a Lean path to prosperity, creating success from everyone's perspective. They have always been open to anyone seeking to learn, whilst also keen to learn from others. Toyota is, quite rightly, highly respected around the world. Manufacturers around the globe often refer to Toyota as the world-class benchmark. Many have sought to copy or adapt Toyota's approaches and practices, in an attempt to gain the level of success Toyota has achieved.

The system behind Toyota is well documented and is commonly referred to as the Toyota Production System (TPS). The basic components of the Toyota Production System are shown in Figure 2.48. It is visually represented as a house, built from firm 'foundations' and consisting of a 'roof' held up by 'pillars'. The pillars signify the means by which Toyota create their desired business outcomes.

In the Toyota Production System, the 'foundations' are laid by smoothing the volume, type and flow of work so that both people and resources are not overburdened (called Heijunka). Continuous improvement, a key principle of Toyota, lies at the

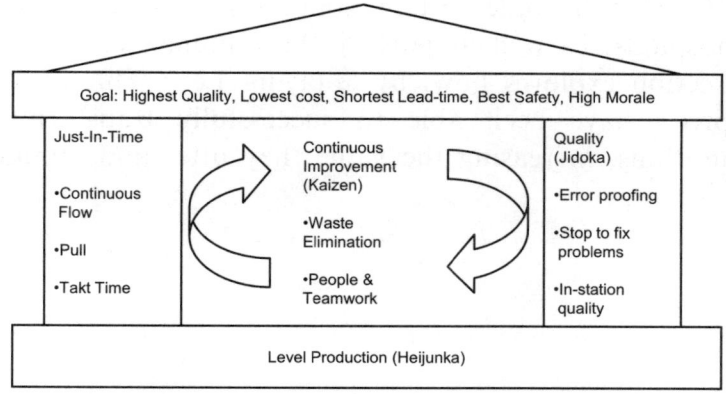

Figure 2.48 The Toyota Production System.

heart of the Toyota Production System. It is the responsibility of everyone, and allows Toyota to repeatedly raise the bar and to expose/eliminate problems. The flow of value (e.g. reducing batch sizes) becomes better and better as 'Just-in-Time' and 'Quality' improvements are progressively implemented. Changes are implemented following careful reflection and in a standard way across the enterprise. This provides a strong foundation for further improvement.

Instead of improving utilisation or reducing waste within individual departments, Toyota focuses upon improving the way materials and products flow through their organisation, delivering value to their customers. This allows them to see value from the customer's perspective. By doing this, Toyota uniquely exposes waste whilst seeking to improve the flow of value, and it is this waste that it removes. This is often described as exposing and removing the 'rocks' (i.e. barriers to the flow) in a river, as shown in Figure 2.49.

For example, this includes the time taken, any excess inventory, over-processing or non-value add activities such as transportation, checking or re-work. It is this approach that has particularly allowed Toyota to continually improve the value they provide to customers and to reduce costs, a combination which has successfully differentiated Toyota from its competitors.

Other companies have sought to emulate Toyota's practices/

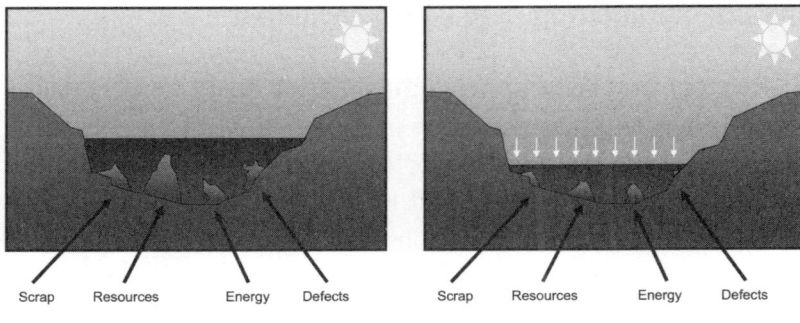

(a) Waste in a Traditional enterprise   (b) Waste removal in a Lean enterprise

Figure 2.49 Exposing and removing waste (i.e. 'rocks') using continuous improvement.

approaches and have implemented production systems of their own. Whilst these have often created positive and relatively dramatic improvement breakthroughs for the companies involved, they have not necessarily resulted in them catching up with the recognised leader. The reasons for this are often two-fold. First of all, Toyota continually re-invests any released resources into creating further improvement and development. In this case, it is like trying to catch a snow ball rolling down a hill, picking up more and more momentum as it goes along. Secondly, the production system and its associated practices are effectively a by-product of their philosophy, strategy and policies. Hence, Toyota's success is actually a result of its strategy, not its production system. This is brought out particularly well in the book, 'The Toyota Way' [6], which describes many of the philosophies, policies and practices within Toyota.

The core strengths of Toyota can be quickly and thoroughly examined using the Lean World Management System. The Lean World Management System is capable of providing a unique and holistic view of Toyota's enterprise model. It provides a complete picture of the enterprise, expanding upon components already contained within the Toyota Production System. It is able to articulate Toyota's strategy, its processes and key outcomes (see Figure 2.50).

Toyota maintains a strong set of values and a long term philosophy. They are primarily based upon continuous improvement, honour and respect [6,24,25], including:

- Respect for the language and spirit of the law of every nation, being open and fair in its dealings and a good corporate citizen of the world,
- Respect for the people, culture and traditions of each region and country in which it operates, promoting economic growth and prosperity in those countries,
- Respect for the natural environment, contributing to regional living conditions and to social prosperity, striving to offer outstanding products and services that are clean, safe and of high quality,

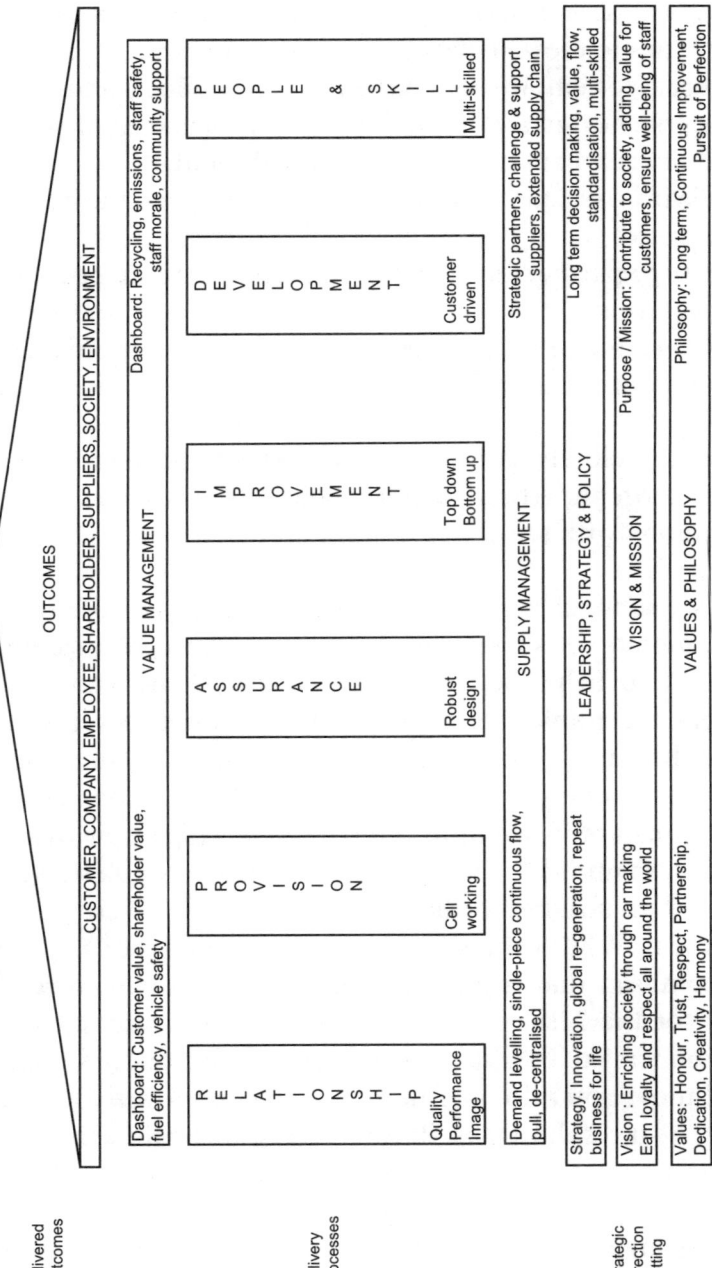

Figure 2.50 Representation of Toyota using the Lean World Management System.

- Respect for customers, fulfilling their needs worldwide, and conducting extensive research and development activities to create new value for customers,
- Respect for employees, nurturing their abilities and inventiveness in a climate of co-operation, so employees and the company realise their full potential,
- To learn from the best in the world to become the best in the world,
- To forge partnerships with customers and to exceed their expectations,
- To welcome new challenges and the opportunity to create,
- To encourage teamwork and excellence in pursuit of goals, and
- To work closely with business partners to achieve stable, long-term growth, with mutual benefits that are in harmony with the global community.

Toyota's vision lies way beyond selling cars for a profit in order to make money for shareholders [24]. It seeks to enhance quality of life and to help societies to grow, by adding value for its customers and employees, as well as the communities in which it operates. In Toyota's own words, whilst aiming to enrich society through car making, Toyota's goal is to be a 'good corporate citizen,' constantly 'winning the trust and respect of the inter-national community.' Toyota seeks to create, stable long-term growth, whilst striving for harmony with people, society and the environment. While others aspire to follow in Toyota's footsteps, Toyota realised that it also needed to create a new vision and strategy for the 21st century. In 2002, the company created its new vision, called Toyota Global Vision 2010, centred upon the theme 'Innovation into the Future – A Passion to Create a Better Society'. As a result of this, it now strives, through technological innovation and the manufacturing of value-added products, to create a more prosperous society.

This vision is underpinned by a number of distinct strategic themes, including:

- Becoming a driving force in global regeneration by implementing the most advanced environmental technologies,
- Creating automobiles and a motorized society in which people can live safely, securely and comfortably,
- Promoting the advantages of cars throughout the world and attract more Toyota fans, and
- Being a truly global company that is trusted and respected by all people around the world.

These four themes are already starting to have a significant effect on the company and its products. For instance, the first, 'being true to the earth', involves Toyota becoming 'a leading force in the reduction, re-use and recycling of resources by implementing the most advanced environmental technologies.' This has already seen Toyota introduce hybrid technologies into a range of their vehicles, with over 500,000 of their Prius models already sold. These cars have successfully resulted in higher fuel efficiency and lower exhaust emissions, whilst also providing a superior driving performance. Toyota is also progressively increasing the amount of recyclable materials used within its cars.

Toyota's strategy involves minimizing any negative aspect of motor vehicles on individuals and the environment. These include traffic accidents and the additional impact of traffic congestion. At the same time, Toyota are maximising the positive aspects of automobiles, including their fun, excitement, image and comfort. Combined, such strategies drive the development of new technological solutions, including passive collision safety systems (focused on minimizing damage during collisions) and advanced preventive safety systems (capable of foreseeing collisions and alerting drivers, whilst also offering superior maneuverability). Technology is also being continually developed to increase vehicle functionality and to enhance the overall transport system (e.g. further linking automobile technology with communication networks and road infrastructure). By quickly sensing and responding to potential dangers, whilst avoiding any congested areas, journeys can be completed quickly and safely. They can also be undertaken with increased comfort, whilst maintaining maximum fuel efficiency. Toyota consistently seeks lifetime customers, by adopting a customer-first strategy. By doing this, they aim to remain the most successful automobile company, through a combination of choice and the best purchasing, ownership and transport experience.

The policies of Toyota are highly effective and well documented [6,24]. These policies are deployed both carefully and decisively (using Hoshrin Kanri), providing the structure, standards and consistency needed to carry out all of its processes. They effectively result in the creation and governance of the Toyota Production System. The development of staff has also been key to Toyota's success. Toyota's policies include 'going to see for oneself', 'learning by doing' and 'developing leaders from within'. Multi-skilling and cell-working are also used within teams, to improve the flow of value and increase staff motivation. Front line staff are encouraged to stop production on encountering problems, so they can resolve them and avoid any problems flowing down the line. Technology and automation are also used to support operators in carrying out their work and to free them from any voluminous and repetitive tasks (e.g. detection of quality problems). Teams and suppliers are constantly challenged to identify improvements and are supported in the process of implementing them. Suppliers are classed as partners, with high levels of mutual respect and a common and consistent set of standards, schedules and goals. At the frontiers of Lean, they set the benchmark for a 'no compromise development process' [6,18], which is responsible for implementing new brands such as the Lexus and rapidly creating new products such as the Prius.

Toyota's continued success is testimony to their commitment to the Toyota Way and the impact of Lean Thinking. Whilst others have faltered, Toyota have consistently developed and grown in terms of the value they offer, the revenues they receive and the profits that result. However, more importantly, they continue to grow in stature in terms of their vision – creating a better society. They support the communities they serve in many ways and their level of openness, combined with their visible corporate, social and environmental responsibilities provides a benchmark for others. Their openness is helping other leading companies achieve what should be a common goal for everyone, creating a better society and a more sustainable environment. Toyota have achieved a great deal and have an impressive track record; yet they also realise they have much more to do. If Toyota maintain course, their future success is likely to be limited only by their vision and ambition.

Lean Service – The Rise of Tesco

In the 1990's Tesco were generally classed as a middle ranking player in the UK retail market, operating superstores predominantly selling food and facing growing competition from groups like Wal-Mart (following their acquisition of Asda). Over the past decade, Tesco has undergone a massive transformation and has become one of the most respected global retailers in the world. This success if often attributed to how they manage their supply chains, which are regularly ranked as some of the best in the world. Whilst this is true, their success is due to much more than this. Lean Thinking has been applied within Tesco since the early 1990's and has successfully underpinned their growth over this period. It has involved a more holistic application of Lean Thinking; from setting their strategic direction through to the outcomes their processes create. This can be quickly and easily demonstrated using the Lean World Management System framework (see Figure 2.51).

The strategic direction setting within Tesco has been particularly effective. Its values and philosophy, through to its strategy and policies, provide clear and unambiguous direction for the whole organisation. This has made Tesco highly effective and not simply efficient, at what they do. Tesco are well known for offering their customers choice and this has become a clear differentiator for them. They not only offer choice in the range of products and services they offer, but in the way customers can choose to receive them. Their philosophy of continuous improvement is also very visible and a part of everything they do (i.e. Every Little Helps). Their purpose is simple; to create value for customers to earn their lifetime loyalty.

Their strategy has also been highly successful, driving their development and growth into many new areas through the expansion and extension of their portfolio. The Tesco strategy is currently based upon four themes [13]:

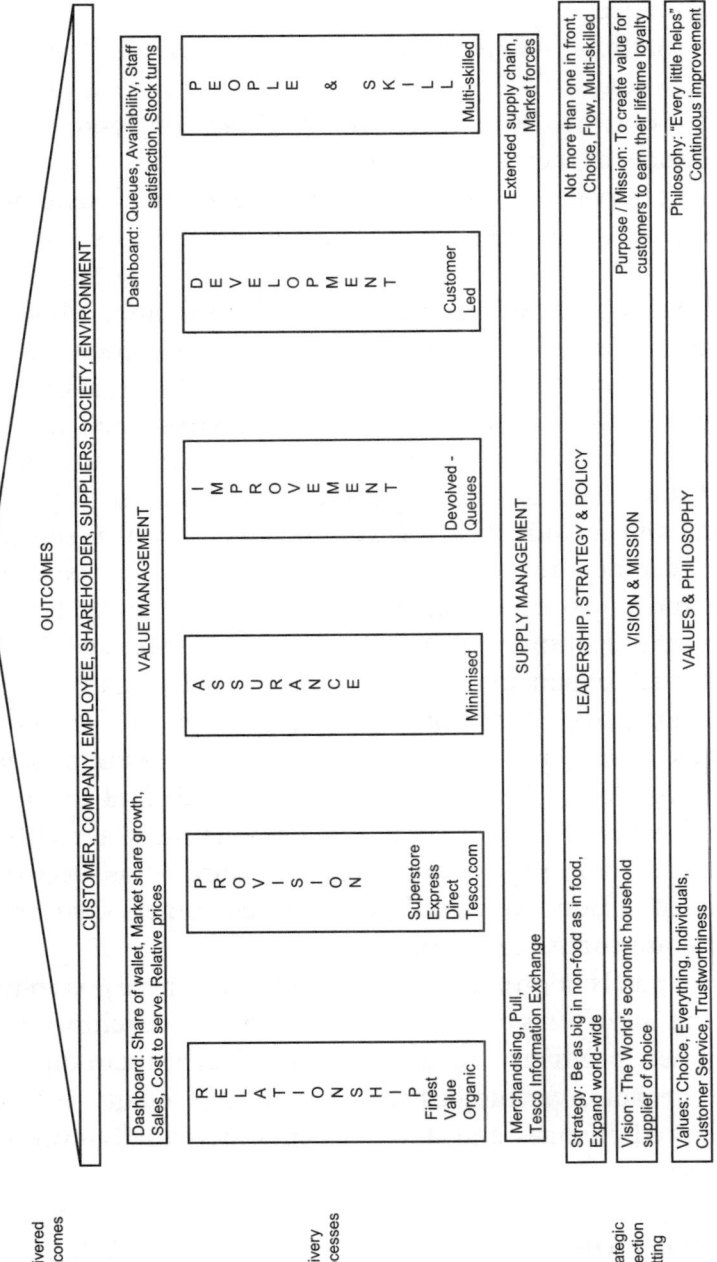

Figure 2.51 Representation of Tesco using the Lean World Management System.

- Core UK – to provide all customers with excellent value and choice,
- International – to focus on giving local customers what they want,
- Non-food – to be as successful at selling non-food products as they are in food,
- Retail Services – to meet the changing needs of customer lifestyles by providing new products and services.

This strategy has helped them to develop more choice for customers, in terms of the products and services they offer and the way customers are able to receive them. For instance, they have successfully expanded into new services such as Tesco Express and Tesco.com. Similarly, their non-food strategy has resulted in an extension of the products and services they offer, including the introduction of Tesco Direct, with Tesco set to shortly become the largest UK non-food retailer. New retail services have also been created, including Insurance, Financial and Communications products and services. Meanwhile, their international expansion has been progressing carefully and successfully across the globe, providing local customers with what they want. This has included recent successful expansion into Japan, China, Malaysia, Turkey, Poland, and the United States of America. Tesco's strategy demonstrates a number of key features required in any Lean strategy. It is holistically constructed around the needs of their customers and created without compromise or conflict.

Tesco spends a great deal of time and energy constantly improving all of its processes. They have also developed a vast range of new products and services and brought them quickly to market. In fact, over the last few years in particular, there have been marked changes and developments in virtually everything Tesco does.

Tesco has been at the frontier of successfully developing relationships with their customers for some time. Whilst many service providers are still grappling with how to improve their customer satisfaction ratings, Tesco have focused on providing customers with exactly what they want and seeking to earn their lifetime loyalty. This is very important, as loyalty can only be earned by being loyal to your customers – it is not something you can either expect or buy. It involves being able to respond to individual customers needs, which themselves can be very different at different times of the day. For Tesco, this is underpinned by their core values, including choice. Tesco has for some time offered product choice from a vast array of suppliers and have also created a number of distinct ranges to satisfy differing customer needs. In the case of food, these include their Finest, Standard, Value, Healthy Living and Organic ranges. The introduction of the Tesco loyalty card has also been a huge success and the envy of many.

Tesco have also recognised that customers have different needs at differing times, opening up a vast array of formats offering products and services to customers. The needs of a customer requiring a pint of milk on the way to work, can be very different to that of the same customer, on a different day, requiring milk and shopping for their family on their way home from work. Likewise, a customer in a rush and in need of just a few items may have very different needs to the same customer, on another day, wishing to complete their weekly shop. Insight and experience gained from understanding what customers want is invaluable to any business. For example, after gaining quite basic information (e.g. sex and age profile) on who were buying products in Japan, 7/11 stores were surprised to find that the main buyers of pantyhose were actually men! This was often due to them receiving a telephone call from their partner whilst at work, requesting various items to be picked up from the store on their way home. Moving pantyhose towards the edge of the women's section and much closer to other items (e.g. the wine and beer), was therefore able to bring richer rewards in terms of additional sales. Likewise, with space at a premium, such stores cannot stock vast quantities of items and change their shelf layouts 2–3 times a day, adjusting stock levels and ranges to match the needs of their customers at different times of the day. With the level of insight created by their loyalty card, Tesco are in a highly enviable position of being able to offer a unique form of convenience to their customers, not simply offering basic convenience (e.g. bread and milk) but providing specialised local convenience (e.g. speciality products) given their knowledge of what customer's actually want down to very localised geographical areas.

In terms of provision, Tesco Express provides one component within a multiplicity of formats. These include Supermarkets, Metro, Tesco.com and Tesco Direct. Recent years has seen the introduction of a number of 24 hour stores as well as a vast array of new provision processes, offering customers both flexibility and choice. For instance, Tesco introduced a variety of options for paying for petrol, from pay at the pump to pay at the till in the shop. Tesco, along with a number of other retailers, have also created check-out lanes for customers purchasing only a few items within their larger superstores. They have also sought to adopt a 'not more than one in front' principle and more recently introduced self service check-outs. Tesco is always seeking ways to improve, for instance, by finding new ways to help customers find the right items (e.g. by using 'rich media' in Superstores). It also includes finding quicker and easier ways to pay for items. This could involve customers going to empty supermarket checkouts (which store staff then open), or moving the check-out closer to the customer (e.g. by paying for items as they are selected and added to the trolley). The latter of these would remove the need for customers to take items out of the trolley and to put them back in again once scanned. Tesco are well known for the many improvements that they have made to their supply chains, including the introduction of the Tesco Information Exchange (TIE) system which provides suppliers, throughout the supply chain, real time information on the level of customer sales of their products. This reduces the risk of any destructive bullwhip effect and allows the levels of inventory to be minimised [19].

Tesco have also carefully developed and improved their formats, including Tesco.com. When introduced, it was initially quite small scale. It involves taking customer orders on-line,

Tesco staff taking trolleys around their local store to collect items and distribution teams finally delivering orders to customers. This approach helped them to learn and develop this new service. As the popularity of the service has grown, Tesco are beginning to industrialise it and scale it to deliver higher volumes. At the same time it is removing any unnecessary steps within the process. For instance, warehouses have recently been introduced within the London area which cater for home delivery only. This reduces the space, inventory, time and resource consumed in providing customers what they need. Over time, this will start to reduce the amount of time spent by Tesco staff in local stores taking items from shelves and grouping them together in readiness for home delivery. Interestingly, when Tesco staff started to collect the items required by their customers for themselves, it began to expose the need for further improvements within their supply chain. Even when individual stock availability is high (e.g. 99% to 99.5%), an individual customer requiring a basket of 40 items may only obtain exactly what they want 60–80% of the time. The rest of the time, they would either have to substitute an out of stock item for a similar item, or go without it completely. This raises the bar once again for all supply chains.

Tesco minimises the need for assurance, providing support through separate and highly visible customer service desks. They seek to multi-skill their staff, to be able to offer a variety of customer services. For instance, people stacking shelves may be asked for their advice by customers. Additionally, they may be requested by colleagues to operate extra check-outs during busy periods. This does not have to be made into an exact science or a military operation. Operators simply need to be able to identify when extra support is required, communicate this to others and to then receive the necessary support. Many retail environments still, too often, have large queues of frustrated customers, trying to be served by highly stressed check-out staff. Worse still, other members of staff, perhaps involved in stacking or tidying shelves, are often available but appear either unable or unwilling to help. Such environments will not survive in a highly competitive world, where customer's time cannot be classed as 'free'. Tesco clearly understands that they will only survive and prosper for as long as customers choose to buy from them. Others, in a far weaker position than Tesco, need to adapt quickly if they are going to survive.

Tesco understands the value of developing relationships with their customers and the impact of loyalty on both future purchases and recommendations to others. For instance, viral marketing was used heavily as part of their advertising campaign for their new internet phone service. Their customers are seen to be recommending the service to their family and friends too. Tesco have also been very successful in providing choice to customers. Supermarkets providing food have had to ensure customers have year round access to a wide range of climate dependent and seasonal foods. Not all of them can be success-fully produced locally and some have to be acquired from around the globe. This naturally increases the average distance food has to travel (known as food miles). Whilst supply naturally moves as close to the point of consumption as possible, consumers should still be given choice and in doing so drive change themselves. For significant change to happen, consumers have to adjust their expectations and behaviours. Enterprises must try to avoid deciding what customers will be able to have or telling them when they can have them. For instance, Tesco are looking at ways to provide better and more meaningful product labelling, so consumers have the ability to make more informed decisions themselves. Tesco, just like other retailers, are also searching for ways for items, such as food, to be supplied more locally, wherever it is practicable to do so. At the same time, they are developing new distribution channels to complement their more traditional ones (e.g. addition of Tesco Direct, Tesco.com). These approaches provide an effective way to increase the range of products they are able to offer their customers, without significantly increasing cost.

Unfortunately, companies like Tesco often become a poten-tial target due to their success. When given a massive choice, individual customers sometimes complain that they cannot get everything they want. This is balanced by those (e.g. lobby groups, other retailers or potential customers) who complain because they are concerned people can get anything from Tesco, and that they are getting too big! In reality, there is almost infinite variety in customer demand and it is this that ultimately allows a plethora of companies to prosper [15]. However, it necessitates a clear vision and robust strategy, if each company is to successfully differentiate itself from others. For instance, Aldi, also a very successful retailer, offers a wide range of products, but with little to no choice of product supplier. This contrasts with the large range of product suppliers found at Tesco. Some customers demand choice, others get easily bogged down when given too much choice. Such differences allow apparently similar companies to live in relative harmony.

Tesco have not simply sought to secure more and more of the food market. Instead, they have focused upon earning customer's lifetime loyalty and increasing their share of the household wallet. This has led them to expand rapidly into non-food items and other retail services, whilst successfully growing their core UK business. Tesco often state that their future success depends purely on whether customers continue to choose to buy from them. This principle has served them well to date and, if they do not falter, it will make them a formidable global player – one very hard to catch. Tesco also recognise the importance of the communities they serve, as well as the environment. For instance, they have created innovative projects, such as computers and sport for schools. They also provide recycling services at many of their sites and now offer additional loyalty points for customers helping to reduce the number of plastic bags they use. They are also investing a great deal of time and money into ways of reducing energy consumption and in renewable sources of energy. Tesco have made huge steps forward over the last decade and should be proud of their achievements. Just like Toyota, they have helped to chart a successful path any other enterprise can choose to take. Relatively, Tesco's Lean journey is still in its infancy when compared to a company like Toyota. Involving everyone and harnessing the ingenuity of all staff, are crucial stages in any Lean journey. By developing deeper and more purposeful relationships with customers and suppliers, the creativity within the whole value chain is also utilised. These are powerful ingredients for continuous improvement and help to ensure complete success. They are responsible for supplying the 'fuel' (i.e. ideas for change) and determining the size of the 'engine' (i.e. people creating change). The strategy determines the 'direction' taken, but continuous improvement determines the rate at which an enterprise is able to catch up or accelerate away from any rivals. Supply chains are continuing to re-configure all around the world and opportunities are abound [26]. The reality is that Tesco's current success, great as it is, could be just the beginning. Tesco is in a good position to capitalise upon the foundations it has laid and the many opportunities now before it. They have much still to do, but if they continue along a Lean Way then they are likely to have a prosperous future ahead of them.

Lean Government – a new Criminal Justice System

There is increasing pressure for government agencies to increase the value they offer whilst minimizing any tax burden upon society. Given the proven success of Lean Thinking in creating such outcomes, there is increasing attention being given to applying Lean within government agencies. There are currently many small pockets of application in the UK, including within the health service, police forces, local government and other national government departments. Here, we explore the application of Lean Thinking to the Criminal Justice System, an area currently under much scrutiny. The criminal justice system is generally responsible for minimizing crime, dealing with crime and reducing the fear of crime. The process for dealing with crime, together with those typically involved, is schematically shown in Figure 2.52.

There are perpetrators of crime (i.e. criminals) and victims of crime. There are also those who represent the different parties, including witnesses and solicitors. There are judges and jurors (often members of the general public), who decide the fate of those directly involved, guided by the law created by government. Individual victims (and families) suffer the initial impact of crime. Everyone suffers the residual impact of crime,

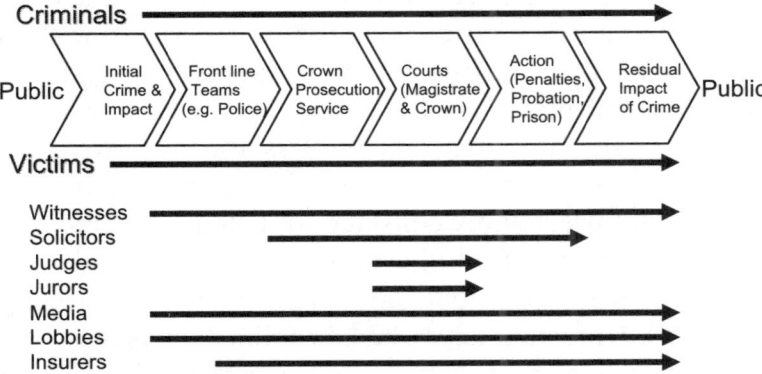

Figure 2.52 Schematic representation of UK criminal justice system.

including the increased fear of crime and all direct and indirect costs associated with it. The financial cost of crime includes any actual financial losses incurred, increased insurance premiums that result and the cost of running the criminal justice system itself. It also includes the costs of helping and supporting individual's emotional, mental and physical recovery.

There is a great deal of improvement activity within the Criminal Justice System, but to date, most of this has been contained within individual departments. A leading police force has been successfully using Lean Thinking and Deming's philosophies to develop a Lean Way [27]. At the start of their journey, they have mainly focused on improving what they can within their sphere of control. The operation of their initial system was typical of many enterprises prior to starting a Lean journey. Traditional management approaches were commonplace and often very similar to those represented by the Lean World Management System in Figure 2.53. Measures and targets existed for individual departments, with league tables used to compare different forces and bonuses given to officers, based upon their clear up rates. This had previously driven some police officers to report linked crimes separately if they knew they could be easily cleared up [28]. It had also led to some police officers offering known criminals the opportunity to reduce their sentences in return for admitting to further crimes (even if they didn't actually commit some of them!). Whilst improving the figures, this type of activity was effectively hiding the activity of other criminals and leaving them on the streets. Whilst wishing to be 'tough on crime and the causes of crime', the system was beginning to fall into a common trap, starting to struggle to process crime and becoming less and less able to prevent crime. Reporting systems wishing to show the crime situation improving, would predictably consider adjusting or excluding any measures making reported figures worse (e.g. criminal damage offences), offering apparent improvement without changing anything [27]. Unfortunately, whilst headline figures may be seen to improve, it does not change what is actually happening or remove what the public sees around them everyday.

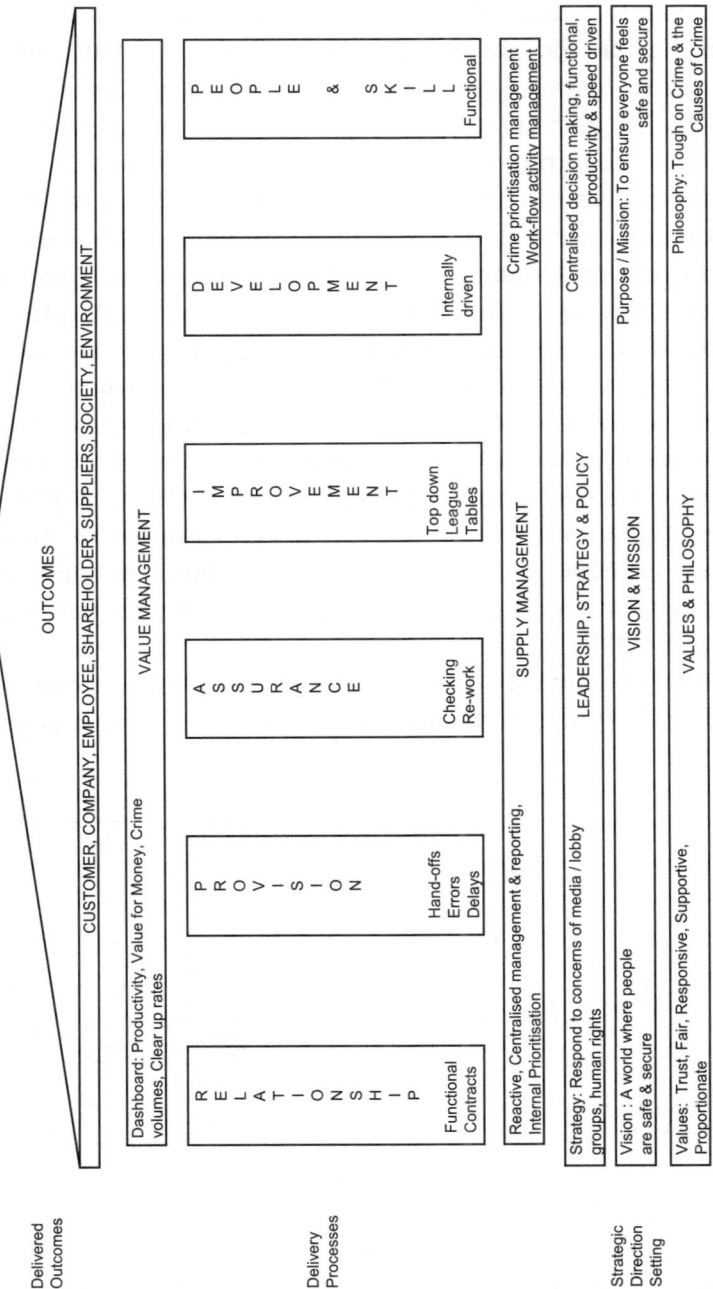

Figure 2.53 Representation of 'Traditional' criminal justice using the Lean World Management System.

Police forces, employing Lean Thinking, start to focus on what really matters to the public. The public generally want to see crime, as well as the fear of crime, minimized. They also want to see different types of offences dealt with appropriately and effectively, as part of a justice system that makes sure crime doesn't pay. Lean police forces seek to learn far more about the systematic nature of crime they are faced with. They understand the nature of crime and the causes of crime. They focus on managing improvement (not numbers) and finding innovative and effective ways to deter potential criminals, catch criminals and stop them from committing offences again. An example control chart used to understand and reduce burglary in one particular region is shown in Figure 2.54. It shows how burglary was progressively reduced by adopting a process of continuous improvement. It also serves to highlight the effect that prolific offenders have on levels of crime, with the number of monthly burglaries reducing significantly every time one was successfully stopped (e.g. arrested using 'trick and trap' techniques such as 'housetrap') [27].

Approaches capable of tracking a complete supply chain involved in criminal activity are also increasingly used. By

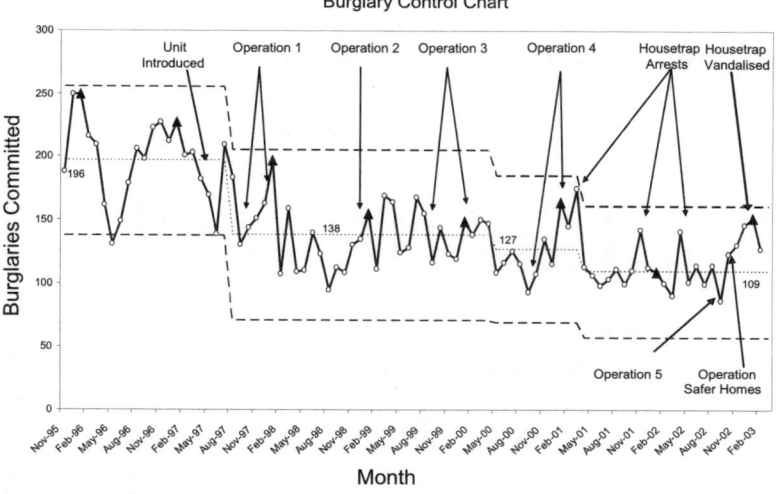

Figure 2.54 Example control chart used for systematically reducing burglary.

reducing crime in one area, police often find that it moves to another – albeit sometimes into an area which is the responsibility of a different force! Lean police therefore need to work holistically across a nation and as part of an overall criminal justice system, to reduce crime and minimize the impact of crime. However, they also need to work closely with other agencies to help remove the causes of crime (see Figure 2.55). They seek to find out how and why crimes are committed, ensuring methods are put in place not only to detect them, but to prevent them. Lean police particularly focus on removing those offences that result in further crime being created (e.g. drug trafficking creating more burglary). They also play their part in reducing the number of offenders committing further crime once they are released. Clearly there is still a lot more to do in all of these areas.

In the UK, whilst certain police forces have started to use Lean strategies to successfully reduce crime, its current application is still somewhat limited (e.g. crime moves to a different region not applying Lean). For the Criminal Justice System to become truly effective, Lean now needs to be adopted holistically and at a strategic level, across the whole value chain and including all departments and teams. At present, operational strategies of the various participants and groups differ widely in their nature. Instead of 'eliminating crime', some are effectively 'processing crime', or worse still, 'profiteering from crime'. However, what all groups do have in common is a disproportionate number of functional measures and targets, as well as increased levels of paperwork and micro-management (e.g. national, regional or departmental). Until everyone in the system is heading in the same direction, and front line staff are given increasing responsibility for continuously improving the way that public outcomes are achieved, there is little chance of providing an overall service that is effective. In the UK, traditional approaches are creating more criminals and overcrowded prisons. It's also raising public frustration and creating higher levels of employee stress. Improvement has to be holistic. A Lean Way involves continually improving the entire system, creating

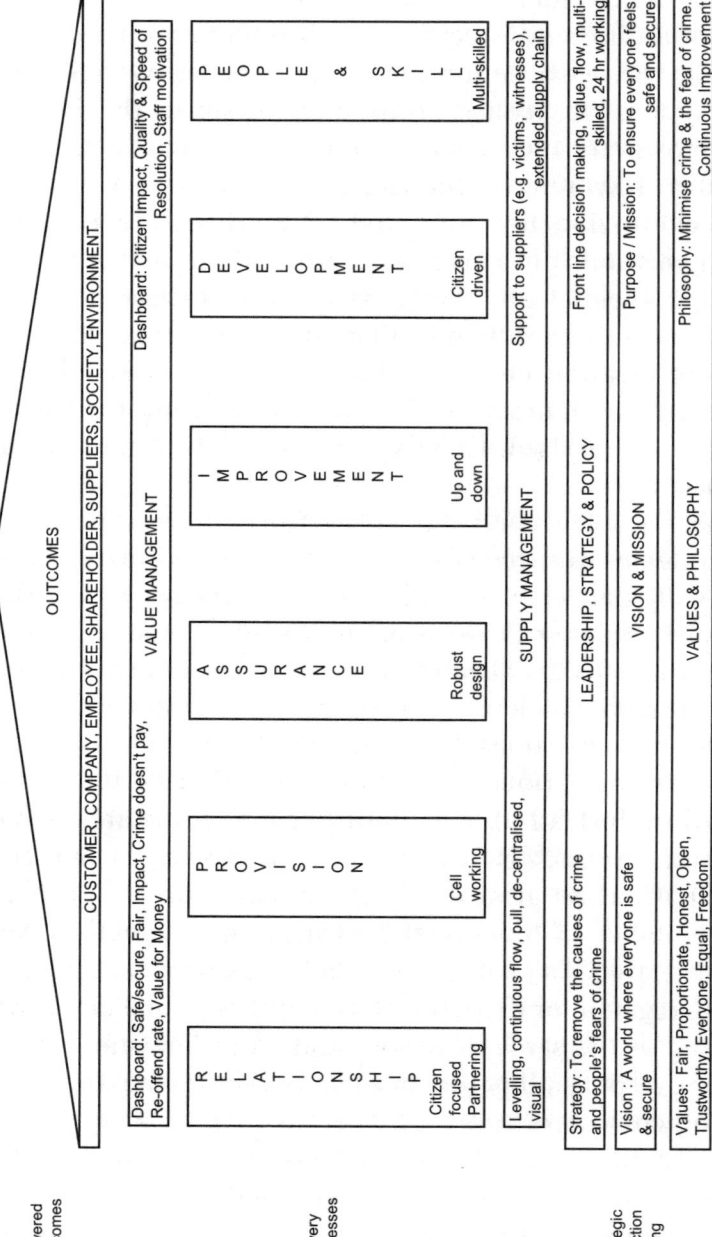

Figure 2.55 Representation of 'Lean' criminal justice using the Lean World Management System.

better and meaningful outcomes for everyone – except those attempting to profiteer from crime.

The police force provides a crucial role within a Lean criminal justice system. However, the front line in the criminal justice system is not the police, but the public themselves. The public need to recognize and take responsibility for their role in making sure crime is identified, reported, detected and minimised. They cannot simply devolve this responsibility to others. In doing so, the public must feel safe in the knowledge that they have the full support of the community and will be protected from any potential harm. Likewise, governments have a key responsibility in making sure that the laws are appropriate, proportionate, fair and workable. The system as a whole must ensure the rights of everyone are maintained. The rights of the criminal to be classed as innocent until proven guilty needs to be equally balanced by the rights of all law abiding people to be protected. Communities do not like to feel that they are, effectively, 'paying' for the crimes other people choose to commit. Rather than criminals being offered more lenient sentences for admitting to more crimes (that they perhaps did not do), or simply offering it in return for good behaviour, they could be offered leniency but only for helping the criminal justice system reduce crime. The criminal justice system, as a whole, must ensure criminals are punished appropriately and that crime does not pay. Without this, crime will never go away. Today, many criminals refuse to pay the fines imposed on them by the courts, leaving the criminal justice system to try to locate them again in order to recover the money due. Lean criminal justice systems simply lock the criminal up until they pay their fine. Contrary to initial thinking, this does not require additional cell space as criminals, knowing how the system works, will tend to pay fines immediately. The criminal justice system must ensure that places, such as prisons, do not become a training ground for developing further and more sophisticated crime. Currently, many criminals re-offend again soon after they leave prison, either because nothing has changed or circumstances have become even worse. A family member, particularly a parent, going to prison can create great strain on families and relationships. It can also result in children being placed in care, particularly when it involves a child's mother going to prison. Many people, currently in prison, also suffer from mental health problems but these often go untreated. The criminal justice system as a whole needs to help rehabilitate individuals and support them to successfully adopt a new law abiding future on entering back into society. It is not commonly known that it costs far more to lock a prisoner in jail for a year than it does to send them to Harvard – not that people should be encouraged to commit crime in order to go to Havard!

Resources need to be focused based on actual crime, the impact of crime and the causes of crime. If crime in certain areas or within certain communities are known to be particularly prevalent, then resources need to be proportionately focused towards these. This is nothing to do with nationalism, racism or any other 'ism' – it's simply common sense and an effective use of time and resources needed to secure the safety and security of everyone. Areas or communities, where this is necessary, should not seek to condemn agencies actively trying to help them. Instead, their energy would be far better spent supporting them in changing the environment in which they also have to live. If crime in an area or community is actually reduced then resources will also naturally migrate to those where it is more greatly needed.

Implementing a Lean World Management System involves robustly integrating top down strategy (including policy deployment) with bottom up continuous improvement, across the whole value chain. It focuses the entire system on eliminating crime and minimizing the fear of crime. The fear of crime is often greater than the actual crime itself. Whilst focusing on eliminating actual crime, increased use of communications technology, such as the internet, must also be used to bring public perception of crime closer to reality. By making the true facts about crime more readily available, it reduces the impact of otherwise sensationalist stories capable of distorting the perceptions of the public. In a similar way, by understanding customer's perception over time, it also highlights what the priorities should be and what needs to be improved. For instance, simple measures of public opinion can be obtained by asking a few questions, such as:

1. 'On a scale of 0–10, how safe and secure do you feel?' and
2. 'On a scale of 0–10, do you think crime pays?'

These would provide a useful set of reporting statistics. However, only by asking and then listening to why the public have given their scores, are real insights, priorities and ideas for improvement obtained. Measurements are used for improvement, not for setting targets and rewards. For instance, it would highlight the influence criminal damage has on the public's perception of crime and fear of crime. This is partly because it is highly visible. It would also demonstrate the level of public concern about those offenders who persistently commit offences and are not being dealt with effectively. Likewise, it would draw attention to those offenders for whom crime does appear to pay. On the other hand, it will also highlight situations where perceptions are completely different to reality, for instance showing temporary distortions caused by individual crimes that have been sensationalized by the media. These should not be ignored. Instead, a Lean criminal justice system needs to intelligently use its knowledge to ensure that the public receives a more balanced account of crime, by providing more information currently contained within the criminal justice system itself and building up public confidence. It also avoids the risk of becoming heavily driven by the media or deflected away from those things that really matter to the public by exceptional events. It also ensures a Lean journey which involves a clear and steady migration away from processing crime, to eliminating the causes of crime and removing the fear of crime. By doing this, governments ensure that their communities start to receive what they want at its most basic level – to feel safe and secure, with little fear of crime. As well-being improves within communities, attention

can increasingly focus on other positive outcomes, such as contented communities, prosperous enterprises and a sustainable
environment. Combining these together can then help to create
individual well-being and happiness.

Part Three

The Lean World

Chapter 7

Components of the Lean World

The philosophy of the Lean World Management System is to use 'Continuous Improvement' to create 'Complete Success'. The outcomes that result help to develop a Lean World – a world where individuals, communities, enterprises and the environment all flourish together. It involves ensuring the sustainability of our planet and its resources, improving the happiness and well-being of individuals, as well as increasing the level of contentment in our communities (previously shown in Figure 2.33, Chapter 3).

In the Lean World, minimal amounts of the world's resources are wasted or extracted. Natural, renewable and recyclable resources are harnessed. Lean enterprises flourish by offering services which create the most value and the least waste, whilst requiring the minimum of effort and resources. In the Lean World, enterprises focus on reducing the overburdening of employees, reducing stress and continually developing the skills of individuals so they can innovate and add more value.

The Lean World is considered to be made up of four elements; individuals, communities, enterprise and the environment (as shown in Figure 3.1). The elements in the Lean World are highly interconnected, with individuals at its heart. Individuals live within the environment and as part of communities. They obtain value from enterprises and most individuals work for at least one of them too; whether they are public, private or third sector organisations (i.e. charities).

Each element can be considered in its own right, but in reality they are all dynamic and connected to one other to create the whole. For instance, the Enterprise System, otherwise known

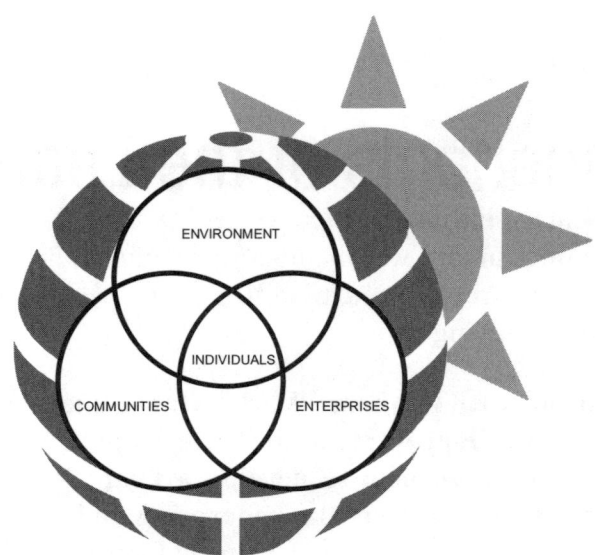

Figure 3.1 The Lean World.

as the Lean World Management System, plays a key role in supporting individual well-being, community contentment and a more sustainable environment. By doing this, the role of enterprise is viewed more holistically and avoids any disconnect between the purpose of enterprise and the world around it.

Individuals

Individuals are central to the Lean World. They have the ability to learn, make decisions and enact change. Increasing attention is being given by individuals, communities and governments, to creating contentment, well-being and happiness [29]. Well-being and happiness are believed to result from four main elements, which include having:

1. Basic needs being fulfilled,
2. Social relationships,
3. Enjoyable and meaningful work, and
4. Personal contentment.

The first element involves having ones basic needs fulfilled. This covers a multitude of areas, including; health, food, water, warmth, shelter, trust, safety and security. These are often referred to as 'hygiene' factors [30]. Our health can affect our overall feeling of well-being and happiness. At the same time, our overall happiness can affect the rate at which our body's age and the risk of us becoming unwell. Without the basic needs of life in place, it is hard to build fruitful relationships or carry out meaningful work. In poorer countries the lack of basic needs can result in a great deal of stress, anxiety and unhappiness. For instance, in war torn areas of the world it is not easy for individuals to live their lives in a happy and meaningful way when their main focus is to stay alive.

The second element, relationships, relates to how people share their lives with their family, friends, social groups, communities and even their pets. The closeness and level of support obtained from these relationships are critical to personal well-being and happiness. For instance, the ability to share problems and responsibilities can have a huge impact on well-being, which is underlined by the well known saying 'a problem shared is a problem halved'. When a family break-down occurs, or a family suffers bereavement, it can prove hugely stressful and take a long time for an individual's well-being to recover. In some cases it can continue to spiral downward and result in depression and other health problems.

For an individual's well-being to improve further, they also need to be happy and contented in their work. This can be paid or unpaid, working either as an employee or helping out a local community or charity. Just as importantly, it also includes being a home-maker for the family. Whilst money can help to provide the basic needs in life, it is not the key to happiness. Well-being and happiness are derived from the enjoyment gained from carrying out the work and because the work itself is meaningful. Leading companies realise that money does not motivate people in the long run, but the intrinsic meaning and value of the work does. The euphoria of a pay rise or bonus tends to be rather short lived and quickly forgotten. Individuals have a natural instinct to learn and improve. People want challenges and to carry out activities that build on their strengths, but they also need supportive management that nurtures this environment and allows them to develop as individuals. Individuals like to be able to think for themselves, and do not like having to just do what they are told.

The final contributor to well-being and happiness is personal contentment and outlook. As individuals, our personal outlook and tendency towards happiness varies. This is due to our natural physical and psychological disposition, but it is also formed through life events and experiences. Individuals tend to view a glass as either half full or half empty. Contentment not only relates to our satisfaction as individuals, but also as groups within a wider community and as part of the overall environment. For instance, we are unlikely to feel happy or contented if we know we are causing others harm. People often want to be connected to something larger than themselves, such as a culture, religion, social or an environmental cause. Many people also spend a significant amount of their time supporting good causes, such as recycling, fair trade or healthy living.

The four contributors to well-being and happiness fit very well into the overall model of the 'Lean World'. Our individual happiness and well-being is dependent on how we co-operate together, as part of communities and enterprises, whilst living in a shared environment. Once an individual's basic needs are met, individuals can spend more time developing relationships. They can get involved in additional activities that have more meaning to them and which increase their self esteem. Communities will build upon the growing understanding of the factors that affect well-being and happiness. As they learn more they will seek additional ways to improve it. It is likely to impact many aspects of our lives in the future, from the way we teach in our schools to the way we act in our communities. As individuals gain more choice, personal well-being and happiness will become key drivers of change.

Communities

Communities, within which individuals live, are made up of families, friends, local communities, societies, regions, nations and global communities. Communities join together common interests and goals, share knowledge and responsibilities, and create change.

The primary unit of communities are families. The deeper these relationships, the better it is for everyone. It includes sharing values, knowledge and responsibilities. It's about working as a single unit with common goals, taking ownership and responsibility for all the different activities required, not just to survive, but to prosper. It begins by ensuring the basic needs of the family are met; from food and water, to warmth and shelter. It involves sharing out tasks and co-ordinating activities for the good of everyone (some search for food and water, whilst others create warmth and shelter). It is about nurturing the young in the values of the family group and providing them with the ability to learn and develop, as individuals and as a group. In very close family communities, elders act as role models and pass on their values and knowledge to the younger generation – they teach their young how to catch fish for themselves, rather than continually supply them with food. However today, families are finding it increasingly difficult to stay together, with more marriages than ever breaking down. This is partly due to the levels of stress placed upon relationships by pressures created within society (e.g. desire for wealth and material goods) and from work (e.g. for more productivity). Family breakdown can be devastating to all those directly (and indirectly) involved and for many individuals their personal well-being and happiness can take a long time to recover. It can also result in health problems and create stress in other areas of people's lives, including their work and other relationships. Some cultures focus heavily on the role of the family, whereas other cultures believe that personal independence is the key to future well-being and happiness. By studying latest research, the importance of the role played by families cannot be underestimated. From cradle to grave, families set the environment in which we learn, shape the values by which we live and the way we nurture our offspring.

Friendships are also a key part of society. They link individuals to communities who share similar values and interests. They can also widen a person's understanding and tolerance. Recent research has shown how friendship can have a much bigger influence on our well-being and happiness than personal income [29]. Friends listen and help one another, without judgement or favour. They understand the value of friendship and respect people as individuals. They trust each other and just like a family unit, they can be relied upon to offer support in times of need.

Society is made up of many communities, based on their location, values, cultures and beliefs. They also develop through people's interests (called communities of interest), for instance from the sports they like, the music they listen to or the hobbies they enjoy. Society has an almost infinite number of permutations, which is arguably what makes life so varied and fulfilling.

Technology such as communications and the internet are spreading both the meaning and boundaries of communities further. People are now able to make new friends across the world and not just locally. They can date on-line and trade on-line. Every day individuals can get involved in millions of small communities around the world. No longer are people in a local community finding themselves isolated in either their hobbies or their views, as the internet is able to connect individuals who share similar ideals and interests.

New communities and groups spring up every day, some with a temporary existence and some permanently. Some do so to share information, knowledge, values and interests. Many do so just to have fun. Others use their connectivity to trade or to engender change. For example, there has been huge growth in the use of web sites, chat rooms and blogs. Individual creativity has been released and similar minded people are joining forces to create change. Modern communications, and in particular the internet, allows information to traverse easily across any border; be it geographic, cultural or editorial. This has far reaching implications on the future role of governments and on future policy. It has the ability to allow individuals to collectively understand and change society, enterprise and the environment, for the better. For example, governments and enterprise will need to increasingly take into account the well-being of individuals and contentment within society, as well as the sustainability of the planet. Nurturing the role of the family and of friendships, developing people's individual skills at work and listening once again to the voice of the majority, will become a priority.

3.1.3 Enterprises

Enterprises, including governments, charities and other agencies, are focused on providing products and services to individuals, communities and to other enterprises. They only exist to provide value to their customers, changing resources provided by suppliers into products or services for others to use or consume. In the process they also create waste, including excess raw materials, defective products/services or other unwanted by-products/pollution (e.g. materials, chemicals and gases). The overall role of an enterprise is summarised in Figure 3.2. 'Transformed resources' include all the materials, inventory, information and energy consumed in the transformation process to create the products or services. 'Transforming resources' include the facilities and staff used to transform the materials into the goods and services. Any waste created is processed, recycled and disposed of.

In a car plant, the transformed resources include body panels, wheels, nuts, bolts and energy whilst the transforming resources include the staff, equipment, tools and the production plant carrying out the transformation process. In an insurance company, the transformed resources include customer specific

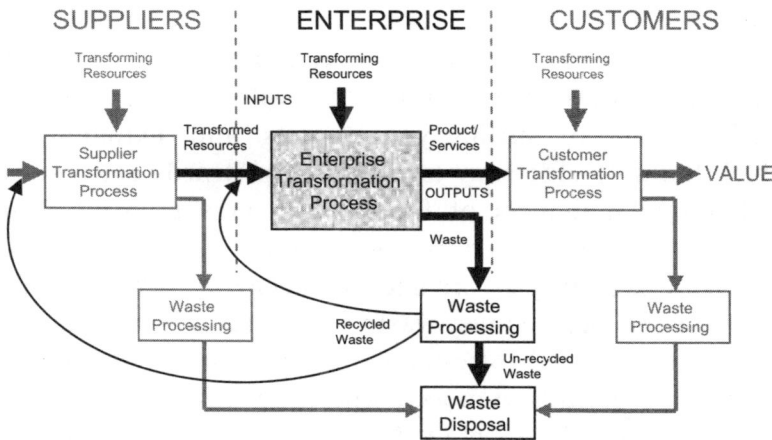

Figure 3.2 Enterprise transformation and waste processes.

information which is transformed into an insurance policy, by the staff using IT equipment and their knowledge about different types of risks.

The ability of an enterprise to grow its revenues and profits is determined by how well it delivers more and more value to its customers, so customers continue to purchase from it and recommend its products/services to others. Minimising waste within value creating processes also ensures that value is provided quickly and with minimum effort (and cost!). By doing these things, stakeholders and shareholders investing in the company can expect to see their shares rise in value and for dividends to grow. With increasing choice, individuals are also looking to work for, and purchase from, enterprises that maintain similar moral, social and environmental principles to their own. The company they work for and companies they purchase from, invariably says something about them and individuals are increasingly voting with their feet.

Enterprises must therefore have a clear vision and goal, operate world class management practices but also attract, nurture and develop staff. They must seek not to overburden their employees and yet challenge, develop and support them to achieve their true potential; adding more value for customers and carrying out more meaningful work. Hence, the Lean World Management System classifies the development of staff as a primary goal.

Many enterprises still operate practices which, in effect, separate management from the work, with the job of management being one of 'hitting your targets' and 'managing your people'. Sales or efficiency targets are arbitrarily set and given to individual managers of functional teams to meet. Rather than breaking down barriers, these tend to increase functional specialisation, quality errors and management overheads. From the customer's perspective, waste is generated, not eliminated. Such companies need to re-focus their attention onto the capability of their organisation as a whole, so they can improve the delivery processes providing value to their customers. They need to move away from driving front line staff harder, to a situation where they can support them to continuously improve the enterprise.

Herzberg's Motivation-Hygiene Theory [30] has for some time, highlighted the key factors that lead to job satisfaction and job dissatisfaction respectively (see Figure 3.3). These factors were understood back in 1959, yet many companies today have a lot to do if they want to apply such principles.

Hygiene Factors (Dis-satisfiers)	Motivators (Satisfiers)
Company policy	Achievement
Supervision	Recognition
Relationships with boss	Work itself
Working conditions	Responsibility
Salary	Advancement
Relationships with peers	Growth

Figure 3.3 Hygiene and Motivating factors.

The dis-satisfiers are referred to as hygiene factors and the satisfiers are referred to as motivators. Once hygiene factors are satisfied, including individual's obtaining a sufficient salary to satisfy their basic needs (e.g. food and shelter), it is possible for staff to become motivated. Pay is not a motivator, but personal development and meaningful roles are. In a Lean Enterprise, pay is related to the breadth and depth of skills successfully applied. Individuals are also motivated by the ability to improve, to be challenged, to achieve, and to receive recognition for a job well done (not necessarily financial).

The hygiene factors also point towards the causes of unnecessary stress; highlighting the importance of company policies, working conditions and the relationships with managers and peers. The working conditions (e.g. plant, office and buildings) clearly play a part, but the majority of hygiene factors relate to the type of work being carried out and the interaction with others. In fact, recent research into the condition nicknamed Sick Building Syndrome [31] concluded that the problem had very little to do with the building or environment, and far more to do with the work, the management and the level of support provided. This research comes too late for those companies that have already spent millions, knocking down buildings or recruiting expensive consultants to redesign their work places and completely re-fit their premises. Research into the physiological impact of stress also shows that one stressful encounter can impair the ability to think rationally for up to two hours [32]. This means that if we are continually being stressed it is not only bad for our health; it's bad for business too!

Stress, within public and private enterprises, has been growing at an increasing rate for some years. The impact of this on an individual's well-being and happiness can be great. It filters into people's social lives too; creating more family turmoil and potential marital breakdowns. Stress has often been classed as a necessary evil when working for an employer, but we now know it does not have to be so. With overall well-being and happiness being increasingly linked to factors other than money, employees will become more demanding of their employers. As individuals in the future are given more choice, an enterprise choosing to maintain policies that generate high levels of stress should not be surprised if they lose their best staff, most of their once loyal customers and with them, most of their revenue.

Environment

The environment in which we live consists of everything that exists on the planet. It includes the earth, atmosphere, mountains, volcanoes, trees, rivers, seas and oceans. It encompasses all the natural and man-made resources in the world. It also includes mankind, all species of animals and plants, as well as all natural habitats and man-made structures existing on earth. In such a complex environment, entities can often be symbiotic, or reliant, upon each other. For instance, animals rely on plants and other animals to live. Trees and plants consume CO_2 and give out O_2, whilst animals consume O_2 and give out CO_2. Balance within an environment is essential if the overall system is to remain stable.

The environmental conditions which we enjoy today on earth are due at least in part to the 'Greenhouse Effect'. Simplistically, the atmosphere around us has the ability to successfully let through most of the sun's energy (e.g. mainly as the light we can see), but the energy is readily absorbed by the earth and mainly converted to heat (infra-red). The atmosphere is less transparent to infra-red energy and hence, some of it is reflected back down to earth again. The net effect of this is to significantly raise the temperature of the earth compared to what it would otherwise be. The most important anthropogenic gas responsible for this is CO_2. Others include water vapour, methane and nitrous oxide. CO_2 is the gas that mankind and animals give out, but which trees and plants remove. CO_2 is also the gas given off when fossil fuels such as coal, oil, petrol, diesel, bio-fuels or natural gas are burnt. Over many decades, we have seen increasing levels of CO_2 entering the atmosphere [33,34], alongside growth in other greenhouse gases such as methane.

Scientific research into climate change has revealed evidence that growing levels of CO_2 could have a significant impact on our future climate and environment [33,34]. Whilst most people have become more aware of climate change over recent years, scientific knowledge on the likely causes of it, and the outcomes that will result from it, are still the subject of much debate and controversy. Some scientists point out that other factors, ones outside of mankind's control, are in fact far more influential on the earth's temperature than levels of CO_2 (e.g. sun, cyclic variations, water vapour, clouds). At the same time, other scientists suggest levels of water vapour and CO_2 will increase as temperatures rise, which will exacerbate the problem further. Others highlight that the permafrost (frozen peat bogs) around the world are going to add to the problem as they melt, giving off large amounts of methane with over 20x the potential power of CO_2. All these factors are likely to have an impact on our climate and mankind is not in a position to influence all of them.

Common sense and prudence would suggest that mankind should seek to do all it reasonably can to support the future sustainability of the environment and to conserve natural resources. Otherwise, mankind, by its own doing, could quickly consume many of the world's natural limited resources, as well as make their local and global environment worse. Enterprises need to minimise the amount of resources they consume, the energy they use and the waste products they create. The volume and impact of any waste needs to be minimised and enterprises need to recycle as much as they can. Waste is generated during transformation processes and whilst it does not add to value, it does add to cost! Reducing waste therefore does not just make environmental sense, it makes business sense too! Enterprises can help to create a more sustainable environment and reduce unnecessary costs at the same time. Enterprises are beginning to take on this greater responsibility, partly in response to growing demand from communities, customers and staff. However, for Lean enterprises it is an integral part of their strategy.

Chapter 8

The Lean World System

The world we live in is never static – it's a living entity which is highly dynamic. Individuals, communities, enterprises and the environment are all integrated together and continually changing. As such, the development of the world needs to be explored using four dynamic systems; an individual, community, enterprise and an environmental system. These four components join together into an overall dynamic system, called the Lean World System. This is visually represented in Figure 3.4.

For Lean enterprises, the 'Enterprise System' is in fact the 'Lean World Management System', generically described in chapter 3. It is a system capable of creating improved outcomes for individuals, communities and the environment (See Figure 3.5).

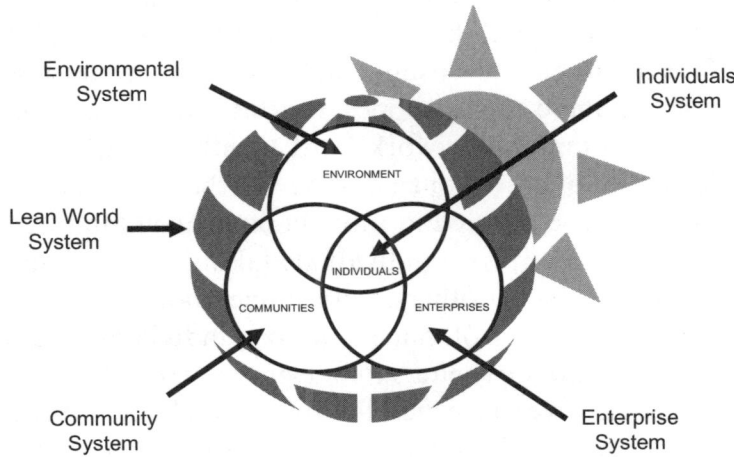

Figure 3.4 The Lean World System™.

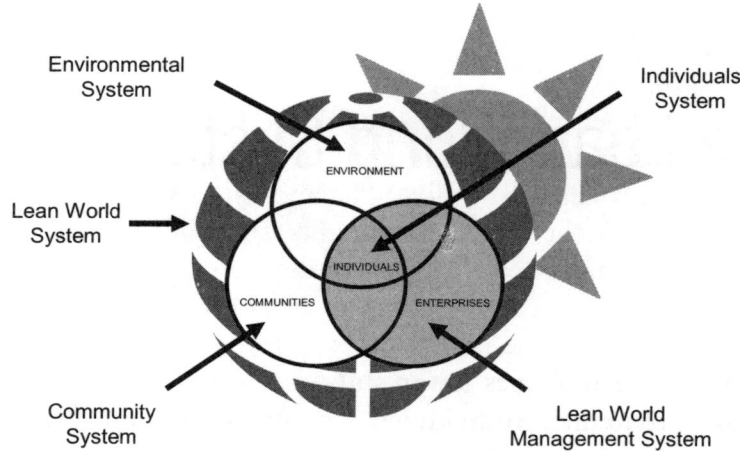

Figure 3.5 The Lean World Management System as part of the Lean World System.

Individuals play a pivotal part within the Lean World System, as they heavily participate in all of the systems. They work for and buy from enterprises (e.g. providing value to one another), play their part in communities (e.g. in families) and interact with both the local and global environment (e.g. resources, nature, climate).

Environmental conditions often dictate the number of individuals in a given region and the types of communities created. For instance, areas with limited resources (e.g. food and water) often find it difficult to sustain high levels of urbanisation or enterprise. In these areas, money has little to no meaning, as families and communities work hard together to maintain the basic necessities of life (e.g. in a desert). On the other hand, where environments have allowed it, more complex communities have been able to develop, with individuals taking on differing roles and providing value to others, with money becoming a way of transacting the transfer of value from one individual to another (e.g. from one building shelters to one growing food).

As individuals we are generally able to make a considerable number of choices. Indeed, mankind is one of the few species that has been able to harness its natural intelligence and creativity, to learn how to improve and, as communities, create solutions capable of improving the environment in which we live (see Figure 3.6).

The intelligence gifted to mankind has the ability to be positively used, in a virtuous circle of continuous improvement. We are able to learn as individuals and as a society, understand our impact on the environment and, through innovation and enterprise, harness opportunities to develop in sustainable ways. This includes the ability to create clean water and sanitation facilities to reduce the risk of disease. It also includes the ability to develop technologies capable of harnessing natural sources of energy, and to tackle other environmental challenges.

Alternatively, one could also take the view, that the intelligence of mankind is currently being negatively used, creating a continuous negative spiral of destruction. With a predominant focus upon economies, enterprise and wealth, the world is increasingly consuming its natural resources, burning fossil fuels and destroying rainforests. However, even within this system, individuals have choice and the ability to enact change. Individuals can both singularly and collectively demand change

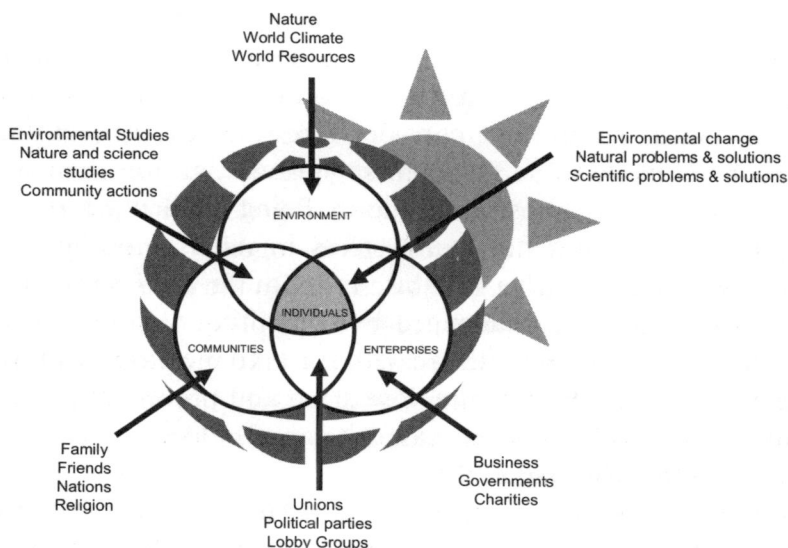

Figure 3.6 Individuals within the Lean World System.

from enterprise (including government), driving them to provide solutions with more positive outcomes. They have the ability to choose what they want to do, what they buy, who they work for and who they buy from. With technology, such as communications and the internet, globally connected communities share knowledge, trade and join together to create change (e.g. through lobby groups).

Technology, developed by mankind, will play a big part. For instance, modern communications technology can be used by individuals at home, in society and at work. It can provide instant communication with family, friends, colleagues, customers and other service providers. It connects communities all around the world, without the need for travel. It also provides access to knowledge around the world wherever we may be. Technology can therefore help to create more communities and increase contentment (e.g. communications solutions). It can also help to improve individual well-being (e.g. healthcare solutions) and help to improve the environment (e.g. renewable energy solutions). This trend will continue, with technology playing its part in blurring the boundary between enterprise and individual/community activity [15].

The combined Lean World System is complex and highly dynamic, but Systems Thinking can be used to visualise and explore many of the relationships and behaviours within it. For instance, let us first consider stress. Stress is something everyone is likely to suffer from at various times in their lives, but for some it's almost continuous. Being challenged and put under pressure does not cause stress in itself – indeed many people enjoy and thrive on this. Individuals only suffer from stress when they are challenged by something they do not feel they can cope with and their anxiety starts to increase as a result. It can cause them to perspire, lose sleep and prevent them from thinking rationally. In some cases, it can also lead to depression and losing the will to live.

Moving house, changing job and getting married have, for some time, been well known for creating stress. However, stress can also be generated by numerous much smaller events, such as finding a long queue at a check-out, or as a result of a car being driven dangerously. However, on a day to day basis, stress is often caused by having to complete apparently impossible tasks at work, or as a result of problems within family relationships. The body secretes a number of chemicals from the brain every time high levels of stress are experienced. Whilst some of these go on to stimulate other hormones such as adrenaline (which help in 'fight' or 'flight'), others make rational thought processes extremely difficult and can persist for a number of hours [32]. This means that staff who are subjected to increasingly impossible challenges or targets, with little to no support, live within an environment of continual stress at work. This could, for instance, include employees who have to continually deal with complaints from customers, or have to try hard to sell products to customers who do not want them. The inability to think/act rationally under stress leads to increased errors (i.e. failures), more failure demand to process and growing pressure and targets from management to process work more quickly. This results in more stress (as shown in Figure 3.7).

In a traditional workplace, all relationships re-enforce one another (NB they are supporting relationships, with no opposing ones) and stress continues to build up. Levels of stress continually increase whilst a company maintains a strategy of managing by

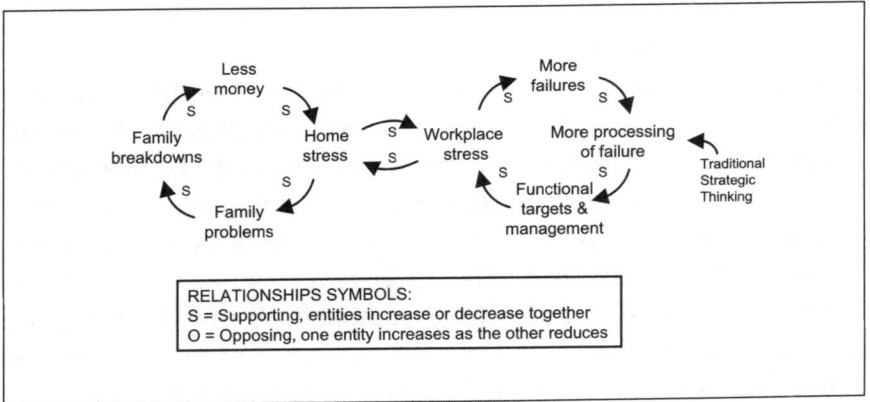

RELATIONSHIPS SYMBOLS:
S = Supporting, entities increase or decrease together
O = Opposing, one entity increases as the other reduces

Figure 3.7 Basic causal loop diagram showing stress within the traditional workplace and home environment.

numbers and driving people to hit increasing functional productivity targets. Some traditional companies now offer employees stress management courses, partly to reduce absenteeism and also to minimise the risk of being sued. However, rather than help employees to find ways to better manage stress, Lean companies adopt strategies that focus on eliminating it (e.g. providing effective support and reducing overburden).

Stress can also transcend across work and home life. After a stressful drive home in rush hour traffic, one may still be highly stressed and unable to think rationally. This may make it difficult for one to listen, converse or empathise effectively with other family members in the home. This can then create additional stress within the family environment, leading to more family problems, potential marital breakdown, less money and even more stress. This additional stress is then returned back into the workplace (see Figure 3.7). Again, these are re-enforcing loops, causing stress to continually increase (i.e. they are all 'S's'). It doesn't really matter where stress begins; the problem lies in the fact that stress is continually re-enforced.

As stress in the workplace grows, more mistakes are made and products & services get poorer. Costs go up, revenues & profits go down. This places further stress on individuals, as more jobs are lost and family incomes reduce. At the same time, more family breakdowns increases the demand and cost of housing, reducing family budgets still further and increasing levels of stress (See Figure 3.8).

Traditional companies reduce jobs in an attempt to survive and maintain profitability. Others fail completely. These all result in reduced levels of income & corporation tax. The causal loop diagram in Figure 3.9 shows how overall levels of personal taxation increase as a result, which generates more stress. Between 2001 and 2006, the UK government, unlike many other countries during this time, managed to avoid a recession due, at least in part, to a dramatic increase in expenditure on public services. Notably, this creates the first balancing loop in the system (due to their being one opposing relationship, labelled 'O'), creating more work and jobs for those freed up by

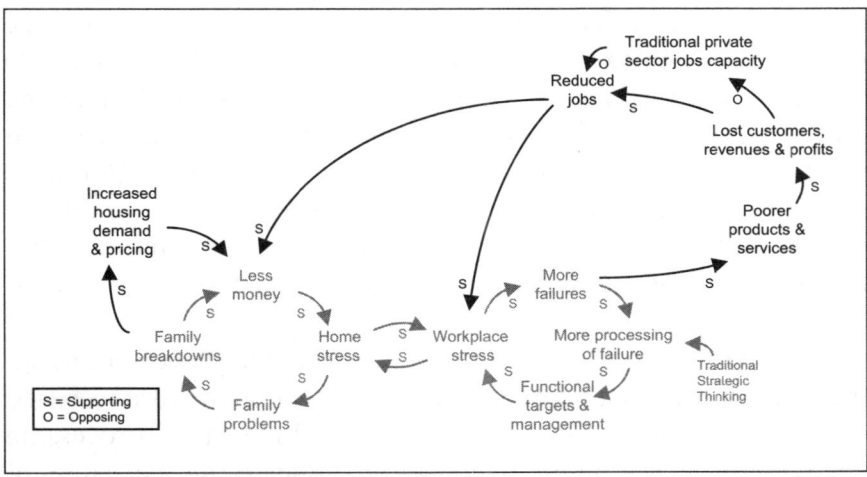

Figure 3.8 Causal loop diagram showing stress within traditional organisations and families.

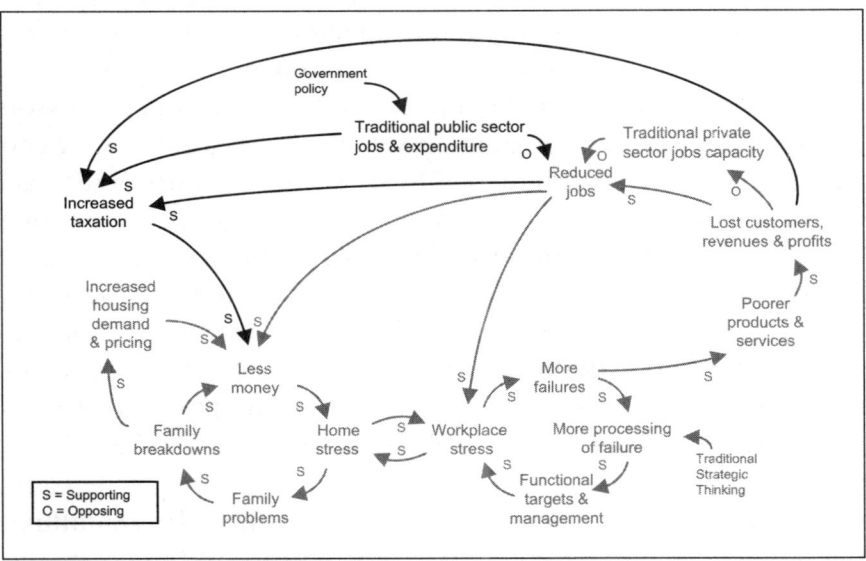

Figure 3.9 Causal loop diagram showing stress and job losses within traditional organisations.

traditional companies. It was successful in maintaining economic growth during this particular period, but it also resulted in a wide variety of tax increases, as well as increased levels of borrowing and a growing trade deficit. Increases in personal taxation reduce the amount of money available to individuals/families and increases levels of stress. Offering targeted support (e.g. tax relief/credits) to families with children helped to minimise this, although this placed additional burden upon those individuals/families without them.

By understanding the system as a whole, the power of changing the strategy of an enterprise and government, to one based on Lean Thinking can be clearly seen. Instead of processing all demand, Lean Thinking seeks to understand the cause of failure demand and eliminates it (see Figure 3.10). In doing so, it uniquely removes functional targets and goals, minimises the level of management and empowers the workforce to improve the way the work works (NB the 'S' between 'more processing of failure' and 'more targets and management' changes to an 'O'). It also minimises the amount of stress and overburden placed on its employees. By developing a policy of learning from successful Lean enterprises, providing investment/education in Lean Thinking, and by introducing Lean strategies into enterprise and government, the whole model transforms itself into one capable of creating Lean jobs, increasing global competitiveness, attracting inward investment and providing more public services. Such changes would also result in less stress, family breakdowns and the need for additional housing. They are also capable of reducing the overall tax burden, increasing personal happiness and improving overall well-being too – goals well worth striving for!

In a similar way, useful insight can be gained by examining the impact of humans on the environment. A basic causal loop diagram is shown in Figure 3.11, showing how humans have a direct impact upon their environment. Humans consume all types of resources, including limited natural resources (e.g. oil, gas, coal, metal ores), renewable resources (plants, water, solar energy) and man-made resources (e.g. metals, chemicals,

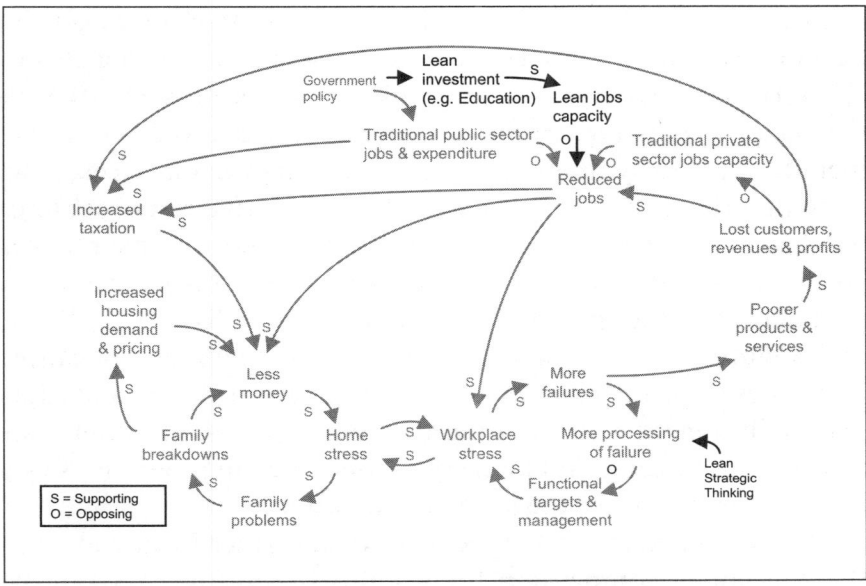

Figure 3.10 Causal loop diagram showing stress reduction and job creation using Lean Thinking.

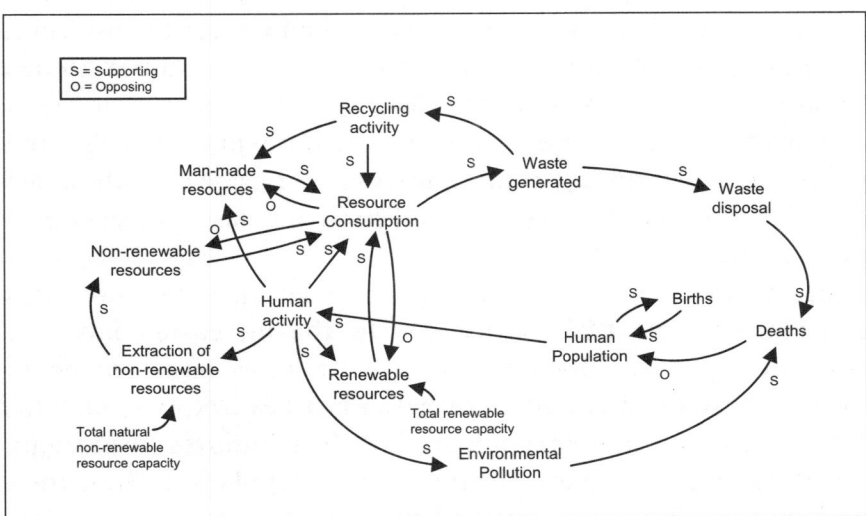

Figure 3.11 Basic causal loop diagram showing the impact of humans on resource consumption and the environment.

synthetic materials, products and structures). As more resources become available, humans tend to consume more (hence the 'S's'). Human activity results in consumption of resources (hence the 'O's'), but it creates man-made resources too ('S'). These include metals, synthetic materials and man-made structures; including those used to generate other renewable resources (e.g. wind/solar power). Human activity and resource consumption generate pollution and waste as by-products ('S'). These by-products are either processed and re-cycled, or discarded. Waste and pollution result in increased disease and death. For instance, in less developed countries this can occur due to poor sanitation and pollution of the environment (e.g. sources of water and food). This creates a balancing loop (odd number of 'O's') limiting the growth of the human population.

This simplified model can be developed further by introducing the concept of competition for resources (See Figure 3.12). As demand grows and availability drops, more activity is devoted to locating further non-renewable resources, creating additional man-made ones and harnessing renewable ones. It also increases the need for recycling. If additional resources are not made available then they become more limited and fewer births occur, as families find it more difficult to obtain the resources needed to support additional children. Worse still, conflict can break out over critical scarce resources, creating more deaths and potentially devastating communities/countries. All of these act to balance population growth and limit the size of the human population.

In the world today, the human population is growing at a considerable rate [35], partly due to the increasing levels of education and health-care. Whilst birth rates have tended to drop in developed countries over the last few decades, humans tend to live far longer compared with a hundred years ago, resulting in a net increase in the human population. Education and farming have also resulted in an ever increasing capacity to support mankind. Improvements to sanitation and water purification have also reduced the levels of death due to disease (see Figure 3.13). Population growth is creating further demand

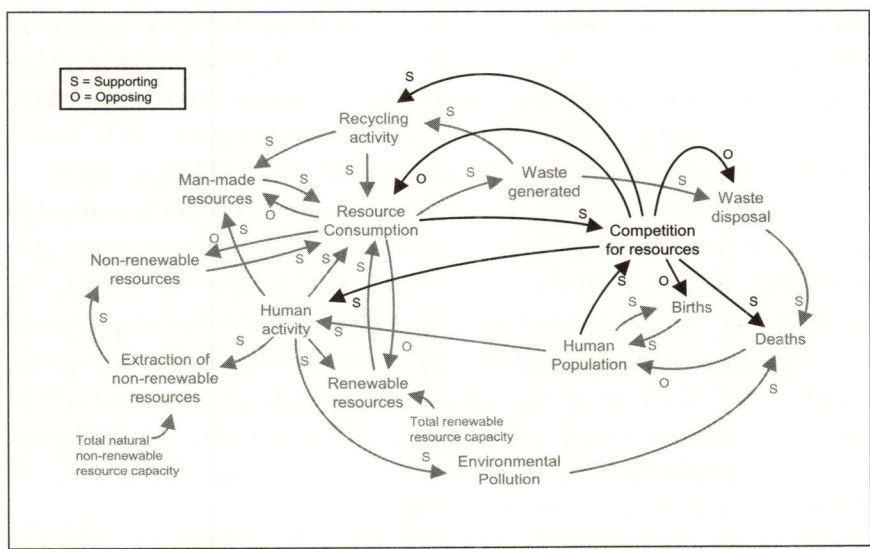

Figure 3.12 Causal loop diagram showing the impact of humans on consumption and the environment with competition for limited resources.

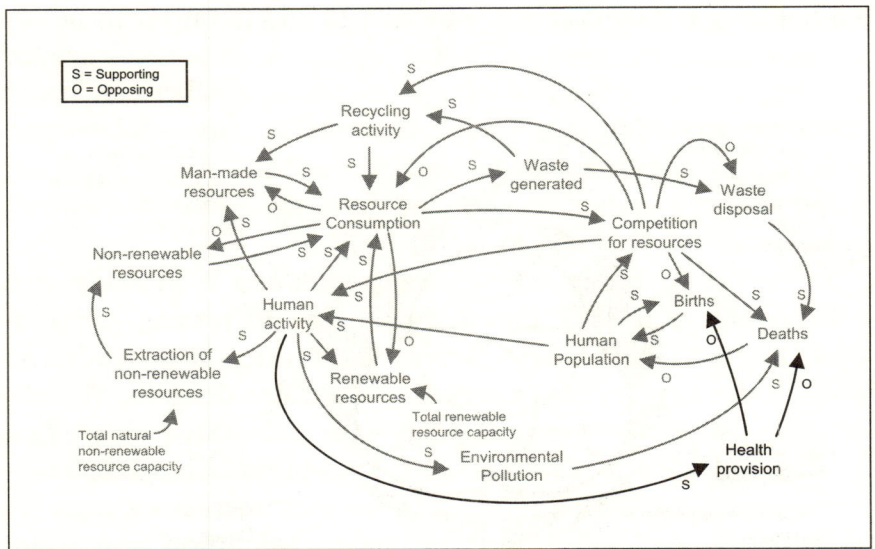

Figure 3.13 Causal loop diagram showing the impact of humans on the environment with increasing levels of healthcare provision.

for resources and a need for solutions which are able to conserve the planet's limited natural resources more. It is placing more and more importance on being able to reduce the amount of over-processing and the levels of waste created in the first place. All of these things are directly addressed by Lean Thinking.

Mankind will continue to thrive if it develops the knowledge and ability to create sustainable solutions. By doing this, mankind will also help to improve the future well-being of individuals and communities. If the human population grows in an apparently unsustainable way, then a mixture of pollution, conflict or worsering environmental conditions will start to limit the development of mankind. Individuals, communities and enterprises can all play a part in improving the situation. They are all able to create value and enjoy their existence, whilst improving the well-being of others and looking after the environment they all share together.

In its entirety, the Lean World System begins to de-code the 'DNA of Prosperity' for Enterprises, the 'DNA of Contentment' for Communities, 'The DNA of Sustainability' for the Environment and the 'DNA of Well-being & Happiness' for everyone as individuals (see Figure 3.14). Individuals sit at the

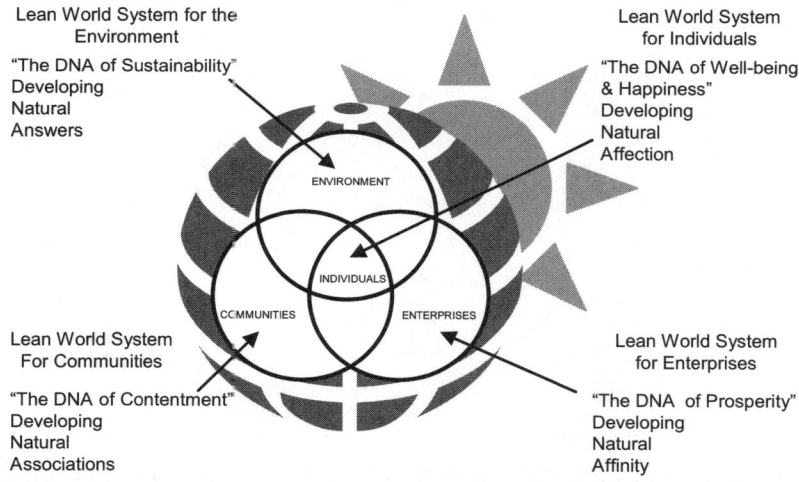

Figure 3.14 The DNA of Success™ in a Lean World.

centre, connecting all the systems together. The choices they make, individually and collectively, have the ability to affect the dynamics of the overall system; from the products they buy to the enterprises they work for. We all can and do make choices every minute of every day. To that end, individuals hold the responsibility and key to the success of enterprises, the contentment within communities, the sustainability of the world, as well as to their own personal happiness and well-being. Whilst most communities and enterprises have historically been relatively localised, mankind has increasingly introduced technologies and solutions that allow global enterprises and communities to form. This is no accident, but a result of mankind's intrinsic desire to learn and improve. These attributes are also complimented by mankind's instinct for survival, to seek pleasure and to search for greater meaning in life.

Chapter 9

Towards a Lean World

On steering a path towards a Lean World, transformation is likely to occur in almost every aspect of life. Leaders in every walk of life become much closer to the people they represent, articulate a clear desirable direction and devolve decision making as much as possible. As a result, individuals and groups are given greater responsibility and choice.

A new era of continuous improvement and creativity result, as well as new ways of governing enterprises and communities. Governments make many critical decisions on behalf of us all which affect us all; collectively as individuals, communities and enterprises. In many countries governments, elected by communities, take overall responsibility for collective decision making which influences much of the social fabric in which people live and work (e.g. law and order, education, health care, transport). In a Lean World, collective decisions are made following thorough consultation, reflection and co-operation; involving the communities actually affected and those with whom invaluable knowledge resides. Decisions are made more and more on a local basis. They are also underpinned by a strong set of values and a clear direction. This makes sure that any decision made is effective and improves overall success. Individuals and communities take more personal responsibility for the decisions they make and the actions they take; from determining their own destiny through to helping to conserve the planet's limited natural resources.

Successful enterprises and communities will be those that respond precisely to the real needs of people as individuals and together as groups. A new criminal justice system, described in chapter 6, provides one example of this. Changes to law, policies, strategies and priorities are still necessary, but the whole environment becomes far more people centric and less politically driven. Governments and service providers start to spend more time understanding the real needs of citizens and harnessing the wealth of knowledge people are more than willing to provide. At the same time, governments must avoid setting arbitrary targets for service providers to hit or micromanaging how services are actually delivered. Instead, they need to focus on setting a clear overall direction and supporting the service providers addressing the key barriers they face to improving the services.

A number of localised healthcare service providers have recently begun Lean journeys and are already reporting significant breakthroughs. Hospitals are starting to dramatically reduce mortality rates, waiting times and cycle times [36,37]. At the same time, they are also reporting significant increases in resource effectiveness. Lean is creating initial improvement gains of between 30–40%, when previous hospital change programmes struggled to achieve a 3–4% change. At the same time, minor changes to working practices in local General Practitioner (GP) surgeries are starting to allow patients to speak directly to their own doctor and to see them the same day, whilst also reducing costs! This was partly due to the fact that around 50% of patient demand could easily be handled through direct dialogue with their doctor, without the need to visit the surgery at all. Such changes are just the beginning of a Lean journey and the opportunity exists for all healthcare providers to migrate more time and resources towards prevention rather than treatment. This type of change will start to occur a lot more rapidly once a Lean management system is put in place and arbitrary targets have been replaced.

Enterprises successfully adopting a Lean management system, start to prosper and grow, benefiting from the knowledge their customers' offer, the purchases they continue to make and the marketing they provide to others. On the other hand, those with business models which thrive upon failure demand will find it increasingly difficult to survive. This includes companies that currently offer pure maintenance services, such as roadside assistance, car repairs, IT maintenance (e.g. technology, software) or infrastructure maintenance (e.g. water pipes, communication networks, roads, rail). Products are becoming increasingly reliable, making breakdowns less frequent (e.g. cars). As concerns about the environment and the consumption/waste of limited natural resources grow, more sustainable solutions will naturally be sought. Components will be increasingly manufactured to ensure their longevity and their ability to be recycled. More resources will be reused, rather than disposed of and product companies will expand their horizons to providing more of the services people want from the products that they make (e.g. automobile companies into transportation services). This creates a variety of challenges and opportunities for many companies in terms of how they operate today.

For instance, whilst one water company in the UK has become one of the fastest enterprises to be able to respond to leaks, another has focused more upon eliminating leaks, so there is no need to respond to them at all [38]. Which one is properly applying Lean Thinking? Given the first company is processing problems and the latter is eliminating problems, it is only the latter company that's applying Lean Thinking. For instance, by intelligently managing flow, they are able to supply water using minimum pressures which dramatically reduces the risk of burst pipes and levels of water leakage. This minimises the cost of producing clean water, only to lose it, which will be very important particularly in those parts of the world where water is scarce. In a Lean World, a water company will look more holistically at supplying a multiplicity of services to households (e.g. infrastructure, heating). It is this that allows a gradual migration of resources away from maintaining water pipes, to providing more value customers want and are willing to pay for. It also creates increased growth and prosperity, as well as more motivating work and further opportunities for staff to develop.

Also, a more recent and well-documented set of failures occurred when the dot com bubble burst at the turn of the century. It left many people, directly and indirectly, nursing heavy financial losses. Huge amounts of money speculated on technology and internet stocks were lost. A few start-ups had relatively robust business models and have since become highly successful (e.g. Amazon, Google, eBay). The majority of others did not. Many companies did not offer a great deal of value to customers and for others, there were few barriers to prevent other businesses copying them. From a Lean perspective, it does not take long to identify those that are likely to win and those that will not survive. Making sure the company provides products and services which add real value in the eyes of the customer is an obvious first step. For instance, search services, comparison services and trading services have helped people to obtain information, find the best supplier and to exchange goods respectively. All of these services have helped to drive down prices in many markets, offering small levels of profit for those providing basic products and services. Whilst patents help protect a number of companies, many others are at real risk from competition, innovation and advances in technology. Ultimate value is provided when companies create effective relationships with their customers, provide them with what they want and partnering with them, to steadily increase the value they provide. These companies are successfully able to grow and accelerate away from any potential competitors. They avoid an otherwise negative downward spiral, trying harder and harder to sell commodity products and services to more customers, whilst seeking to find more commodity products or services to sell (at commodity prices)!

Technology will continue to be a critical aspect of change, supporting Lean Thinking. This applies to almost every area, including communications, information technology, trans-portation, manufacturing and energy production. It also includes areas such as medicine (e.g. vaccines, genetics), energy con-servation (e.g. efficiency and insulation) and environmental management (e.g. natural resource management, waste reduc-tion, pollution and nature conservation). Technology will help mankind to build knowledge and to free them from more mundane tasks. Artificial Intelligence will also allow technology to interact more personally with humans, as well as other computers, where it is advantageous to do so. This will help speed up and improve decision making processes. For instance, personal virtual assistants will obtain information, negotiate on our behalf and present options for us to choose what we would like. These will become common in real life (e.g. televisions in our homes) as well as within virtual lives (e.g. within cyberspace). The internet is already starting to make the world a lot smaller place and allowing more relationships to be formed. The internet and world wide connectivity of communities, is going to increasingly drive change, with the needs of the vast majority starting to overcome the vested interests of a small minority. Enterprises will struggle if they treat customers badly. Everyone finds out about it and people can then choose not to buy from them. In a similar way, there is little value continuing to spend money on advertising poor products, when the first few people to purchase it will go and tell everyone else. On the other hand, if you have a fantastic product you will not have to heavily advertise it, as people will start to tell others for you. Trusted companies will create the ability to search quickly and effectively through the infinite variety available in order to obtain what they need. Many retail enterprises will fall by the wayside. Customers will continue to have choice, but they won't want to spend all their time choosing! They need help to turn information into knowledge – finding the right things for them in a world of infinite variety (e.g. information, products, services and fun).

Technology is creating infinitely sized 'shop windows'. These will, over time, naturally impact on the number of aggregators (e.g. pure retailers and niche retailers) and 'middle-men'. The internet has made traditional retail constraints such as geography and floor space less relevant (e.g. Amazon, eBay and Google) and markets are now global. Niche/local retail products and services are not only more likely to be economic, but also more likely to be successful on a global scale. Overall, the range of

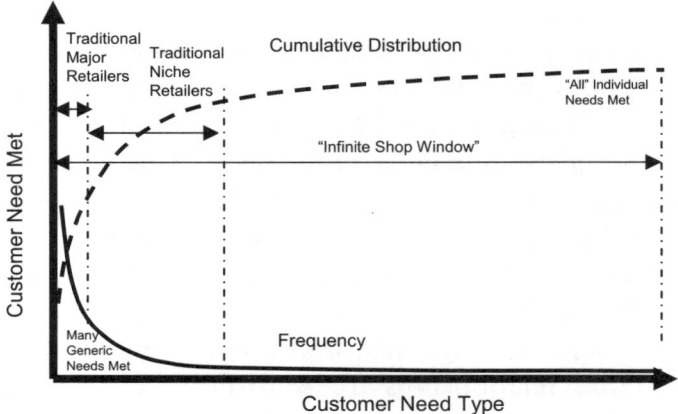

Figure 3.15 Frequency & cumulative distribution of customer needs met, showing the traditional boundaries of enterprise and infinite 'shop windows'.

products and services available to satisfy individual consumer needs gradually become infinite, through 'shop windows' of the future (See Figure 3.15).

Technology is unleashing 'creators' (i.e. those creating and providing value directly to others) and is expanding their numbers exponentially. This is yet another positive outcome in a Lean World. In many areas, the internet is blurring the boundaries between the amateur and the professional, as well as the individual and the institution. For instance, consumption of video and music are now a complex mix of traditional popular artists (e.g. via Radio, TV or Cinema) and little known niche ones (e.g. via YouTube or MySpace). Aggregators, such as YouTube, are looking to offer amateurs an opportunity to share in the advertising revenue they generate. A myriad of other creators are also selling their own products and services on sites such as Amazon and eBay. Some enterprises are already starting to use these types of arenas to spot emerging ideas and talent. They are also using them to test, develop and promote their own product / service offerings [15]. The current explosion of creativity is only the beginning, as these environments become a key nurturing ground for talent and enterprise. The creativity and knowledge economy are going to develop and grow out of all recognition, changing the landscape of enterprise forever. However, at a global level there is growing recognition that a number of issues need to be addressed. The first is the digital divide. Most of the world's population currently does not have access to the technology or skills to become a part of this emerging world [39]. If this is left unresolved then individuals, communities and nations risk falling behind and finding it difficult to catch up. The second is the issue of intellectual property rights, where information can be provided seamlessly around the world without the risk of it being misused.

People will become increasingly selective, not only about what they purchase, but who they are associated with and who they work for. Many people will offer their skills to a number of companies at the same time – but when they do, they will always maintain honour and mutual respect. The risk to a company from the loss of one individual (and their knowledge) is reduced, as business outcomes result more from the unique cohesion of the enterprise, not one individual. Workers in a Lean World have a new and far more exciting role to play, one which creates far more value for their communities and the environment in which they live. They take responsibility for driving change and continuous improvement. They no longer see knowledge as power and something to be kept to oneself. Instead, they realise that their ability to listen and to learn, to share and work collectively as a team, are the real sources of power. They understand and share with others the benefits of a Lean World. They seek forgiveness rather than permission and they support each other in order to create change. Lean Navigators help companies to ask the right questions and to follow a Lean Way from the very outset. They chart a path to a successful future, a Lean future, without the need to cross difficult oceans or mountains (see Figure 3.16).

Through advances in communications, communities (both local and global) are more capable of creating new relationships, reducing levels of isolation and increasing levels of collective responsibility. In environments where free speech and democracy

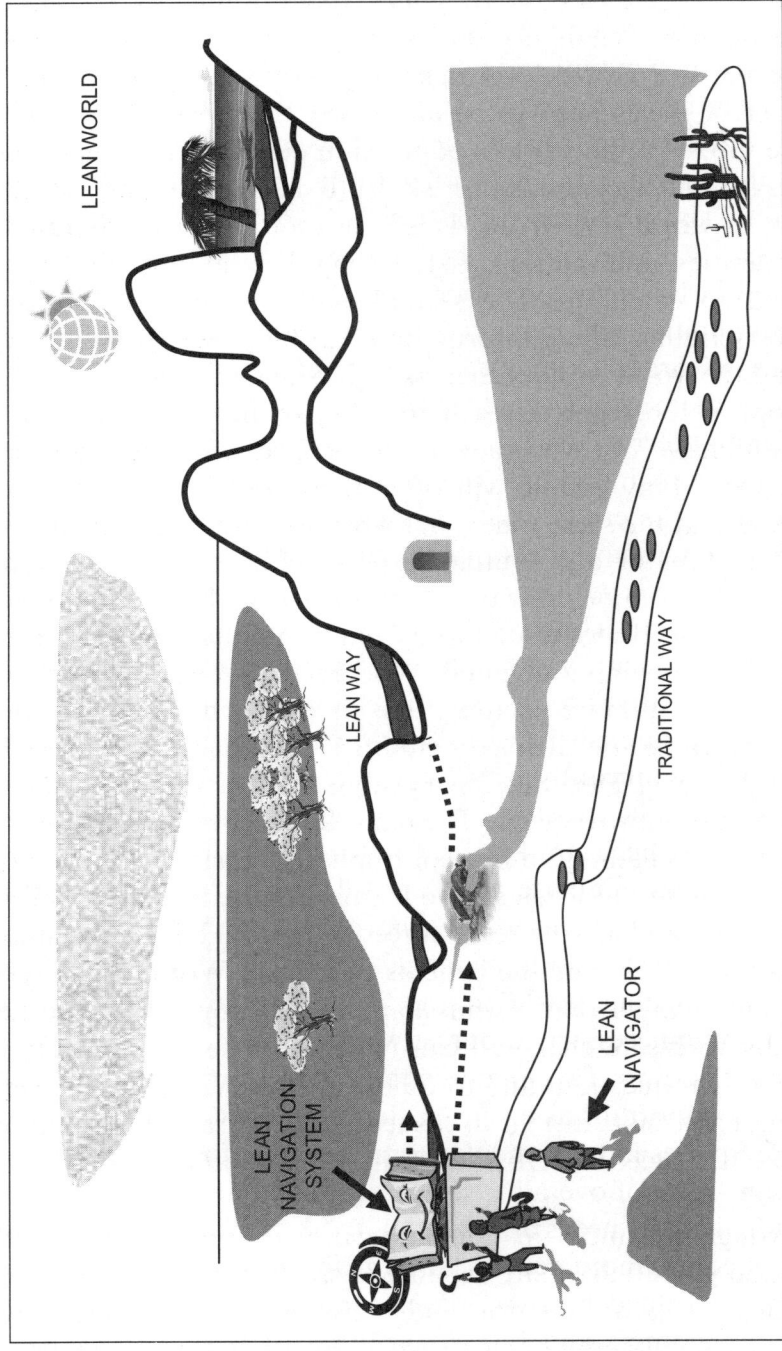

Figure 3.16 A Lean Navigator helping to create a Lean Start™ along a Lean Way.

flourish, social responsibility and collective decision making take place. Information is turned into knowledge by everyone involved, allowing individuals and whole communities to make more informed choices. As the ability to communicate becomes easier, information from groups such as media, political parties and lobby groups is augmented by people directly providing opinions and experiences themselves. As more information becomes available, it can be progressively transformed into knowledge. However, popularity must not be mistaken for fact.

Communities will start to come together and support one another in order to tackle some of the significant challenges ahead. These include challenges such as famine and disease, conflict and terror, drugs and crime. Drugs are often associated with a lack of individual well-being and happiness and result in much of the crime and anti-social behaviour we see in our communities today. Collectively, communities need to start to tackle the root cause of such problems and not just treat the symptoms. Lean Thinking has a major role to play in helping communities identify the true causes of problems, helping to formulate creative, robust solutions and gaining the consensus necessary to implement them. Concern about the environment has grown significantly over the last few years. Limited natural resources need be treasured, not squandered. In the Lean World, communities need to find ways to reduce the rate they're consumed and minimise any harmful waste created. Recycling and waste management services have developed in recent years, but it's not just about managing waste more effectively. It's about minimizing waste in the first place and reducing the amount of unnecessary resources we consume.

The well-being of communities and the happiness of everyone, is just as important as ensuring the future sustainability of our planet. Studies have found economic growth does not provide a good indicator of overall well-being and happiness [30]. Once an individuals basic needs are met (e.g. food, warmth, shelter), well-being becomes more dependent on being a part of a community and being valued by others (i.e. social capital). This involves supporting others and being supported by others at the same time. Individuals, enterprises and communities have a lot to do and everything to gain if they embrace Lean Thinking. Stress management and counselling will gradually reduce as new ways of systematically reducing (and eliminating) stress are adopted. As more enterprises begin their Lean journey, overall stress levels will reduce and motivation and opportunity will increase. Enterprises will be rewarded by the customers and communities they serve, not just in the short term but in the long term. This isn't wishful thinking – it's Lean Thinking! Enterprises that fail to hear the starting pistol risk being left behind. As these companies struggle to survive, their employees will naturally migrate to those companies that are successfully changing and growing. Individuals will play a pivotal role in creating change, as they take on more responsibility and make reasoned choices, both individually and collectively.

Success in a Lean World comprises of contented communities, prosperous enterprises and a more sustainable environment (see Figure 3.17). With individuals situated at its heart, overall individual well-being and happiness also improves too.

Figure 3.17 Success in a Lean World.

In summary, this book has primarily focused on describing Lean Thinking and a Lean World Management System; one capable of generating sustained prosperity for enterprise and helping to create complete success for everyone. The role of a Lean Navigator has also been introduced; one capable of guiding enterprise successfully to a Lean Way and a better World. The book has also sought to provide a more holistic picture of a Lean World and the roles enterprise play within it. Finally, it has looked ahead towards a Lean World and the role technology is likely to play. By doing these things, the book has been written to provide additional guidance and encouragement to all those seeking to create a better world, as well as to those already embarking on a Lean Journey. As a result, I hope it heralds, for everyone, the dawn of a new 21st Century world – a Lean World.

References

1. 'Leading Change: Why transformation Efforts Fail';
   Kotter, J.P., Harvard Business Review, March-April 1995.
2. 'Out of the Crisis'; W. Edwards Deming, 2000.
3. 'The New Economics for Industry, Government,
   Education', W. Edwards Deming, 2000.
4. 'The Machine That Changed the World: The Massachusetts
   Institute of Technology 5-million-dollar, 5-year Report on
   the Future of the Automobile Industry', James P. Womack,
   Daniel Roos, Daniel T. Jones, 1990.
5. 'Lean Thinking: Banish Waste and Create Wealth in Your
   Corporation', James P. Womack & Daniel T. Jones, 2003.
6. 'The Toyota Way', Liker, J.K. 2004.
7. 'Lean Solutions: How Companies and Customers can
   Create Value and Wealth Together', James P. Womack and
   Daniel T. Jones, 2005.
8. 'The Stupid Company – How British Businesses Throw
   Away Money by Alienating Consumers', Philip Cullum,
   National Consumer Council, 02/2006.
9. 'Sense & Respond: The Journey to Customer Purpose',
   Susan Barlow, Stephen Parry and Mike Faulkner, 2005.
10. 'Seeing the Forest for the Trees: A Manager's Guide to
    Applying Systems Thinking'; Sherwood, D., 2002.
11. 'How to Prevent Lean Implementation Failures', Rurich. L,
    2004.
12. 'Total Strategy', Rakesh Sondhi, 1999.
13. http://www.tescocorporate.com/, 01/03/2007.
14. 'Beyond Re-engineering: How the Process Centred

Organization is Changing our Work and our Lives',
Hammer M., 1988.

15. 'The Long Tail', Anderson, C., 2006.
16. 'Freedom from Command and Control', Seddon, J. , 2003.
17. 'I Want You to Cheat', Seddon, J. , 1992.
18. 'The Toyota Product Development System', Morgans,
    J.M, Liker, J.K., 2006.
19. 'The Bullwhip Effect In Supply Chains', Lee, H, et al,
    Sloan Management Review, 1997.
20. 'The Ultimate Question'; Reichheld, F., 2006.
21. 'Practical Lean Accounting', Maskell. B, Baggaley. B, 2003.
22. 'The New Lean Toolbox', Bicheno. J, 2004.
23. 'Seven C's of Consultancy', Cope. M, 2000.
24. http://www.toyota.co.jp/en/vision/, Toyota web site,
    1/3/2007.
25. http://www.toyota-industries.com/corporateinfo/
    philosophy/basic/index.html, Toyota industries web site,
    1/3/2007.
26. '2016: The Future Value Chain', Global Commerce
    Initiative Report, 2006.
27. 'Life on Mars'; Mark Sheasby, M. et al, Deming
    Transformation Forum, June 2006.
28. 'Undercover Copper', Dispatches, Channel 4, April 2006.
29. 'The Happiness Formula', BBC Series, April-May 2006.
30. 'The Motivation of Work', Herzberg, 1959.
31. 'Building Health: An Epidemiological Study of 'Sick
    Building Syndrome' in the Whitehall II Study', Marmot,
    A.F., Eley, J., Stafford, M., et al, British Medical Journal,
    Occupational and Environmental Medicine, Volume 63,
    P283–289, 2006.
32. 'How to Reduce Workplace Conflict and Stress',
    Maravelas, A., 2005
33. 'The Economics of Climate Change', Stern Review, UK,
    Oct 2006.
34. 'Climate Change 2007: The Physical Science Basis:
    Summary for Policy Makers', International Panel on
    Climate Change, Feb 2007.

35. 'World Population: The 2004 Revision', Population Division of the Department of Economic and Social Affairs of the United Nations Secretariat, 2004.
36. 'What You Measure is What You Get: Measuring the Impact of Lean', Fillingham, D., Lean Healthcare Forum, Oct 2006.
37. 'Going Lean in the NHS', NHS Institute for Innovation and Improvement, Feb 2007.
38. 'Winning Line', NCE Water Supplement, Oct 1994.
39. 'Living the Digital World', Utsumi, Y., ITU Telecom World 2006 Forum, Hong Kong, Dec 2006.